HIKE LIST

MENASHA RIDGE PRESS
Birmingham, Alabama

60 HIKES
WITHIN 60 MILES

DALLAS/
FORT WORTH

INCLUDES
**TARRANT, COLLIN,
AND DENTON COUNTIES**

JOANIE SÁNCHEZ

DISCLAIMER

This book is meant only as a guide to select trails in the Dallas/Fort Worth area and does not guarantee hiker safety in any way—you hike at your own risk. Neither Menasha Ridge Press nor Joanie Sánchez is liable for property loss or damage, personal injury, or death that result in any way from accessing or hiking the trails described in the following pages. Please be aware that hikers have been injured in the Dallas/Fort Worth area. Be especially cautious when walking on or near boulders, steep inclines, and drop-offs, and do not attempt to explore terrain that may be beyond your abilities. To help ensure an uneventful hike, please read carefully the introduction to this book, and perhaps get further safety information and guidance from other sources. Familiarize yourself thoroughly with the areas you intend to visit before venturing out. Ask questions, and prepare for the unforeseen. Familiarize yourself with current weather reports, maps of the area you intend to visit, and any relevant park regulations.

Copyright © 2008 by Joanie Sánchez
All rights reserved
Printed in the United States of America
Published by Menasha Ridge Press
Distributed by Publishers Group West
First edition, third printing 2009

Library of Congress Cataloging-in-Publication Data
Sánchez, Joanie
    60 hikes within 60 miles : Dallas and Fort Worth, including Tarrant, Collin,
    and Denton counties / Joanie Sánchez. — 1st ed.
    p. cm.
    Includes index.
    ISBN-13: 978-0-89732-649-0
    ISBN-10: 0-89732-649-0
    1. Hiking—Texas—Dallas Region—Guidebooks. 2. Hiking—Texas—Fort
Worth—Region—Guidebooks. 3. Trails—Texas—Dallas Region—Guidebooks.
4. Trails—Texas—Fort Worth Region—Guidebooks. 5. Dallas Region (Tex.)—
Guidebooks. 6. Fort Worth Region (Tex.)—Guidebooks.
    I. Title. II. Title: Sixty hikes within sixty miles.
    GV199.42.T492D35 2008
    917.64'28120464--dc22
                                                    2007031158

Cover and text design by Steveco International
Cover photo Andrew Sánchez
Author photo by Andrew Sánchez
Cartography by Scott McGrew, Lohnes+Wright, and Joanie Sánchez

Menasha Ridge Press
P.O. Box 43673
Birmingham, AL 35243
www.menasharidge.com

**TO MY MOTHER AND FATHER,
FOR TEACHING ME MY FIRST FEW STEPS AND GUIDING ME ON EACH ONE
THEREAFTER.**

— JOANIE SÁNCHEZ

TABLE OF CONTENTS

ACKNOWLEDGMENTS

Throughout these hikes, I was unfailingly greeted by park rangers, office staff, and volunteers whose infectious enthusiasm had me eagerly lacing up my boots and seeking out their trailheads. Many went above and beyond in suggesting trails, providing maps, and relaying history—as they do every day with everyone who enters their doorway ready to explore their domain. My greatest thanks go to these watchful custodians whose tips, insights, recommendations, and knowledge were not only helpful but inspiring.

I would also like to thank my father, Orlando Sánchez, who tirelessly requested updates on each and every hike and unquestioningly picked up a hiking stick during vacation; Bob Shauchunas, whose knowledge and tips were always available and invaluable; and my mother, Joan Shauchunas, whose fresh energy and company made each hike an adventure.

And finally, a very special thanks to my brother, Andrew Sánchez, who was always up for a hike, whether through mud, meadows, or flying insects; these hikes would not have been nearly as easy or as fun to explore without his assistance, advice, and companionship.

—JOANIE SÁNCHEZ

FOREWORD

Welcome to Menasha Ridge Press's *60 Hikes within 60 Miles.* Our strategy was simple: First, find a hiker who knows the area and loves to hike. Second, ask that person to spend a year researching the most popular and very best trails around. And third, have that person describe each trail in terms of difficulty, scenery, condition, elevation change, and all other categories of information that are important to hikers. "Pretend you've just completed a hike and met up with other hikers at the trailhead," we told each author. "Imagine their questions, and be clear in your answers." An experienced hiker and writer, author Joanie Sánchez has selected 60 of the best hikes in and around the Dallas/Fort Worth metropolitan area. From the greenways and urban hikes that make use of parklands to flora- and fauna-rich treks along the cliffs and hills in the hinterlands, Sánchez provides hikers (and walkers) with a great variety of hikes—and all within roughly 60 miles of Dallas/Fort Worth.

You'll get more out of this book if you take a moment to read the Introduction explaining how to read the trail listings. The "Topographic Maps" section will help you understand how useful topos will be on a hike, and will also tell you where to get them. And though this is a "where-to," rather than a "how-to" guide, those of you who have hiked extensively will find the Introduction of particular value. As much for the opportunity to free the spirit as well as to free the body, let these hikes elevate you above the urban hurry.

All the best,
The Editors at Menasha Ridge Press

ABOUT THE AUTHOR

JOANIE SÁNCHEZ

An avid hiker, camper, and traveler, Joanie Sánchez's love of the outdoors began with an opportunity to work one summer with the Youth Conservation Corps in Yosemite National Park. That summer led her to serving as a leader within the group the following year, teaching and mentoring as she shared her passion for nature. Since then her adventures have taken her backpacking across Europe, on a state-to-state bike tour across New England, and hiking through the Caribbean islands. She has

traveled extensively throughout Mexico and has written an adventure guidebook to Mexico's Gulf Coast. Sánchez is a graduate of Yale University. She grew up and lives in the Dallas area and spends her free time showing fellow hikers the beauty that Texas trails have to offer.

PREFACE

According to the U.S. Census Bureau, the Dallas–Fort Worth–Arlington metropolitan area is the fourth-largest metropolitan area in the United States, home to more than 6 million people. For those of us who have lived here and watched the area blossom into the world-class destination it has become, its growth has had both benefits and drawbacks. On the one hand, we thrive on the diverse cultural, entertainment, and dining offerings of our cosmopolitan city; on the other hand, we long for the open prairies, wooded creeks, and wildflower fields that the freeways, shopping centers, and gas stations have replaced. When I tell people that I'm working on a book describing hikes within 60 miles of Dallas–Fort Worth, most have two responses—"Really! I love the outdoors, and I love to hike!" inevitably followed by a shake of the head, and the sad comment "but there just isn't anyplace nearby for me to go." I find that many have overlooked the parks and green-belts in their neighborhoods, and the nature preserves in their towns—beautiful spots dismissed mostly because they find it hard to believe there can be any worthwhile natural areas left in such an urban setting.

In writing this book, I've had the pleasure of searching out these and many other hidden gems—and was surprised with what I found in the unlikeliest of spots. Nestled adjacent to freeways, hidden behind apartment complexes, and sitting quietly near busy town centers, I found patches of wilderness where animals and plants thrive, and where for a few hours you can forget the hassles of urban life and act as explorer—hiking through woods and prairies, listening to birds, and identifying animal prints. Within 60 miles, there's something to appeal to everyone. Woodland treks, grassland paths—and there are even plenty of hikes along water—thanks in part to the Trinity River and its four forks—the Clear Fork, Elm Fork, West Fork, and East Fork—which spider throughout the region. You'll also find many trails along lakes. Interestingly, the only natural lake in Texas is Caddo Lake (located in East Texas); all the rest are man-made, created mostly by damming rivers to make reservoirs.

I've done my best in this book to describe the trails I've found, but don't be surprised if, on your own explorations, you discover something slightly different. A trail you've been on before (or heard about) can be an entirely new experience in another season. If you don't like a trail in the winter, come back in the spring when the flowers are in bloom and the trees are budding. Conversely, a hot prairie path can be a delight on a sunny winter day, but probably not as pleasant at the peak of summer.

Regardless of when you go, or where you go, it's important to get out there. If you've heard of a hike, but don't see it mentioned here, that doesn't mean it's not great—I was unable to include some hikes because of weather or logistics; don't be afraid to check them out. If you've thumbed through this book and found a hike you'd like but that is too short or too long, go anyway—any hike can be shortened, and many of these hikes can be lengthened. And when you're done exploring the hikes in this book—keep going! There are many more trails out there just waiting for you to discover them. I hope you enjoy them as much as I have.

—*Joanie Sánchez*

HIKING RECOMMENDATIONS

HIKES 1–2.9 MILES

HIKES 3–5 MILES

HIKES 3–5 MILES *(continued)*

HIKES > 5 MILES

BEST FOR CHILDREN

BEST FOR CHILDREN *(continued)*
39 Ray Roberts Lake State Park, Isle du Bois Unit:
    Lost Pines Trail (page 179)
59 Post Oak Trail (page 272)
60 Samuell Farm Trail (page 276)

BEST FOR SOLITUDE
25 Trinity River Trail (Northside) (page 119)
42 Walnut Grove Trail (page 191)
55 Lake Mineral Wells State Park: Cross Timbers Trail (page 252)
57 Lost Creek Reservoir State Trailway (page 261)
58 Lake Tawakoni Nature Trail (page 268)

BEST-MAINTAINED TRAILS
11 Spring Creek Park Nature Trail (page 59)
14 Bear Creek–Bob Eden Trail (page 74)
29 Breckenridge Park Trail (page 139)
32 Cicada–Cottonwood Loop (page 151)
53 Waxahachie Creek Hike & Bike Trail (page 241)
59 Post Oak Trail (page 272)

BUSIEST TRAILS
1 Bachman Lake Trail (page 18)
8 Katy Trail (page 47)
9 L.B. Houston Nature Trail (page 51)
10 Rowlett Creek Nature Trail (page 55)
13 White Rock Lake Trail (page 67)
19 Horseshoe Trail (page 95)
21 North Shore Trail (page 103)
27 Arbor Hills Loop (page 130)

EASIEST HIKES
4 Duck Creek Greenbelt (page 31)
6 Fish Creek Linear Trail (page 39)
15 Benbrook Dam Trail (page 79)
18 Fort Worth Nature Center: Prairie Trail (page 91)
22 River Legacy Trail (page 107)
30 Carrollton Greenbelt (page 143)
32 Cicada–Cottonwood Loop (page 151)
38 Ray Roberts Greenbelt (page 175)
39 Ray Roberts Lake State Park, Isle du Bois Unit:
    Lost Pines Trail (page 179)

EASIEST HIKES *(continued)*

FLAT HIKES

HIKES ALONG CREEKS AND RIVERS

HIKES FOR RUNNERS

HIKES FOR RUNNERS *(continued)*

BEST FOR DOGS

LAKE HIKES

LAKE HIKES *(continued)*

MOST DIFFICULT HIKES

MOST SCENIC HIKES

STEEPEST HIKES

URBAN HIKES

URBAN HIKES *(continued)*

WHEELCHAIR ACCESSIBLE TRAILS

WILDFLOWER HIKES

WILDLIFE HIKES

WILDLIFE HIKES *(continued)*

BIRDING HIKES

HIKES FOR HISTORICAL INTEREST

60 HIKES
WITHIN 60 MILES

DALLAS/FORT WORTH
INCLUDES
TARRANT, COLLIN, AND DENTON COUNTIES

INTRODUCTION

Welcome to *60 Hikes within 60 Miles: Dallas/Fort Worth*. Whether you're new to hiking or are a seasoned trekker, take a few minutes to read the following introduction. We explain how this book is organized and how to use it.

HOW TO USE THIS GUIDEBOOK

THE OVERVIEW MAP AND OVERVIEW MAP KEY

Use the overview map on the inside front cover to assess the exact locations of each hike's primary trailhead. Each hike's number appears on the overview map, on the map key facing the overview map, and in the table of contents. Flipping through the book, a hike's full profile is easy to locate by watching for the hike number at the top of each page. The book is organized by region, as indicated in the table of contents. A map legend of the symbols found on trail maps appears on the inside back cover.

REGIONAL MAPS

The book is divided into regions, and prefacing each regional section is an overview map of that region. The regional map provides more detail than the overview map, bringing you closer to the hike.

TRAIL MAPS

Each hike contains a detailed map that shows the trailhead, the route, significant features, facilities, and topographic landmarks such as creeks, overlooks, and peaks. The author gathered map data by carrying a Garmin eTrex Legend GPS unit while hiking. This data was downloaded into the Topo! State Series digital mapping program and processed by expert cartographers to produce the highly accurate maps found in this book. Each trailhead's GPS coordinates are included with each profile.

1

ELEVATION PROFILES

Corresponding directly to the trail map is a detailed elevation profile for each hike. The elevation profile provides a quick look at the trail from the side, enabling you to visualize how the trail rises and falls. Key points along the way are labeled. Note the number of feet between each tick mark on the vertical axis (the height scale). To avoid making flat hikes look steep and steep hikes appear flat, height scales are used throughout the book to give an accurate image of the hike's climbing difficulty.

GPS TRAILHEAD COORDINATES

To collect accurate map data, each trail was hiked with a handheld GPS unit (Garmin eTrex series). Data collected was then downloaded and plotted onto a digital USGS topo map. In addition to providing a highly specific trail outline, this book also includes the GPS coordinates for each trailhead in two formats: latitude/longitude and UTM. Latitude/longitude coordinates tell you where you are by locating a point west (latitude) of the 0° meridian line that passes through Greenwich, England, and north or south of the 0° longitude line that belts the Earth, AKA the equator.

Topographic maps show latitude/longitude in addition to UTM grid lines. Known as UTM coordinates, the numbers index a specific point using a grid. The survey datum used to arrive at the coordinates in this book is WGS84 (versus NAD27 or WGS83). For readers who own a GPS unit, whether handheld or onboard a vehicle, the latitude/longitude or UTM coordinates provided on the first page of each hike may be entered into the GPS unit. Just make sure your GPS unit is set to navigate using WGS84 datum. Then you can navigate directly to the trailheads.

Most trailheads, which begin in parking areas, can be reached by car, but sometimes one must walk a short distance from a parking area to reach the trailhead. In those cases, a handheld unit is necessary to continue the GPS navigation process. That said, readers can easily access all trailheads in this book by using the directions given, the overview map, and the trail map, which shows at least one major road leading into the area. But for those who enjoy using the latest GPS technology to navigate, the necessary data has been provided. A brief explanation of the UTM coordinates from Rocky Point Trail follows.

UTM Zone	14S
Easting	672767
Northing	3656549

The UTM zone number 14 refers to 1 of the 60 vertical zones of the Universal Transverse Mercator (UTM) projection. Each zone is 6 degrees wide. The UTM zone letter S refers to one of the 20 horizontal zones that span from 80 degrees south to 84 degrees north. The easting number 672767 indicates in meters how far east or west a point is from the central meridian of the zone. Increasing easting coordinates on a topo map or on your GPS screen indicate that you are moving east; decreasing easting coordinates indicate that you are moving west. The northing number

3656549 references in meters how far you are from the equator. Above and below the equator, increasing northing coordinates indicate you are traveling north; decreasing northing coordinates indicate you are traveling south. To learn more about how to enhance your outdoor experiences with GPS technology, refer to *GPS Outdoors: A Practical Guide for Outdoor Enthusiasts* (Menasha Ridge Press).

HIKE DESCRIPTIONS

Each hike contains seven key items: an "In Brief" description of the trail, a key at-a-glance box, directions to the trail, trailhead coordinates, a trail map, an elevation profile, and a trail description. Many also include a note on nearby activities. Combined, the maps and information let you assess each trail from the comfort of your favorite reading chair.

IN BRIEF

This section gives you a taste of the trail. Think of this as a snapshot focused on the historical landmarks, beautiful vistas, and other sights you may encounter on the hike.

The information in the key at-a-glance boxes gives you a quick idea of the statistics and specifics of each hike.

LENGTH This indicates the length of the trail from start to finish (total distance traveled). There may be options to shorten or extend the hikes, but the mileage corresponds to the described hike. Consult the hike description to help you decide how to customize the hike for your ability or time constraints.

CONFIGURATION This information tells you what the trail might look like from overhead. Trails can be loops, out-and-backs (trails on which one enters and leaves along the same path), figure eights, or a combination of shapes.

DIFFICULTY The degree of effort an average hiker should expect on a given hike is provided here. For simplicity, the trails are rated as easy, moderate, or difficult.

SCENERY This short summary gives an overview of the attractions offered by the hike and what to expect in terms of plant life, wildlife, natural wonders, and historic features.

EXPOSURE A quick check of how much sun you can expect on your shoulders during the hike helps you plan when to go and what to wear.

TRAFFIC How busy is the trail on an average day? Trail traffic, of course, varies from day to day and season to season. Weekend days typically see the most visitors. This part tells you what kinds of other trail users may be encountered on the way.

TRAIL SURFACE The path may be paved, rocky, gravel, dirt, boardwalk, or a mixture of elements.

HIKING TIME You'll want to know how long it takes to hike the trail. A slow but steady hiker will average 2 to 3 miles an hour, depending on the terrain.

ACCESS A notation of any fees or permits that may be needed to access the trail or park at the trailhead is given here.

If you plan to do a lot of hiking, consider buying a Texas State Parks Pass, which will waive the daily entrance fee to the state parks and historic sites within the state, allowing pass holders unlimited free access. The annual pass costs $60 for a one-card membership, or $75 for a two-card membership (with the stipulation that both pass holders live at the same residence), and allows everyone in the vehicle admittance. If you do not have a State Parks Pass, you will need to pay the daily entrance fee, which varies from park to park (most within 60 miles of Dallas/Fort Worth cost $5). Passes can be purchased at the visitor centers at most state parks. Folks aged 65 and older, and veterans, may be eligible for reduced or free entry. For more information on the Texas State Parks Pass, visit **www.tpwd.state.tx.us/spdest/parkinfo/passes.**

MOST OF THE PARKS I've listed that are operated by the Army Corps of Engineers do not require any admission or parking fees, but most city parks offering recreation areas, such as camping, boating, and picnicking, typically do have a small entrance fee.

MAPS Here you'll find a list of maps that show the topography of the trail, including Green Trails Maps and USGS topo maps.

FACILITIES This lets you know what to expect in terms of restrooms and water at the trailhead or nearby.

DIRECTIONS

Used in conjunction with the overview map, the driving directions will help you locate each trailhead. Once at the trailhead, park only in designated areas.

GPS TRAILHEAD COORDINATES

The trailhead coordinates can be used in addition to the driving directions if you enter the coordinates into your GPS unit before you set out. See page 2 for more information on GPS coordinates.

DESCRIPTION

The trail description describes the heart of each hike. Here, the author provides a summary of the trail's essence and highlights any special traits the hike has to offer. The route is clearly outlined, including landmarks, side trips, and possible alternate routes. Ultimately, the hike description will help you choose which hikes are best for you.

NEARBY ACTIVITIES

Look here for information on activities or points of interest in the area. Sites might include nearby parks, museums, restaurants, or even a brew pub where you can get a well-deserved beer after a long hike. Note that not every hike has a listing.

WEATHER

There is an old saying – "If you don't like the weather, wait 5 minutes, it'll change"— and nowhere is that more true than in North Texas. You can find yourself wearing a winter jacket one day, and shorts the next—or be dismayed by severe thunderstorms with lightning, thunder, and heavy rain wreaking havoc on your day, only to find the sun shining only an hour later. In April of 2007, snow showers sprinkled the Dallas area—uncommon for winter there, and even rarer in spring; of course, five minutes later, they were gone. But there are month-to-month trends, of course.

Winters are usually mild, with average daily temperatures in the 50s during December and January. Occasionally, much colder weather sets in, and you'll have a few days of below-freezing temperatures. Although winter storms rarely bring snow, a few times each year storms combine with overnight freezing temperatures to cause black ice to form on roads and bridges, temporarily immobilizing the city. The coldest month of the year is January, with temperatures rising around 7 to 8 degrees each subsequent month before finally peaking in July, the hottest month of the year.

Spring peaks around mid-April, when Texas's favorite wildflower—the bluebonnet— blankets highway medians, parks, and undeveloped fields. Daytime temperatures during this time are typically in the high 70s, and it's not uncommon for showers and severe thunderstorms to threaten at least a couple of days a week. In conjunction with the storms, threats of tornados also increase in the spring.

Summers are typically hot, with temperatures in the 90s and include an average of two weeks when readings are above 100—typically during July and August.

Average Temperature by Month

	Jan	Feb	Mar	Apr	May	Jun
High	55°	61°	69°	77°	84°	92°
Low	36°	41°	49°	56°	65°	73°

	Jul	Aug	Sep	Oct	Nov	Dec
High	96°	96°	89°	79°	66°	57°
Low	77°	76°	69°	58°	47°	39°

WATER

How much is enough? Well, one simple physiological fact should convince you to err on the side of excess when deciding how much water to pack: A hiker working hard in 90-degree heat needs approximately 10 quarts of fluid per day. That's 2.5 gallons—12 large water bottles, or 16 small ones. In other words, pack along one or two bottles, even for short hikes.

Some hikers and backpackers hit the trail prepared to purify water found along the route. This method, while less dangerous than drinking it untreated, comes with risks. Purifiers with ceramic filters are the safest. Many hikers pack the slightly distasteful tetraglycine-hydroperiodide tablets (sold under the names Potable Aqua, Coughlan's, and others) to debug water.

Probably the most common waterborne bug hikers face is giardia, which may not hit until one to four weeks after ingestion. It will have you living in the bathroom, passing noxious rotten-egg gas, vomiting, and shivering with chills. Other parasites to worry about include E coli and cryptosporidium, both of which are harder to kill than giardia.

For most people, the pleasures of hiking make carrying water a relatively minor price to pay to remain healthy. If you're tempted to drink found water, do so only if you understand the risks involved. Better yet, hydrate before your hike, carry (and drink) six ounces of water for every mile you plan to hike, and hydrate after the hike.

CLOTHING

The most important thing to remember is that you want to be comfortable on the trail, and being comfortable—especially in Texas, where temperatures can be extreme—means keeping yourself cool in summer and warm in winter. In warmer weather, a cotton T-shirt and shorts are great for urban hikes; cargo shorts are popular for their loose, comfortable fit. If you'll be in the grasslands or woodlands, consider opting for a pair of hiking pants; they'll protect your legs from ticks and snakes commonly found in these areas. You can find lightweight, quick-drying, UV-protective pants at many outdoors shops; these will keep you suitably cool. Consider a pair that converts into shorts so you can unzip them when you're done with the trail.

Hiking in cooler weather brings its own set of problems because even though it might be cold out, after a little exertion, you'll find yourself sweating. Layering is a good solution and an important part of keeping you comfortable. Wear a T-shirt or, better yet, a moisture-wicking shirt under your clothes, and top it with a lightweight fleece or sweater. In winter, wear an outer jacket. It's more than likely you'll find yourself taking off and putting on layers throughout the hike.

Year-round you'll want to be sure you have a good pair of hiking shoes. Day hikers are a great choice for most North Texas trails. They come in both low-top and high-top and are lightweight but have good tread and support. Tennis shoes are suitable for any of the paved trails but are not ideal for the dirt paths. A hat is an essential at any time of year and not only keeps the hot Texas sun from burning your face but also doubles as protection against insects and low-hanging limbs. Another useful item is a rain jacket that can be compressed small enough to be stuffed in your pack; if you're caught out in the rain, you'll be thankful for it.

THE TEN ESSENTIALS

One of the first rules of hiking is to be prepared for anything. The simplest way to be prepared is to carry the Ten Essentials. In addition to carrying the items listed below, you need to know how to use them, especially navigation items. Always consider worst-case scenarios like getting lost, hiking back in the dark, breaking gear (for example, a broken hip strap on your pack or a plugged water filter), twisting an ankle, or weathering a brutal thunderstorm. The items listed below don't cost a lot of money, don't take up much room in a pack, and don't weigh much, but they might just save your life.

Water: durable bottles, and water treatment like iodine or a filter
Map: preferably a topo map and a trail map with a route description
Compass: a high-quality compass
First-aid kit: a good-quality kit including first-aid instructions
Knife: a multitool device with pliers is best
Light: flashlight or headlamp with extra bulbs and batteries
Fire: windproof matches or lighter and fire starter
Extra food: you should always have food in your pack when you've finished hiking
Extra clothes: rain protection, warm layers, gloves, warm hat
Sun protection: sunglasses, lip balm, sunblock, sun hat

FIRST-AID KIT

A typical first-aid kit may contain more items than you might think necessary. These are just the basics. Prepackaged kits in waterproof bags (Atwater Carey and Adventure Medical make a variety of kits) are available. Even though there are quite a few items listed here, they pack into a small space.

Ace bandages or Spenco joint wraps
Antibiotic ointment (Neosporin or the generic equivalent)
Aspirin or acetaminophen
Band-Aids
Benadryl or the generic equivalent, diphenhydramine (in case of allergic reactions)
Butterfly-closure bandages
Epinephrine in a prefilled syringe (for people known to have severe allergic reactions to such things as bee stings)
Gauze (one roll)
Gauze compress pads (a half dozen 4 x 4-inch pads)
Hydrogen peroxide or iodine
Insect repellent
Matches or pocket lighter
Moleskin/Spenco "Second Skin"
Sunscreen
Whistle (it's more effective in signaling rescuers than your voice is)

HIKING WITH CHILDREN

No one is too young for a hike in the outdoors. Be mindful, though. Flat, short, and shaded trails are best for infants. Toddlers who have not quite mastered walking can still tag along, riding on an adult's back in a child carrier. Use common sense to judge a child's capacity to hike a particular trail and always expect that the child will tire quickly and need to be carried. A list of hikes suitable for children is provided on **page xiv.**

When packing for the hike, remember the child's needs in addition to your own. Make sure children are adequately clothed for the weather, have proper shoes, and are protected from the sun with sunscreen. Kids dehydrate quickly, so make sure you have plenty of fluid for everyone.

GENERAL SAFETY

While many folks hit the trails full of enthusiasm and energy, eager to begin their adventures, others may find themselves more reserved about potential outdoor hazards. Although potentially dangerous situations can occur anywhere, as long as you use sound judgment and prepare yourself before hitting the trail, your hike will be as safe and enjoyable as you hoped. Here are a few tips to make your trip safer and easier.

- **Hike with a buddy. Not only is there safety in numbers, but a buddy can help you if you twist an ankle on the trail, help if you get lost, assist in carrying lunch and water, and be there to share in your discoveries. If you're hiking alone, be sure you've left your hiking itinerary with a friend or relative. It's best to bring a buddy not only to infrequently traveled or remote areas but also to urban areas.**

- **Stay hydrated. North Texas heat can be brutal, and a little exertion can quickly have you sweating. Don't wait until you feel thirsty, instead drink plenty of water throughout the hike, and at regular intervals.**

- **Always carry food and water, whether you are planning to go overnight or not. Food will give you energy, help keep you warm, and sustain you in an emergency until help arrives. You never know if you will have a stream nearby when you become thirsty. Bring potable water or treat water before drinking it from a stream. Boil or filter all found water before drinking it.**

- **Stay on designated trails. Most hikers get lost when they leave the path. Even on the most clearly marked trails, there is usually a point where you have to stop and consider in which direction to head. If you become disoriented, don't panic. As soon as you think you may be off track, stop, assess your current direction, and then retrace your steps to the point where you went astray. Using a map, compass, and this book, and keeping in mind what you have passed thus far, reorient yourself, and trust your judgment on which way to continue. If you become absolutely unsure of how to continue, return to your vehicle the way you came in. Should you become completely** lost and have no idea of how to return to the trailhead, staying where you are and waiting for help is most often the best option for adults and always the best option for children.

- Be especially careful when crossing streams. Whether you are fording the stream or crossing on a log, make every step count. If you have any doubt about maintaining your balance on a foot log, go ahead and ford the stream instead. When fording a stream, use a trekking pole or stout stick for balance and face upstream as you cross. If a stream seems too deep to ford, turn back. Whatever is on the other side is not worth risking your life.

- Be careful at overlooks. While these areas may provide spectacular views, they are potentially hazardous. Stay back from the edge of outcrops, and be absolutely sure of your footing; a misstep can mean a nasty and possibly fatal fall.

- Standing dead trees and storm-damaged living trees pose a real hazard to hikers and tent campers. These trees may have loose or broken limbs that could fall at any time. When choosing a spot to rest or spend the night, look up.

- Know the symptoms of heat exhaustion. Excessive sweating, faintness or dizziness, clammy skin, vomiting, and paleness are all common symptoms. If symptoms arise, cool the person off by removing extra clothing, moving them to the shade, and hydrating them.

- Know the symptoms of hypothermia. Shivering and forgetfulness are the two most common indicators of this insidious killer. Hypothermia can occur at any elevation, even in the summer, especially when the hiker is wearing lightweight cotton clothing. If symptoms arise, get the victim shelter, administer hot liquids, and dress them in dry clothes or a dry sleeping bag.

- Take along your brain. A cool, calculating mind is the single most important piece of equipment you'll ever need on the trail. Think before you act. Watch your step. Plan ahead. Avoiding accidents before they happen is the best strategy for a rewarding and relaxing hike.

- Ask questions. Visitor center and park employees are there to help. It's a lot easier to get advice beforehand than to have a mishap away from civilization when it's too late to amend an error. Use your head on the trail and treat each area as if it were your own backyard.

ANIMAL AND PLANT HAZARDS

TICKS

Ticks like to hang out in the brush that grows along trails. Hot summer months seem to explode their numbers, but you should be tick-aware all months of the year. Ticks, which are arthropods and not insects, need a host to feast on in order to reproduce. The ticks that light onto you while you hike will be very small, sometimes so tiny that you won't be able to spot them. Primarily of two varieties, deer ticks and dog ticks, both need a few hours of attachment before they can transmit

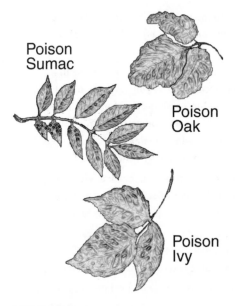

Poison
Sumac

Poison
Oak

Poison
Ivy

any disease they may harbor. Ticks may settle in shoes, socks, or hats, and may take several hours to latch on. The best strategy is to visually check every half hour or so while hiking, do a thorough check before you get in the car, and then, when you take a post-hike shower, do an even more thorough check of your entire body. Ticks that haven't attached are easily removed but not easily killed. If you pick off a tick in the woods, just toss it aside. If you find one on your body at home, kill it and then send it down the toilet. For ticks that have embedded, removal with tweezers is best.

SNAKES

The majority of the snakes you might encounter on your hikes are nonvenomous and pose no threat to humans. Many folks even consider the most common snake in the area—the Texas rat snake—a welcome visitor. This snake, as its name implies, feasts on rats and rodents; and though it may rear and act defensive if you antagonize it, its bite is harmless. Of the more than three dozen types of snakes in the area, only a handful of them are venomous, the most common of these being the cottonmouth and the copperhead. On many of the trails, you'll spot signs warning that you're in a snake habitat. As long as you stay on the trail and out of tall grasses, however, you're unlikely to have a problem. In fact, of the 60 hikes here, I've only met a snake on the trail two or three times, and those encounters were uneventful and brief.

POISON IVY/POISON OAK/
POISON SUMAC

Recognizing poison ivy, oak, and sumac and avoiding contact with them is the most effective way to prevent the painful, itchy rashes associated with these plants. In the South, poison ivy ranges from a thick, tree-hugging vine to a shaded groundcover, three leaflets to a leaf; poison oak occurs as either a vine or shrub, with three leaflets as well; and poison sumac flourishes in swampland, each leaf containing 7 to 13 leaflets. Urushiol, the oil in the sap of these plants, is responsible for the rash. Usually within 12 to 14 hours of exposure (but sometimes much later), raised lines and/or blisters will appear, accompanied by a terrible itch. Refrain from scratching because bacteria under fingernails can cause infection and you will spread the rash to other parts of your body. Wash and dry the rash thoroughly, applying a calamine lotion or other product to help dry the rash. If itching or blistering is severe, seek medical attention. Remember that oil-contaminated clothes, pets, or hiking gear can easily cause an irritating rash on you or someone else, so wash not only any exposed parts of your body but also clothes, gear, and pets.

MOSQUITOES

Although it's not a common occurrence, individuals can become infected with the West Nile virus by being bitten by an infected mosquito. Culex mosquitoes, the primary varieties that can transmit West Nile virus to humans, thrive in urban rather than natural areas. They lay their eggs in stagnant water and can breed in any standing water that remains for more than five days. Most people infected with West Nile virus have no symptoms of illness, but some may become ill, usually 3 to 15 days after being bitten.

In the Dallas/Fort Worth metroplex, the summer months—especially August and September—bring mosquitoes and with them the highest risk for West Nile virus. Mosquitoes are especially prevalent on trails with tall grasses, in marshy/swampy areas, and around dusk and dawn. Anytime you expect mosquitoes to be buzzing around, you may want to wear protective clothing, such as long sleeves, long pants, and socks. Loose-fitting, light-colored clothing is best. Spray clothing with insect repellent. The Centers for Disease Control and Prevention (CDC) notes that repellents that contain the active ingredients DEET or Picardin supply the best protection; they also suggest oil of lemon eucalyptus as an effective plant-based repellent. Remember to follow the instructions on the repellent and to take extra care with children. Within the past few years, insect-repellent clothing, available at most outdoor retailer shops, is another source of protection against mosquitoes and other bothersome insects.

TIPS FOR ENJOYING DALLAS AND FORT WORTH

If you plan on hiking in one of the state parks, Army Corps of Engineers sites, or national grasslands, visit their corresponding Web site for information to help you get oriented to the roads, features, and attractions of where you're going. General and detailed maps of the specific wilderness areas are often available online or, if visiting a state park, at the park office. In addition, the following tips will make your visit enjoyable and more rewarding.

- **Be sure you get out of your car and onto a trail. Auto touring allows a cursory overview of the area but only visually. On the trail you can use your ears and nose as well. Even if you don't use the trails recommended in this guidebook, any trail is better than no trail at all.**

- **North Texas summers can be brutally hot, making a day hike in late July or August seemingly impossible. If there's a nice day and you don't want to miss out on hiking because of the heat, go early in the morning. If you're on the trail at dawn, you can find temperatures 10–20 degrees lower than they'll be later in the day, and there's no better way to start your day than listening to the cheerful singing of birds along the trail.**

- Take your time along the trails. Pace yourself. North Texas is filled with wonders both big and small. Don't rush past a tiny lizard to get to that overlook. Stop and smell the wildflowers. Peer into a clear creek for minnows. Don't miss the trees for the forest. Shorter hikes allow you to stop and linger more than long hikes do. Something about staring at the front end of a 10-mile trek naturally pushes you to speed up. That said, take close notice of the elevation maps that accompany each hike. If you see many ups and downs over large altitude changes, you'll obviously need more time. Inevitably, you'll finish some of the hikes more or less quickly than the estimated time. Nevertheless, leave yourself plenty of time for those moments when you simply feel like stopping and taking it all in.

- We can't always schedule our free time when we want, but try to hike during the week and avoid the traditional holidays, if possible. Trails that are packed in the spring and fall are often clear during the hotter or colder months. If you are hiking on a busy day, go early in the morning; it'll enhance your chances of seeing wildlife. The trails really clear out during rainy times; however, don't hike during a thunderstorm.

- Investigate different areas around the metroplex. The scenery you'll find hiking through meadows and grasslands is pleasantly different from the riparian forest alongside a fork of the Trinity River or lakeside water views. Sample a few of each to see what the area has to offer and what most appeals to you.

- Hike during different seasons. Trails change dramatically from spring to winter, and can transform themselves into something you might not even recognize. If you found a trail you particularly liked—or didn't—try it in a different season.

TOPO MAPS

The maps in this book have been produced with great care and, used with the hiking directions, will direct you to the trail and help you stay on course. However, you will find superior detail and valuable information in the United States Geological Survey's 7.5-minute series topographic maps. Topo maps are available online in many locations. A well-known free service is at **www.terraserver.micro soft.com** and another free service with fast click-and-drag browsing is at **www .topofinder.com.** You can view and print topos of the entire United States from these Web sites and view aerial photographs of the same area at terraserver. Several online services, such as **www.trails.com,** charge annual fees for additional features such as shaded-relief, which makes the topography stand out more. If you expect to print out many topo maps each year, it might be worth paying for shaded-relief topo maps. The downside to USGS topos is that most of them are outdated, having been created 20 to 30 years ago. But they still provide excellent topographic detail.

Digital topographic map programs, such as Delorme's TopoUSA, enable you to review topo maps of the entire United States on your PC. You can download data gathered while hiking with a GPS unit onto the software and plot your own hikes.

If you're new to hiking, you might be wondering, "What's a topographic map?" In short, a topo indicates not only linear distance but elevation as well, using contour lines. Contour lines spread across the map like dozens of intricate spider webs. Each line represents a particular elevation, and at the base of each topo, a contour's interval designation is given. If the contour interval is 20 feet, then the distance between each contour line is 20 feet. Follow five contour lines up on the same map, and the elevation has increased by 1,00 feet.

Let's assume that the 7.5-minute series topo reads "Contour Interval 40 feet," and that the short trail we'll be hiking is two inches long on the map and crosses five contour lines from beginning to end. What do we know? Well, because the linear scale of this series is 2,000 feet to the inch (roughly 2.75 inches representing 1 mile), we know our trail is approximately .8 miles long (2 inches equals 2,000 feet). But we also know we'll be climbing or descending 200 vertical feet because there are five contour lines and each is 40 feet. And the elevation designations written on occasional contour lines will tell us if we're heading up or down.

In addition to the outdoor shops listed in the Appendix, you'll find topos at major universities and in some public libraries; you might try photocopying the ones you need to avoid the cost of buying them. But if you want your own and can't find them locally, visit the United States Geological Survey Web site at **topomaps .usgs.gov.**

BACKCOUNTRY/PRIMITIVE CAMPING ADVICE

Backcountry/primitive camping is available in the LBJ National Grasslands and in many state parks and wildlife-management areas. Practice low-impact camping and adhere to the adages "Pack it in, pack it out," and "Take only pictures, leave only footprints." Practice "leave no trace" camping ethics while in the backcountry. Some backcountry areas are also public hunting areas, so be sure to research your destination before your visit.

Solid human waste should be buried in a hole at least three inches deep and at least 200 feet away from trails and water sources; a trowel is basic backpacking equipment.

Rules on open fires vary depending on where you go, so you'll want to check before your visit; when collecting firewood, many places ask you to collect downed wood instead of chopping branches. In addition, Texas State Parks allow fires only in fire rings, fireplaces, and campsite grills. Burn bans, especially during drought periods, can restrict fires—including those at campsite grills. Be sure to double-check before your trip because state parks may or may not be affected by a county-wide burn ban.

A fishing license is required if you plan to fish. You can get one from many outdoor retailers, sports stores, and bait and tackle shops, online, or over the phone. Visit the Texas Parks and Wildlife Web site **www.tpwd.state.tx.us** for information on regulations, fees, permits, and how to purchase.

Following the above guidelines will increase your chances of having a pleasant, safe, and low-impact interaction with nature. The suggestions are intended to enhance your experience. Regulations can change over time; contact the appropriate park office to confirm the status of any regulations before you enter the backcountry.

TRAIL ETIQUETTE

Whether you're on a city, county, state, or national park trail, always remember that great care and resources (from both nature and your tax dollars) have gone into creating these trails. Treat the trail, wildlife, and fellow hikers with respect.

- **Hike on open trails only. Respect trail and road closures (ask if not sure), avoid possible trespassing on private land, and obtain all permits and authorizations required. Also, leave gates as you found them or as marked.**

- **Leave only footprints. Be sensitive to the ground beneath you. This also means staying on the existing trail and not blazing new trails. Be sure to pack out what you pack in. No one likes to see the trash someone else has left behind.**

- **Never spook animals. An unannounced approach, a sudden movement, or a loud noise startles most animals. A surprised animal can be dangerous to you, to others, and to themselves. Give them plenty of space.**

- **Plan ahead. Know your equipment, your ability, and the area in which you are hiking—and prepare accordingly. Be self-sufficient at all times; carry necessary supplies for changes in weather or other conditions. A well-executed trip is a satisfaction to you and to others.**

- **Be courteous to other hikers, bikers, equestrians, and anyone else you encounter on the trails.**

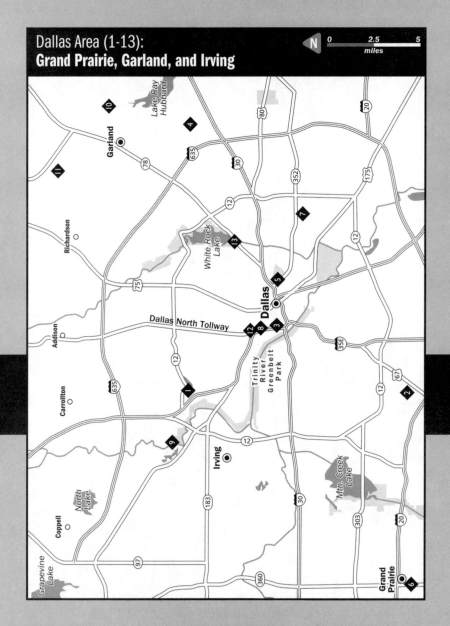

Dallas Area (1-13):
Grand Prairie, Garland, and Irving

N

0   2.5   5
miles

Lake Ray Hubbard

10

4

80

20

Garland

635

78

30

352

175

12

7

12

Richardson

White Rock Lake

13

75

5

Dallas

Dallas North Tollway

12   8   3

35E

Addison

12

67

635

Trinity River Greenbelt Park

12   2

Carrollton

1

9

Irving

12

Mtn. Creek Lake

North Lake

183

30

303   20

Coppell

97

360

Grand Prairie   6

Grapevine Lake

DALLAS AREA (INCLUDING GRAND PRAIRIE, GARLAND, AND IRVING)

01 BACHMAN LAKE TRAIL

KEY AT-A-GLANCE INFORMATION

LENGTH: 3.23 miles
CONFIGURATION: Loop
DIFFICULTY: Easy
SCENERY: Lake
EXPOSURE: Sunny
TRAIL TRAFFIC: Heavy
TRAIL SURFACE: Paved
HIKING TIME: 1 hour 20 minutes
ACCESS: Daily; free
FACILITIES: Restrooms, picnic tables, playground, water fountains
WHEELCHAIR TRAVERSABLE: Yes
SPECIAL COMMENTS: An airport runway nearby is slightly distracting; bring headphones.

IN BRIEF

This hike winds around the perimeter of a small lake in the heart of Dallas that is popular with joggers and others. The setting is open, with mowed grass interspersed with trees, making this a very sunny trail. Without doubt you'll spot at least a few ducks and possibly egrets or herons wading to the lake edge.

DESCRIPTION

Just a stone's throw from Dallas's Love Field airport, the 205-acre Bachman Lake sits in an area that in the 1840s used to be farmland owned by the Bachman Brothers. The lake was created in 1903 by damming a portion of Bachman's Creek to use it as a reservoir for Dallas. The larger White Rock Lake (about four times Bachman's size), however, took over this duty, leaving Bachman for recreation.

Today, the lake sits in a commercial area along Northwest Highway. Although it's not the most scenic spot, the trail encircling the lake is well maintained, and provides a nice day hike for city dwellers. Because of its rather plain shoreline and shorter length, it's not as popular as the nearby White Rock Lake, which also has a trail. It is, however, frequented by nearby residents, especially families, kids, and couples who find the short loop around the

GPS Trailhead Coordinates

UTM Zone (WGS84) 14S
Easting   699272
Northing   3637006
Latitude   N 32° 51' 11"
Longitude W 96° 52' 14"

Directions ———————→

Bachman Lake is located just east of Texas Stadium. From I-35E toward Denton, you'll exit Harry Hines Boulevard. Immediately bear right on Webb Chapel Ext, and after 0.5 miles turn right onto Northwest Highway. Turn right onto Bachman Drive, and park in the lot next to the playground.

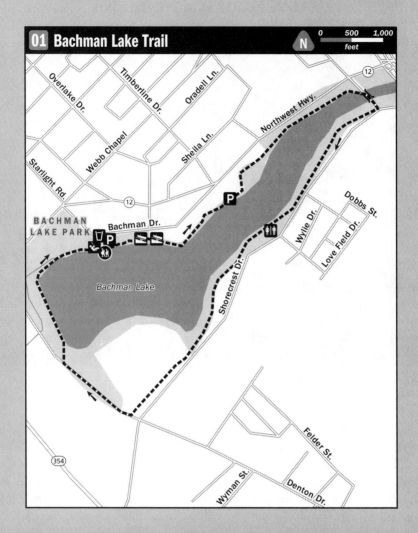

01 Bachman Lake Trail

N

0   500   1,000
feet

Overlake Dr.

Timberline Dr.

Oradell Ln.

Webb Chapel

Sheila Ln.

Starlight Rd.

Northwest Hwy.

12

12

P

Dobbs St.

BACHMAN
LAKE PARK

Bachman Dr.

P

Wylie Dr.

Love Field Dr.

Bachman Lake

Shorecrest Dr.

Felder St.

354

Wyman St.

Denton Dr.

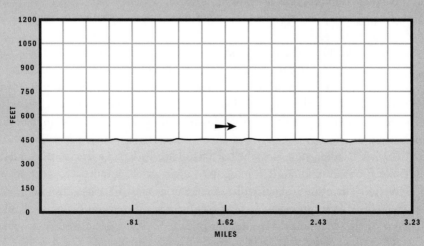

An exercise station abutting Bachman Lake

lake an easy and fun one to tackle on a weekend outing. Exercise stations on the southeastern shoreline also attract a few people.

The trailhead is located adjacent to the busy fenced-in playground next to the recreation center and parking lot. Just ahead of you, the sun glints off the lake's dark waters. From this vantage point, the lake looks very small—the grassy slopes of the opposite side within clear view. As you turn left onto the trail and head northeast rounding the first curve, however, you'll notice that it's actually slightly bigger than you first thought—continuing northeast in a narrow band as far as you can see.

As you head down the trail, keep an eye out for ducks congregating in the shade around a grove of bald cypress trees growing along the shoreline. Ducks like to nestle into the roots of the trees, which grow up out of the water to form knobs or "knees." On the left, you'll see a park with picnic tables and barbecue pits, which is often busy. A little farther down, some shaded benches complete the park setting.

Continue heading along past the Bachman Lake Park picnic area at 0.75 miles. You're likely to hear loud music coming from open-air restaurants across the street off to the left. The noise is slightly distracting but actually fits right into the urban vibe of the hike. Even the seagulls, of which there are dozens on the grassy banks off to your right, seem unfazed by the ever-present rumbling of the nearby cars and music. The noise fades into the background as you continue on.

At 1 mile, you'll bear right and cross the bridge to reach the other side of the lake, where, farther from Northwest Highway, you'll find it much quieter. Across the bridge, turn right, following the trail southwest. Off to your left is a secondary road that leads to parking places. Just across the road, behind an embankment, is Love Field airport; you will undoubtedly already have seen the planes rising low over the lake after takeoff. Keep an eye out for herons and egrets standing quietly in the shallow waters on the shoreline. Signs placed along the banks discourage feeding the abundant birdlife—birds can pose a risk to landing aircraft.

As you continue, you'll pass a few exercise stations placed at regular intervals along both sides of the trail. The stations are put to good use, and I noticed a couple of folks jogging and biking between them. Unfortunately, none of them include instructions, so although the purpose of some is clearly identifiable (such as log-hops or pull-up bars), the use of others is lost to many.

The trail climbs slightly. On the skyline just beyond the lake, you'll have a good view of Texas Stadium in the distance. At 2 miles, you'll reach a shady picnic area beneath a grove of huge old trees. To your left, you'll see a hangar for Southwest Airlines. To your right, just beyond the picnic area, is the boathouse for the Dallas Rowing Club. You'll probably already have noticed some of its members sculling or sweep rowing on the lake.

From here, the trail bends away from the lake for 4 miles. Follow it along the sidewalk as it winds in front of the Bachman Water Treatment Plant. It then curves northwest along Denton Drive and past a small electric grid before rejoining the lake again at 2.7 miles. From here, you'll cross the dam, which forms the lake's western side. At the far end, the trail bears back to the northeast. You'll pass a couple of recreational buildings used by the YMCA, and reach the playground to complete the loop.

NEARBY ACTIVITIES

Just 8 miles away, the Dallas World Aquarium includes more than 85,000 gallons of saltwater displays, a walk-through tunnel, and exhibits on the Mayan world, South Africa, and the rainforest. For hours and fees, visit their Web site at **www .dwazoo.com**. To get there, take I-35E south 6 miles, then take Exit 429A (I-45/US 75) toward Houston. Take the Griffin Street exit. The aquarium is at 1801 North Griffin Street.

02 BOULDER PARK TRAIL

**KEY AT-A-GLANCE
INFORMATION**

LENGTH: 2.26 miles
CONFIGURATION: Loop
DIFFICULTY: Easy
SCENERY: Woodlands
EXPOSURE: Sunny
TRAIL TRAFFIC: Moderate
TRAIL SURFACE: Dirt
HIKING TIME: 50 minutes
ACCESS: Daily; free
FACILITIES: None
WHEELCHAIR TRAVERSABLE: No
**SPECIAL COMMENTS: Do not park in
the church parking lot.**

IN BRIEF

A fun hike that twists and turns haphazardly through dense, shaded woodland. Many junctions provide ample opportunity for exploring, and color-coded trails prevent you from getting too lost.

DESCRIPTION

I am always wary of hikes with no established parking; because of their awkward locations, they are often overly wild and little used, not to mention overgrown and unkempt—or sometimes even closed. So it was with some skepticism that I finally visited Boulder Park, only to be pleasantly surprised with a well maintained and clearly labeled trail network. Even better, the trail is quite pretty—offering a few deeply wooded sections that are especially lovely in the springtime, when everything is green. The park was purchased in 1967 by the city of Dallas and is located near Red Bird Airport, north of Duncanville. It's maintained by DORBA—the Dallas Off Road Bicycle Association—which has built about 6 miles of trails through its woodlands.

As previously mentioned, there is no lot to park at, so you'll have to jockey for position on one of the side streets that fill up on Sunday with churchgoers' cars. It's easy to spot the

GPS Trailhead Coordinates

UTM Zone (WGS84) 14S
Easting   699344
Northing   3616578
Latitude   N 32° 40' 8"
Longitude   W 96° 52' 27"

Directions ⟶

Boulder Park is adjacent to Dallas's Executive Airport, just north of Duncanville. To get there, take US 67, and exit west onto Red Bird Lane, then turn south onto Pastor Bailey Drive. The trailhead is located opposite the small side street Hallett Avenue, and usually has a clustering of cars parked along the street near it. There is no parking lot.

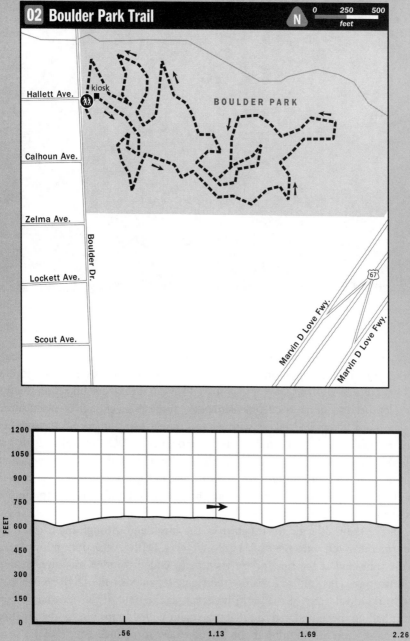

Hand-painted signs mark trail junctures.

folks who are here visiting the trail; they tend to cluster together a few car lengths away from the churchgoers and are easily identifiable by their bike racks. Although this is a favorite DORBA spot, and you are likely to meet some bikers on the trail, don't let this discourage you from visiting; the trail is long enough to easily accommodate both hikers and bikers without too much inconvenience for either. The only downfall of this trail—and this is common among DORBA trails—is that the trail sometimes loops around itself pointlessly (for hikers), this feature being aimed more at mountain bikers who enjoy the twists and turns. Once you get into the woods, you may actually appreciate this, however, as it adds mileage and interest to the route.

From the trailhead, go straight past the kiosk and through the break in the trees then turn left onto the trail. In recent years, DORBA has done a lot of work on the trail, and at the time of my visit, color-coded wooden trail signs marked the junctions. This trail follows the red signs. If you visit the DORBA Web site, you'll find a trail map of the park; however, at the time of this writing, I found that it had not been updated to reflect the color-coded loops nor all the junctions you'll pass. Keep this in mind if you intend to use it to guide you.

Heading down the path, you'll immediately enter the woods. Above you, the trees have intertwined their limbs, welcoming you into a tunnel-like entrance. A couple of small clearings are interspersed throughout the trail, and you'll soon leave the woods and enter the first of these, where cactus dots the open ground.

Be aware that DORBA has been combining and rerouting some of the older trails within the park, and you're likely to pass at least a couple of junctions that have been blocked off with branches and rocks. Just keep your eye out and bypass any that have been closed.

As you head back into a grove of hardwood trees, the trail twists and turns a few times. The ground is relatively flat in this section, but as you continue, the terrain changes and you'll encounter a couple of small up and downs—nothing extensive, just enough to give the trail some interest.

At the next junction, go right, following the red arrow. The woods grow thickly around you, and though you're near the road (which you'll hear faintly, just beneath the bird calls and leaves rustling, if you listen closely), you'll have no idea in which direction it is, thanks to the dense wood cover. Turn right at 0.82 miles. You'll head slightly uphill then back west away from the back perimeter of the park. At the next junction, continue straight; the woods part to welcome a couple of small grassy fields dotted with yellow and white wildflowers before enveloping you once again. Go straight to get back into the woods, then right at 1.62 miles, continuing to follow the red signs. The trail winds down a small rocky hill and enters a pocket of woods where the trees tower high above, sheltering an understory of shrubs and saplings. The ground, rich with the remains of bark and leaves, becomes soft and cushy, making a comfortable path.

Continue straight at 1.8 miles. The trees become shorter and thinner, until they finally break and you find yourself once again in a cactus- and tree-dotted grassy clearing. No longer soft and welcoming, the ground has changed with the scenery, hardening into a white-chalky mixture that reflects the sunlight. At 2.1 miles, bear right, following the blue arrow. You'll wind back into the woods, and soon the sounds of the roadway will become audible. A few hundred feet farther, you'll finally reach the western boundary fence of the park. Turn left to follow the trail just alongside the fence and back south to the trailhead.

NEARBY ACTIVITIES

Just down the street on Camp Wisdom Road, you can do some retail shopping in the Southwest Center Mall (AKA Red Bird Mall), whose anchoring department stores include Dillard's, Macy's, and the Burlington Coat Factory. A brand new mall in nearby Cedar Hill, called the Uptown Village at Cedar Hill, is set to open in March 2008 and will be a big attraction as well. To get to Southwest Center Mall, head south on US 67, then turn right onto Camp Wisdom Road. Cedar Hill is another 7 miles south on US 67.

03 **DOWNTOWN DALLAS URBAN TRAIL**

 KEY AT-A-GLANCE INFORMATION

LENGTH: 3.08 miles
CONFIGURATION: Loop
DIFFICULTY: Easy
SCENERY: Historic landmarks, cityscape, bronze statues, fountains
EXPOSURE: Sunny
TRAIL TRAFFIC: Light
TRAIL SURFACE: Paved
HIKING TIME: 2 hours
ACCESS: Free
FACILITIES: None
WHEELCHAIR TRAVERSABLE: No
SPECIAL COMMENTS: You won't need to feed the meters on Sundays.

IN BRIEF

This urban hike beneath the glistening skyscrapers of the Big D combines the walking routes suggested by the city's visitor center into a loop of some of the best points in the downtown jungle. Though you will not see traditional nature sights along the hike, you will be impressed as you trek past urbanized versions, including a herd of cattle stampeding over a brook, a multilevel waterfall, a sculpture garden, and an infamous grassy knoll.

DESCRIPTION

Start your hike in front of the Old Red Courthouse. One of the most recognizable buildings in downtown, the beautiful red sandstone building, built in the late 19th century, also houses the Visitor Information Center. Be sure to stop inside and pick up brochures, pamphlets, and maps of the area. From here, head east on Main Street. At about 150 feet, you'll pass the Kennedy Memorial Plaza, an open grassy space in the center of which sits a huge square monument designed by the architect Philip Johnson and erected in honor of the late president John F. Kennedy. Across the street to the left, construction of an underground parking lot is ongoing; however, once

GPS Trailhead Coordinates

UTM Zone (WGS84) 14S
Easting 705344
Northing 3628934
Latitude N 32° 46' 45"
Longitude W 96° 48' 27"

Directions ————————————➤

Follow I-30 east toward Dallas and take Exit 44 (Industrial Boulevard). Turn left onto Industrial Boulevard and right onto Commerce Street, then continue straight onto Main Street. The Old Red Courthouse is on the right, just in front of Dealey Plaza. Park at any metered spot along the street.

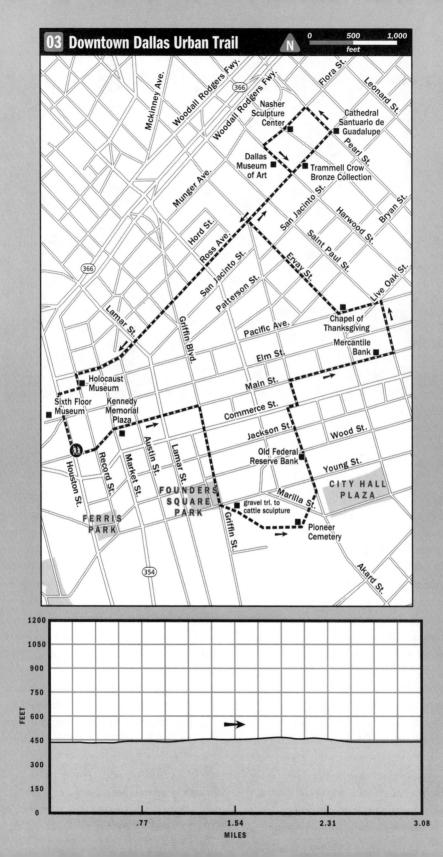

Bronzed sculptures depict a cattle drive in Pioneer Plaza.

it is completed, the John Neely Bryan Cabin, a reconstructed log cabin from Dallas's founder will once again sit on the site.

Cross Market Street, and at about 0.25 miles, just in front of the Bank of America Tower, you'll see the creation of the sculptor Alexander Liberman—a huge, bright-red sculpture of circular tubes stacked atop each other. You'll then reach Griffin Street, where you should turn right, following the road 0.25 miles to the Convention Center District. At 0.53 miles, you'll reach Young Street, where you should turn left and head toward the four-acre grassy hill where the heads of dozens of longhorn cattle are just visible.

Follow the gravel trail toward the steer, which are part of the Pioneer Plaza Cattle Drive, an amazing creation of 70 bronze longhorn cattle being driven down a hill and over a stream by three mounted cowboys. Shawnee Trail, an old route along which cowboys herded cattle in the 1800s, ran near the plaza, which is meant to commemorate this heritage. Continue along the gravel trail, cross the stream, then turn left, heading uphill alongside the cattle. The sculptures are impressive; you can see the veins bulging in their necks, and the muscles rippling beneath their bronze skin. Take a moment to examine the intricately detailed cowboys before continuing back onto the gravel path and toward Pioneer Cemetery.

Turn left onto the short dirt path through the cemetery, which honors Dallas's founders. Many of the names, such as Harwood, Stemmons, and Flynn, have been bestowed on Dallas streets. At about 0.7 miles, the dirt path ends; turn left and cross Marilla Street. Join the sidewalk heading diagonally through a two-acre grassy park that is home to the Dallas Police Memorial. This stainless-steel sculpture is designed to cast shadows on the ground to reveal the badge numbers of fallen officers.

At 0.75 miles, turn left onto Akard Street. To the right, you'll see the U.S., Texas, and city of Dallas flags flying in front of City Hall. To the left is an excellent view of a famous Dallas landmark, Reunion Tower—a 55-story tower topped with a dome in which there is a revolving restaurant and an observation deck. Cross Young Street and follow the tree-lined Akard Street. You'll pass the historic old Federal Reserve Bank on the right. Straight ahead, if you look up you'll see a huge statue of Pegasus resting atop another famous Dallas building, the Magnolia Hotel. The building—and its logo, the winged horse—originally belonged to the Magnolia Petroleum Company and is now listed on the National Register of Historic Places. Across the street, you'll see another ornate and historic old building that has been here since 1912, the Adolphus Hotel.

At about 0.9 miles, Akard ends. Cross the street and head through the brick plaza toward and past the Magnolia. Just beyond some patio tables where folks are enjoying the outdoors, you'll cross Commerce Street and then continue back onto the northern section of Akard Street. Next, turn right onto Main Street. You'll pass Pegasus Plaza on the right, Nieman Marcus at 1.1 miles, and then a skyscraper—the Mercantile Bank building—at 1.18 miles.

Next, turn left onto St. Paul Street. You'll pass the historic old Titche-Goettinger department store. When you reach Elm, look to the right to see the vertical sign of the historic Majestic Theatre, which has been around since the 1920s. Continue one block farther, where you'll head west (left) down Pacific Avenue, and at 1.43 miles, make a right onto Ervay. Thanks-Giving Square, which celebrates the world's thanksgivings, is on the left and is a nice spot for a break. Enjoy the courtyard, the outdoor fountains, and the prominent white spiral tower, which is actually the Chapel of Thanksgiving, inside which you can view a beautiful stained-glass design entitled the "Glory Window."

Continue over the trolley tracks and past the post office, until you reach Ross Avenue, at 1.7 miles. Turn right. On the left, you'll pass the Dallas Museum of Art, fronted by a huge orange–red steel sculpture. A few hundred feet farther down on the left is the Trammell Crow Bronze Collection, dozens of sculptures surrounding a tall office building. Finally, you'll reach the Cathedral Santuario de Guadalupe, a cathedral dating to the 19th century, featuring stained-glass windows and a bell tower housing 49 bells. Turn left just in front of the cathedral onto North Pearl Street, and at 2 miles make another left onto Flora.

Continuing along, you'll see the Nasher Sculpture Center on your right and the Crow Collection of Asian Art on your left, which has a magnificent sculptural waterfall entrance. The road dead-ends in front of the Dallas Museum of Art; turn left onto Harwood. At the next intersection, at 2.18 miles, turn right to get back onto Ross Avenue.

At 2.4 miles, you'll walk past Fountain Place on the right—a prism-shaped skyscraper at the base of which is a waterfall with ledges and pools. This is a nice place to explore, offering a few acres of fountains and waterfalls. Continuing on, you'll cross Lamar Street and then see red-brick buildings, indicating you've reached the West End Historic District, an attractive area of old warehouses that have been converted into stores and restaurants. At 2.83 miles, turn left onto Record Street and pass the Holocaust Museum, then turn right onto Pacific Avenue, following the trolley tracks.

A block down, turn left onto Houston Street. On the right is the former Texas School Book Depository, where on November 22, 1963, Lee Harvey Oswald shot at and killed President John F. Kennedy from its sixth floor. Today, the building houses the Sixth Floor Museum, which harbors exhibits on the life and death of President Kennedy. A few steps farther, and you're at the entrance to Stemmons Freeway, and in the middle of Dealey Plaza, a National Historic Landmark. Here you'll find the infamous grassy knoll, the controversial hill where some theorize another shooter in the Kennedy assassination was hidden. Crowds are always gathered in this spot, reading brochures and pamphlets of the incident. An X in the street marks where the motorcade was at the time of the shooting.

Continuing on, you'll cross the street and find a reflecting pool and a statue honoring George Bannerman Dealey, the Dallas businessman and civic planner after whom the plaza is named. From here, turn left back onto Main Street to reach the trailhead.

NEARBY ACTIVITIES

A few blocks east of downtown, visit Deep Ellum, Dallas's arts and entertainment district, where you can find retail shops selling artsy and unusual items, and an array of restaurants where you can grab a bite to eat. In the evenings, the area is a popular bar and nightclub spot. To get there, head east down Elm Street. Deep Ellum is just past Central Expressway.

DUCK CREEK GREENBELT 04

IN BRIEF

This trail winds through a greenbelt alongside the murky green waters of Duck Creek and is a great hike for bird-watchers.

DESCRIPTION

Part of the Garland Parks and Recreation Department, the Duck Creek Greenbelt cuts a green swath of wilderness through a populated urban area, offering locals a pleasant hike through the woods alongside the creek. I've started this hike on the southeastern end of the greenbelt, although a couple of different parking areas provide alternate access along its length. Adjacent to the parking area, a huge pavilion offering shade and tables is available for rent; contact the parks department. This is not the most scenic hike you'll find in this book and should be considered most attractive for folks who live in the area and are looking for a quick outdoor escape.

The trailhead is on the north side of the parking area, next to a box offering cleanup baggies for folks who have brought their dogs. It heads northwest, following alongside Duck Creek Drive, which peeks in and out of view through the trees off to your right. On your left, trees grow thick alongside a deep gully

KEY AT-A-GLANCE INFORMATION

LENGTH: 2.95 miles
CONFIGURATION: Balloon
DIFFICULTY: Easy
SCENERY: Woods
EXPOSURE: Partial shade
TRAIL TRAFFIC: Moderate
TRAIL SURFACE: Paved
HIKING TIME: 1 hour
ACCESS: Daily; free
FACILITIES: Picnic tables
WHEELCHAIR TRAVERSABLE: Yes
SPECIAL COMMENTS: Dogs are permitted and should be kept leashed.

Directions

Take I-30 east, and exit at 56B onto I-635 north. Go 1 mile and take Exit 9A, turning right onto Oates Drive. Drive approximately 1.7 miles and turn left onto Duck Creek Drive. The parking lot is on the left, at 4917 Duck Creek and is marked with a "Camp Gatewood" sign.

GPS Trailhead Coordinates

UTM Zone (WGS84) 14S
Easting 723478
Northing 3637524
Latitude N 32° 51' 11"
Longitude W 96° 36' 43"

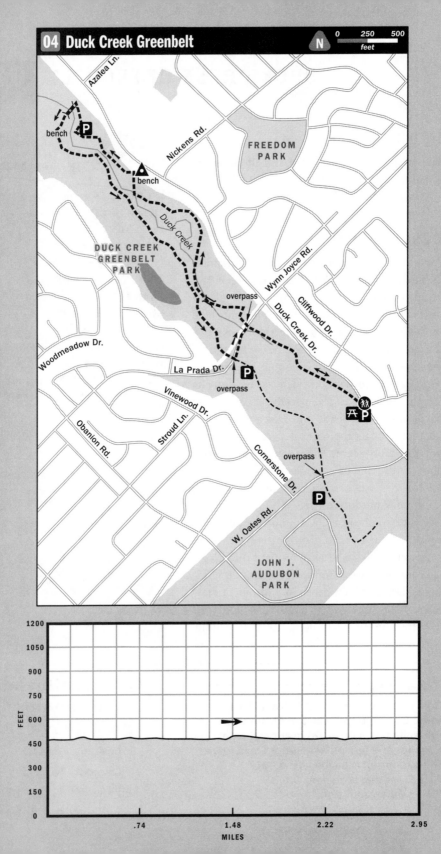

formed by Duck Creek. The low rumble of cars driving by on the nearby roadway is only slightly distracting, and as you walk farther along the path, the cheery chirping of birds flitting through the trees will turn your attention away from the sounds of urban life.

The woods brush the trail, blessing it with partial shade for most of the hike. They also provide an ideal haven for vines, which climb the trunks and hang loosely from the branches of some of the trees. At 0.86 miles, you'll cross a small bridge and continue northwest through the tall trees. You'll catch glimpses of the creek through the woods a couple dozen feet off to the left before reaching an overlook at 1.43 miles. The setting is pretty: a deep gully through which the greenish waters of the creek laze. Trees loom overhead and cling to the creek's edge, creating the ideal haven for birds and frogs—easy to spot here. Although charming, the gully does, unfortunately, collect loose trash blown in by the wind. The trail, however, is still popular among local residents, who look beyond the distracting refuse to see the justifiable charm of the creek. Many come with binoculars to spot birds; others come with strollers and dogs, while still others bring their kids, who dip their feet in the water and hunt for turtles. I also spotted a number of older folks, attracted by the trail's flat, shaded, paved surface. Remind kids that swimming or wading in the creek is prohibited.

At 1.71 miles, you'll pass the parking lot of an alternate trailhead on the right. A few hundred feet farther, a bridge spans Duck Creek, allowing you to cross. Once across the creek, bear left, following the path back the way you came but along the opposite side of the creek. On this side of the creek, the trail is much quieter, as the sound of cars completely fades from hearing. You'll find yourself winding back southwest on the southern side of the woods and creek. A variety of small and large nests in the trees provides evidence of a wide array of birdlife.

Soon, you'll reach a sunny section and, off to your right, you'll pass by a wide field, which abuts a small pond. As I hiked past, dozens of gulls and groups of ducks had taken over the banks of the small oasis, waiting for handouts from a couple of young kids. In the distance beyond the pond, you'll see the backside of local residences. Continue past the field and into the woods. At 2.83 miles, you'll reach an overpass. Cross under the overpass, then bear right (away from the creek) and follow the path as it winds uphill to street level. If you instead continue straight, you'll pass through a section of woods cleared for Frisbee golf, before reaching another access point to the greenbelt, directly across the creek from the pavilion and trailhead where you started. Proximity to the Frisbee area makes this side of the creek a little more trafficked than the opposite side.

Once you're at street level, turn around and head back northeast, crossing atop the overpass along the fenced-in sidewalk on the bridge's side. This will take you back across the creek. Once you've crossed over, you'll turn right, picking the path up again as it heads southeast alongside the creek. This is the path you started on. From here just retrace your steps back to the trailhead.

A shady rest spot on the greenbelt.

NEARBY ACTIVITIES

Just 8 miles north, you can visit the Firewheel Town Center, an open-air complex of department stores, retail shops, and restaurants—a good spot to grab a bite to eat and do some shopping. To get there, take Duck Creek Drive north, where it turns into South 1st Street. Turn right onto TX 78/Lavon Drive and go 3 miles. The mall is at the intersection of TX 78 north and the President George Bush Turnpike (TX 190).

FAIR PARK LOOP

IN BRIEF

This trail loops through the fairgrounds, passing historic Art Deco buildings, the Cotton Bowl football stadium, the Texas Vietnam Memorial, various statues and museums, and a small lagoon.

DESCRIPTION

Listed as a National Historic Landmark, the Fair Park Buildings in Dallas are a group of Art Deco buildings built in the 1930s for the Texas Centennial Exposition. According to the National Historic Landmark Registry, they form one of the largest of such collections in the country. Today the area is the site of the Texas State Fair. Its mascot—Big Tex, a statue more than 50 feet tall depicting a Texan complete with a cowboy hat and a Lone Star shirt—sits at the entrance while the fair is in attendance, greeting millions of visitors each year during its annual three-week run. When the fair is not on the grounds, Big Tex is taken down and the visitors dwindle. The buildings, gigantic Ferris wheel, and permanent exhibits and displays, however, remain; entrance to the area is free, and visitors are welcome to roam around. A pretty lagoon with swan boats and fountain, the Texas Vietnam Memorial, and an esplanade decorated with huge sculptures—not to mention the Cotton Bowl

KEY AT-A-GLANCE INFORMATION

LENGTH: 2.95 miles
CONFIGURATION: Loop
DIFFICULTY: Easy
SCENERY: Lagoon, Art Deco buildings, fairgrounds
EXPOSURE: Sunny
TRAIL TRAFFIC: Moderate
TRAIL SURFACE: Paved
HIKING TIME: 1 hour
ACCESS: Free; daily when fair not in town
FACILITIES: Restrooms, water fountains
WHEELCHAIR TRAVERSABLE: Yes
SPECIAL COMMENTS: There is an admission charge to the grounds when the fair is in town; in the off-season, it is free. Museums are open year-round (with admission), plan for a whole day if you intend to visit some after the hike.

Directions

Take I-30 east to Exit 47, Second Avenue/Fair Park. Continue straight to reach Fair Park. Park at the Grand Avenue entrance in front of the Dallas Museum of History.

GPS Trailhead Coordinates

UTM Zone (WGS84) 14S
Easting 709397
Northing 3628927
Latitude N 32° 46' 42"
Longitude W 96° 45' 51"

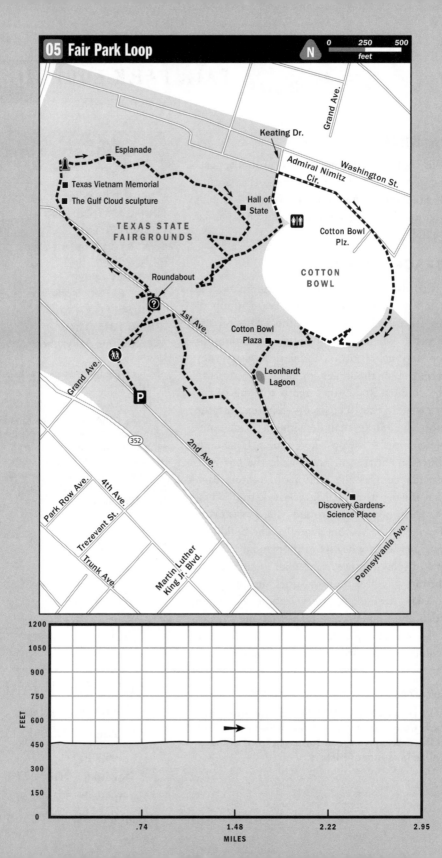

and various museums—make for an enjoyable hike.

From the parking lot, head to the Grande Avenue entrance pedestrian gate. Start the hike by heading northeast onto Grand Avenue and down a wide promenade, keeping the Dallas Museum of Natural History on your right. At 0.1 mile, you'll reach a kiosk with a map of the grounds. Continue straight, then turn left onto First Avenue at the roundabout, keeping the Old Mill Inn on your right. Established in 1936, the building was originally a flourmill exhibit, built to resemble an 1836 mill. Today the structure, complete with waterwheel, houses a restaurant.

Continue along the red-brick path. Ahead you'll see the Dallas skyline in the distance. At 0.42 miles, you'll reach a metal sculpture called "The Gulf Cloud," erected in 1916 in memorial of the first secretary of the State Fair of Texas, Captain Sydney Smith. The sculpture depicts a woman and her daughters, each representing an aspect of Texas's geography—the prairies, the mountains, and the Gulf Coast. Beyond the sculpture is a short field of grass, and beyond that, the Texas Vietnam Memorial. To get there, turn right, heading down the half-circular driveway, and turn left onto the memorial's walkway. The memorial's walls list the names of more than 3,000 casualties of the war.

Continue by turning right, following the walkway out. Ahead is the Women's Museum. You'll walk a few hundred feet then turn right at the statue and head down the walkway. To your left is the Continental DAR House, a small, white, colonial-style house with green trim. During the fair, the DAR (Daughters of the American Revolution) House, is open to the public, displaying exhibits on American history.

Continue straight, and at 0.75 miles you'll reach the esplanade, a long corridor lined with buildings and six huge sculptures surrounding a reflecting pool. At the far end of the esplanade rises the Hall of State. As you walk through the esplanade, you'll find some magnificent murals by the artist Pierre Bourdelle on the buildings. During the winter holidays, the esplanade is lined with lights and Christmas trees.

At 1 mile, you'll reach the Hall of State, a magnificent Art Deco building in front of which stands a gold archer. Along the frieze, the names of dozens of important Texas figures such as Travis, Hogg, Ellis, Lamar, and Milam, adorn the building. A column of statues at the front steps representing Spain, France, Mexico, the Republic of Texas, the Confederate States, and the United States, comprise the Six Flags of Texas.

From the state hall, turn right, heading south. At the end of the building, head left onto the walkway, keeping the Tower Building on your right. Ahead, seemingly out of place, looms the Cotton Bowl, the huge football stadium that hosts the annual Cotton Bowl football game. The game will be moving in 2010 however to the Dallas Cowboys's new stadium in Arlington. At 1.4 miles, turn left onto the drive encircling the Cotton Bowl. After a couple hundred feet, take a left onto Keeting Drive and then the first right onto Nimitz.

Follow Nimitz past some exhibition halls and the Creative Arts Show Place Theatre to head toward the Children's Petting Zoo, which is open during the fair. On your right, you'll see the backside of the Cotton Bowl. Continue walking down the road toward the Ferris wheel. You'll soon see a "Midway" sign atop a closed-off

> **The famous Texas Star Ferris Wheel looms above the last part of the hike.**

entrance to a section holding the fair's amusement rides and games. The road curves to the right and comes out onto a plaza in front of the Cotton Bowl.

Head southwest through the plaza away from the Cotton Bowl and toward the Leonhardt Lagoon. Take a left at the benches in front of the water. Along the water's edges, you'll see oddly shaped red walkways, which is actually a sculpture designed to resemble a fern. Kids can often be seen leaning from its edges looking into the waters for the many turtles that inhabit the lagoon. Among the fish are yellow bluehead and longear sunfish; the plants include lizard tail, water hyacinth, and cattails. Swan boats regularly circle the lagoon, completing the tranquil scene.

Continue following the walkway southeast alongside and past the lagoon. As you walk, you'll get closer to the gigantic Texas Star Ferris Wheel to the left, allowing you to appreciate its beauty and size. The pathway continues past the Science Place and the Discovery Gardens before ending at a parking lot. From here, turn back, retracing your steps to the lagoon, this time turning left to follow the walkway along the opposite side of the lagoon, past the IMAX, and back toward the trailhead.

NEARBY ACTIVITIES

You could easily spend the entire day here after the hike enjoying the sights, including the Dallas Aquarium at Fair Park, the Women's Museum, the African American Museum, and the Texas Discovery Gardens. The Dallas Museum of Nature & Science includes wildlife dioramas and a fossil-bone exhibit. The museum also sells combo packages, which include admission to the museum and admission to the IMAX theater. If you intend to visit multiple museums, ask about purchasing a ticket that allows entrance to all of them. For a bite to eat, stop by the Old Mill Inn, which is open year-round from 11 a.m. until 2:30 p.m.

FISH CREEK LINEAR TRAIL

IN BRIEF

A sunny hike through a cheery wooded green-belt frequented by birds and enjoyed by local residents. A plaque in the middle of the new trail marks the Arlington–Grand Prairie city line.

DESCRIPTION

The neighboring cities of Grand Prairie and Arlington have worked together in an effort to connect their cities with a linear park and trail alongside Fish Creek. The connecting trail was only recently completed, with a dedication ceremony on February 20, 2007. In Arlington, the Fish Creek Linear Park extends from TX 360 west to Craven's Park. The linear park and trail also continue into Grand Prairie, on a previously established section certified as the Nancy Dillon National Recreation Trail. Here, the trail follows Fish Creek about 2.5 miles, heading west past Great Southwest Parkway. Parking spots are plentiful along the entire length of Grand Prairie's trail, allowing access from just about anyplace you'd like to start. I began this hike on the western end of the trail, which is very near the gateway into Arlington.

Folks on this trail are exceedingly friendly —they go out of their way to smile and say hi, ask how you're doing, and give advice. Much

i KEY AT-A-GLANCE INFORMATION

LENGTH: 3.08 miles
CONFIGURATION: Out-and-back
DIFFICULTY: Easy
SCENERY: Trees, birds
EXPOSURE: Sunny
TRAIL TRAFFIC: Moderate
TRAIL SURFACE: Paved
HIKING TIME: 1 hour
ACCESS: Daily, 5 a.m.–midnight; free
FACILITIES: Playground, benches
WHEELCHAIR TRAVERSABLE: Yes
SPECIAL COMMENTS: Bring a hat and suntan lotion.

Directions

Take I-20 toward Grand Prairie, and exit onto South Great Southwest Parkway, heading south. Turn right onto Claremont Drive then left onto Largo Drive. The parking lot is at the end of Largo, adjacent to the trail.

GPS Trailhead Coordinates

UTM Zone (WGS84) 14S
Easting 681953
Northing 3615903
Latitude N 32° 39' 57"
Longitude W 97° 3' 35"

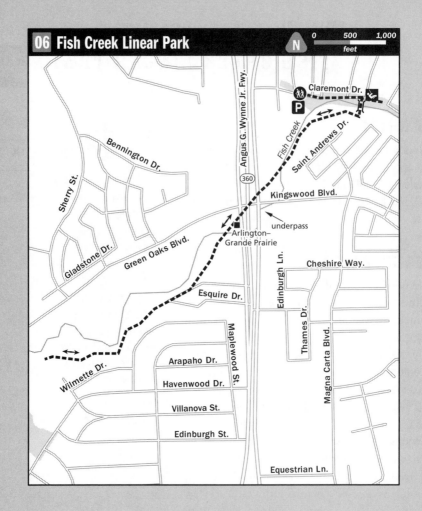

0   500   1,000
feet

Claremont Dr.

P

Angus G. Wynne Jr. Fwy.

Fish Creek

Bennington Dr.

Sherry St.

Saint Andrews Dr.

360

Kingswood Blvd.

Gladstone Dr.

Green Oaks Blvd.

underpass

Arlington–
Grande Prairie

Cheshire Way.

Esquire Dr.

Edinburgh Ln.

Thames Dr.

Magna Carta Blvd.

Maplewood St.

Arapaho Dr.

Havenwood Dr.

Wilmette Dr.

Villanova St.

Edinburgh St.

Equestrian Ln.

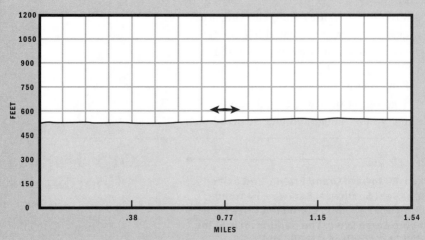

of this is probably due to the fact that the trail abuts the backyards of folks' homes, and residents have taken a personal responsibility for the trail's upkeep. Even at the trailhead, you'll notice that you're just behind a quiet residential neighborhood where local residents simply step out their front doors and onto the trail. This pleasant sense of community sets this trail apart from other greenbelts of its kind.

From the trailhead, turn left onto the trail and head east. To your right, a couple dozen feet off the trail and hidden behind tall trees, is the creek—a sparkling green ribbon of water running parallel to the trail. Peaking down its banks, you're likely to see toads and frogs hopping into the water and out of sight. A large playground to the left offers kids a chance to burn some energy; if it's a sunny day, be sure to coat them with plenty of sunscreen, however, because the play area has no shade.

At 0.23 miles, you'll reach a junction; if you go straight, you'll continue through Grand Prairie. A jogger I met here commented that there was a Mexican bakery with tasty treats at the end, which kept her motivated to finish her run. Although the bakery might sound tempting, you'll want to bear right to get to Arlington. You'll cross over the beautiful, huge, rust-colored bridge spanning the narrow creek. On the other side of the bridge, you'll bear right and follow the trail as it winds onto a sunny peninsula sandwiched between the backyards of residences to your left and the narrow creek to your right. Ahead and above you is a network of crisscrossing overpasses. Here, in the shadow of TX 360, adjacent to the creek, a huge round plaque in the ground marks the Arlington–Grand Prairie city boundary. Around you, the trail is new and well maintained; litter and graffiti you might find beneath other bridges is notably absent. Teenagers jog and skate by, contributing to the trail's friendly vibe.

The trail continues southwest, deeper into Arlington. The smooth, paved path is clearly marked with a yellow stripe down its center. To your right, the creek winds through a deep gully. Just across the gully, you'll glimpse a shopping complex before you head slightly uphill and the woods screen the buildings from view. To your left, the backyards of houses in a small residential subdivision are quickly overtaken by woodland.

On my hike, the unmistakable sounds of woodpeckers pecking the upper trunks of the trees filled the air, outdone only by the chirping of other birds flitting quickly from branch to branch. It's a peaceful, cheery setting, where you'll find friendly older folks out enjoying a walk in the fresh air, and younger ones biking happily along. One cyclist who had stopped for a sip from her water bottle greeted me as I walked by and enthusiastically described how amazed she was that she could bike from Tarrant County in Arlington, where she lived, straight into Dallas County. This was her first foray down the trail, and she was surprised and impressed with its beauty and charm, especially since it runs through such a busy city.

You'll continue heading southwest through much of the same woodland scenery. At 1.54 miles, you'll reach the back fence of an elementary school set

A sun-drenched bridge leads folks towards the Grand Prairie-Arlington city boundary.

a few hundred feet off the trail to the left. This is a nice spot to take a quick breather before turning around and retracing your steps to the trailhead. Alternatively, you can continue straight down the trail through more woodlands. You'll eventually reach Craven's Park at the far western end.

NEARBY ACTIVITIES

Just 7 miles away, the planetarium at the University of Texas at Arlington offers simulated views of the current night sky and constellations in a one-hour star or music show. Their schedule offers afternoon showings on weekends, and discounts for students and seniors. Visit their Web site at **www.uta.edu/planetarium** for more information on show times. To get there, take TX 360 north, exit at Park Row Drive, and go west 3 miles. Turn right onto Cooper Street, then right again onto Mitchell Street. Turn left onto West Street. Two blocks along, you'll find the parking garage. Walk out the opposite side of the garage onto Planetarium Place.

GATEWAY PARK TRAIL

IN BRIEF

This trail winds past the remnants of a historic Indian marker tree—a tree once used by Native Americans to mark an important spot—then continues into a dense woodland that was once Comanche territory. This trail will appeal most to those interested in the area's rich history and able to look past the urbanization to imagine it as it once was.

DESCRIPTION

Intrigued by an article from the November 2006 issue of a *Texas Parks and Wildlife* magazine highlighting Gateway Park in southeast Dallas, I set out to find this small park and hike its wild trail. The article identifies this park as an area once inhabited by the Comanche and discusses how they would shape a young tree into a curve to help mark an important spot. It identifies one such tree in Gateway Park. Only part of the tree remains; most of it was destroyed by a storm in 1998. The article's title, "The Storytelling Place," refers to a natural limestone amphitheater found along the trail.

Excited by the significance of the area, I made my way to the park and was surprised by what I discovered. The historic tree is alongside a paved trail encircling an open field. A separate dirt trail is located on the far

KEY AT-A-GLANCE INFORMATION

LENGTH: 1.5 miles

CONFIGURATION: Figure eight

DIFFICULTY: Moderate to difficult

SCENERY: Historic tree, woods, fall foliage

EXPOSURE: Sunny to shady

TRAIL TRAFFIC: Light

TRAIL SURFACE: Paved path and dirt trail

HIKING TIME: 40 minutes

ACCESS: Free; daily

FACILITIES: Playground, tennis courts

WHEELCHAIR TRAVERSABLE: The first half mile is wheelchair traversable.

SPECIAL COMMENTS: Bring a hiking stick for assistance on the steep rocky sections of the latter half of the trail.

Directions

From I-30 east, exit Jim Miller Road. The entrance to Gateway Park is about 3 miles down on the left.

GPS Trailhead Coordinates

UTM Zone (WGS84)　14S

Easting　715337

Northing　3626742

Latitude　N 32° 45' 27"

Longitude　W 96° 42' 5"

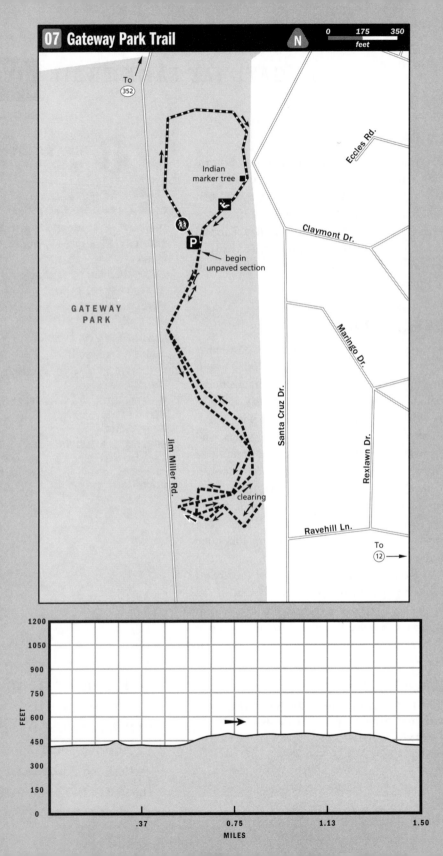

side of the park, opposite the paved trail, and winds through some rugged hilly terrain. The area in this undeveloped section is harsh and woodsy, making it easy to envision it as the tribal grounds it once was. Evidence of its urban location has, however, seeped into the area, and as you hike along, you're likely to see some litter along the trail. With a little effort, however, you can ignore this and immerse yourself in the trail's wildness. Though it's not the prettiest trail in the metroplex, I decided to include it because of the area's cultural history. Hikers should be aware that the trail appears to be only loosely maintained; in some sections, expect to push aside stray twigs that have encroached upon the path. Be sure to wear good hiking shoes—there are a lot of small loose rocks, and there is also a steep section at the beginning that requires good traction.

Start the hike by heading down the paved trail on the north side of the parking lot. You'll follow the loop alongside the field toward a stand of pecan trees on the eastern side. In the center of the group of trees, a tall black metal fence encloses the remnants of the Indian marker tree. The section of this pecan tree's trunk that remains is rooted at one end and bows to the ground at the other. With a little imagination, you can picture how it must once have stood tall, with a distinct artificial curve in its trunk. There is no plaque or other identification marking the site. On April 26, 1997, the tree was entered into the Dallas Historic Tree Registry. In that same year, dozens of pecans were collected from it, blessed by Native Americans, and sent to the American Forests' Historic Tree Nursery, which was able to sell many young saplings grown from them.

Continue the hike by finishing the looped, paved trail and crossing back toward the parking lot, keeping the playground on your left. Head over a small bridge that crosses a tiny creek by the parking area, and walk across the field toward the tennis courts. Head south between the courts on your left and the street on your right, toward a small opening in the woods ahead. At 0.55 miles you'll reach the edge of the field and the trailhead for the dirt path. The path heads into the woods and immediately up a steep, rocky hill. At the top of the hill, a thick wood looms on all sides. Head straight through the trees until you reach a turnoff at 0.58 miles; bear right onto the rocky trail. Stay to the right at the next turnoff, at 0.63 miles. Although the sounds of cars whizzing by on the nearby street to the right drown out the softer sounds of nature, it is not overly distracting. In fact, if you hike the trail during the fall, you'll find yourself immersed in the environment because the mixture of trees along the trail provides spectacular displays of foliage. With the cooler weather, the leaves change to intense shade of reds, purples, and yellows. The wood runs thick throughout the entire hike, with trees such as oaks, pecans, and cottonwoods.

About 100 feet farther, another trail will join the one you're on; just continue straight. At 0.73 miles, stay to the right at the junction and make your way past some overgrown shrubbery. At the next four junctions, stay to your left and you'll eventually come out upon an open clearing at 1 mile. The ground here, and elsewhere along the trail, is white, chalky limestone. If you look carefully at the

The remnants of the historic Indian marker tree.

ground along various sections of the trail, you're likely to notice shell fossils embedded in the limestone, hinting at the age of the area.

From the clearing, circle back by taking the next couple of rights. You'll find yourself back on the trail you came up on. Just retrace your steps north to the trailhead.

NEARBY ACTIVITIES

Dallas's Fair Park, which is open year-round (there is a charge only when the fair is in town) is about 5 miles to the west. You could easily spend the entire day there after the hike, enjoying the various sights, including the Dallas Aquarium at Fair Park, the Women's Museum, the African American Museum, and the Texas Discovery Gardens. If you're interested in a museum, the Dallas Museum of Natural History (now known as the Museum of Nature & Science) is an excellent choice and includes wildlife dioramas and a fossil-bone exhibit. The museum also sells combo packages, which include admission to the museum and admission to the IMAX theater to see a movie. If you intend to visit some of the other museums as well, ask about purchasing a ticket that allows entrance to all of them. For a bite to eat, stop by the Old Mill Inn, which is open year-round from 11 a.m. until 2:30 p.m. To get to Fair Park, go north on Jim Miller Road and left onto Scyene Road. Fair Park is about 4 miles down on your right.

KATY TRAIL 08

IN BRIEF

Popular with a young, urban crowd, this linear trail creates a pedestrian-friendly corridor between downtown Dallas and the Mockingbird DART station. Always lively, this trail will appeal to those who don't mind a constant bustle of activity.

DESCRIPTION

In the late 1800s, the Missouri–Kansas–Texas railroad began operating a passenger and freight line into Texas, connecting it with states to the north. The MKT, nicknamed "Katy," eventually connected St. Louis with Dallas and Fort Worth and extended as far south as Galveston. In the late 1980s, to avoid financial losses, the MKT merged with the Missouri Pacific Railroad Company, part of Union Pacific Railway. Dallas's Katy Trail owes its existence in part to Union Pacific, which donated the abandoned tracks to the city. In Missouri, another old abandoned section of the Katy Trail has been similarly donated and forms a 225-mile trail known as the Katy Trail State Park.

KEY AT-A-GLANCE INFORMATION

LENGTH: 5.64
CONFIGURATION: Out-and-back
DIFFICULTY: Easy
SCENERY: Trees, city views
EXPOSURE: Mostly sunny, some shade
TRAIL TRAFFIC: Heavy
TRAIL SURFACE: Concrete path
HIKING TIME: 1.75 hours
ACCESS: Free
WHEELCHAIR TRAVERSABLE: Yes
SPECIAL COMMENTS: If you can't find a spot near the trailhead, try parking at one of the parks adjacent to the trail.

Directions

To get to the West End from I-35E south, exit Continental Avenue and turn left onto Continental, which turns into Lamar. At the intersection of Lamar and McKinney, the West End will be on the right. Continue one more block to Munger Avenue and turn right. Park in any lot or metered space and walk north down North Houston (which runs parallel to Lamar on its west) toward the American Airlines Center. The trailhead is across the street from the parking lot of the American Airlines Center on North Houston.

GPS Trailhead Coordinates

UTM Zone (WGS84) 14S
Easting 704993
Northing 3630413
Latitude N 32° 47' 33"
Longitude W 96° 48' 39"

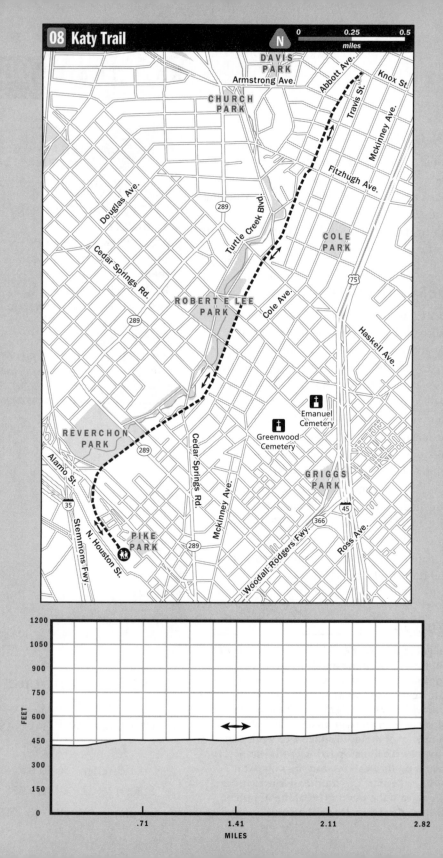

Though I had heard of the trail before, I had never thought of visiting it, not knowing just how nice it was. To my surprise, I found an excellent, well maintained pathway running right from downtown Dallas, near the West End, about 3.6 miles north to Mockingbird.

The Web site of the Friends of the Katy Trail, a nonprofit organization dedicated to the trail's expansion and development, indicates that more than 300,000 people live within 1 mile of the trail. This is not difficult to believe; even on a hot weekend afternoon, the trail is crowded with joggers, hikers, bikers, skateboarders, inline skaters, and folks walking dogs. Many live in the area and access the trail at various points along its length; the trail passes several city parks and intersects a couple of streets. There are about a dozen proposed access points to the trail, and construction is ongoing. As of spring 2007, Friends of the Katy Trail had raised more than $17 million of their $23 million goal for trail construction and improvement. Currently, there is a million-dollar project to connect the trail with the nearby Turtle Creek Trail.

The trailhead is located in Victory Park, right behind the American Airlines Center, across the street from the parking lot. A plaque identifying this entrance point as Victory Promenade marks the trailhead. If you prefer not to drive into downtown Dallas and the West End, you could start your hike from one of the many parks which abut the trail's length. If you choose to do this however, you'll have to consult a map beforehand to get directions, as there is no road which runs alongside the trail. From the primary trailhead, the path starts by heading up a small incline to reach the elevated trail bed, from the top of which you have a decent, though slightly obstructed, view of the Dallas skyline if you turn around.

Because of its old railway status, the trail from here to the end is relatively level, having only a few gentle turns. The scenery is mostly a thick curtain of trees obscuring the highways, streets, and autos only a short distance below. If you're interested in orienting yourself, the trail runs roughly between Oaklawn Avenue and Stemmons Freeway to the left, and the busy Central Expressway to the right. Surprisingly, the sounds of urban life are not overwhelming, and at many points you'll even be unaware of the fact that you're hiking through the busiest part of Dallas.

The trail, which is approximately 12 feet wide and divided into two lanes, is nicely maintained; you'll be hard pressed to find any litter or even a spot where the grass comes close to encroaching on the path. The trail developers have also done an excellent job marking the trail; when you cross over a highway or pass a park, you'll see signs telling you where you are.

You won't find much wildlife along the path, though you may spot a few squirrels scurrying in front of you or a stray cat walking along the path's edge. The backyards of condos and homes abut the trail at various spots along the way, a reminder of the trail's urban location.

At 0.6 miles, just after you pass over Harry Hines and McKinnon, look for Reverchon Park (originally intended as Dallas's version of Central Park) off to the

Weekends will bring many more hikers to the flat, shady trail.

left. The park is named in honor of James Reverchon, a renowned botanist from the late nineteenth century who lived nearby.

From here, the trail passes over Maple and Cedar Springs roads. At about 1.6 miles, just after you cross Lemmon Avenue, you'll pass Turtle Creek Park on the left. As you continue northeast, you'll reach the Highland Park area. The intersection of David's Way and Travis at 2.8 miles is a good turnaround spot. If you need to cool off or grab a drink before the hike back, there are a couple of restaurants and a convenience store just within view. To extend the hike, you can continue straight another mile, where the trail ends at some bike lockers not far from Southern Methodist University and Mockingbird Station.

NEARBY ACTIVITIES

The West End is a pedestrian-friendly walking district with several restaurants. Once the hub of Dallas's commercial activities, today the renovated warehouses make up one of Dallas's main entertainment areas. Listed on the National Register of Historic Places, the West End is also the home of Dealey Plaza, where John F. Kennedy was shot in 1963.

L.B. HOUSTON NATURE TRAIL 09

IN BRIEF

This flat trail through the woods offers glimpses of the Elm Fork of the Trinity River and is a cool, shady hike for a hot summer's day.

DESCRIPTION

To me, this trail is a perfect example of how city dwellers craving the outdoors can turn an otherwise unremarkable location into a happening weekend spot. The sunny weekend day my brother and I arrived, we were greeted by an interesting assortment of folks getting ready for a surprising variety of activities. A group of women in jogging outfits was stretching their hamstrings in preparation for a run, a dozen or so folks (including a few middle-school children) were in various stages of prepping their bikes for a spin along the trail, and an older couple was unloading a kayak from atop their SUV. By the time we parked the car on the street opposite the trailhead (where the overflow of cars had been relegated), the kayakers were on their way down to a small pond and headed toward a spit of beach on which a man with fishing rod and tackle box in hand, had just settled.

Maintained by DORBA, the Dallas Off Road Bicycle Association, the several miles of

KEY AT-A-GLANCE INFORMATION

LENGTH: 1.61 miles
CONFIGURATION: Loop
DIFFICULTY: Easy
SCENERY: Cedar, elm, oak woodlands, river views
EXPOSURE: Shady
TRAIL TRAFFIC: Heavy on weekends
TRAIL SURFACE: Packed dirt
HIKING TIME: 40 minutes
ACCESS: Free; open daily
FACILITIES: None
WHEELCHAIR TRAVERSABLE: No
SPECIAL COMMENTS: Rains cause the trail to become muddy and impassable. If it rained the day before your hike, choose a different trail.

Directions

From TX 183, exit TX 114 toward Grapevine and then exit Tom Braniff Drive/Loop 12. Turn north onto Tom Braniff Drive, which becomes Wildwood Drive. The trailhead is approximately 1 mile down on the right, at the intersection of Wildwood Drive and California Crossing Road, across the street from the National Guard Armory.

GPS Trailhead Coordinates

UTM Zone (WGS84) 14S
Easting   694359
Northing 3638383
Latitude N 32° 51' 59"
Longitude W 96° 55' 22"

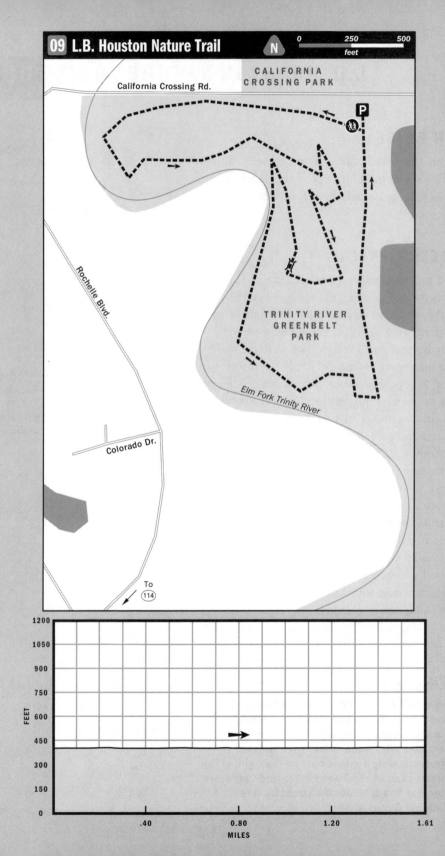

The narrow dirt path winds through dense foliage.

trails here are open to both bikers and hikers. An impressive amount of energy has been put into the trail's maintenance, and though it had a reputation for being in an area prone to vagrants and partiers, the care and maintenance of volunteers has completed turned the area around, and you'll find the trail clean and well maintained.

As you approach from the parking lot, to your left you'll see a pond whose still waters attract birds, such as herons and egrets, searching for a meal. When the water is low, a sandbar attracts local kids looking to hone their fishing skills. Straight ahead, you'll see a tree-lined wide grassy lane down which trickles a steady stream of folks exiting the trail from both sides of the wood.

To the right, you'll see the trailhead. A small kiosk in front of it bears a trail map. The trail is intended to be one long loop, encouraging traffic to flow in one direction. The first part, however, which is ideal for hikers because of its smooth, level terrain, comes back out onto the grassy median before continuing. This allows for a pleasant walk without getting into the more technical sections in the latter half of the trail. If you were to venture on, the trail crosses over the central grass strip into the southeast section. The dips in these sections appeal to mountain bikers.

Begin the hike by entering the trail as it heads right and disappears into the woods. Keep right to follow the main trail. The trail will immediately start to twist and turn gently as it haphazardly makes its way through the trees. Off to the right, you'll catch glimpses of California Crossing Road. At first, you'll hear the background hum of the occasional car, but that quickly gives way to the chirping of birds and rustling of trees. The trees are closely packed all along the trail, bathing most of the path in shade. At some points the branches converge tightly just overhead, enveloping the walkway in lovely tunnels of foliage. In other parts, the trees are a little more spaced apart, allowing wild grass to grow tall and thick at their bases.

The trail itself is narrow, allowing for only single-file walking. It approaches trees, only to curve away at the last minute, keeping the hike interesting as your attention is naturally drawn outward to the cedar, elm, oak, and other trees and plants you pass. Stay to the right, following the outer trail as it makes a rough loop along the banks of Elm Fork of the Trinity River. At a couple of spots, you'll catch glimpses of the river through the trees to the right. Birds can often be seen flying over the water before disappearing into the trees on the far side of the river.

The day of our hike, DORBA volunteers were out on the trail cutting back limbs, clipping bushes, and cleaning debris. Judging from the excellent condition of parts of the trail they had not yet reached, this is not a one-time undertaking but rather a continual effort.

At about 0.95 miles, you'll reach a nice vantage point for viewing the wide expanse of river, whose waters are a muddy greenish-gray. In the spring and summer, you can see colorful butterflies fluttering through the foliage at the river's edge.

The trail crosses a short wooden footbridge, heads slightly uphill, and, at 1.3 miles, exits the woods. There you'll find yourself again on the wide grassy lane just south of the trailhead. Turn left and follow the trail 0.25 miles back to the trailhead. You'll pass the pond on the right before arriving back at the parking lot.

NEARBY ACTIVITIES

In nearby Williams Square in Las Colinas, a section of North Irving, you can visit the Mustangs at Las Colinas, a huge bronze equestrian sculpture of lifelike wild mustangs racing through a fountain in the middle of the plaza. A few restaurants in the area serve lunch. To get to Williams Square, head west on California Crossing and turn right onto Riverside Drive. Turn left onto North O'Connor Boulevard; you'll see the sculptures about 0.5 miles down on the right.

ROWLETT CREEK NATURE TRAIL 10

IN BRIEF

This heavily traveled trail is an excellent choice for a hot, sunny day because most of it is shaded by woods. Because of the dense woodland along the entire length of the trail, this hike would appeal more to those looking for exercise than for scenic views.

DESCRIPTION

When I arrived at the Rowlett Creek Preserve in Garland early one sunny Sunday morning, I expected to be one of the first to head out onto the trails. I was amazed to discover, however, that I would be lucky to find a parking space—the lot was already packed with cars. Upon closer inspection, bike racks, helmets, and fashionable aerodynamic clothing revealed that most of the folks heading down, or coming back from, the various trailheads were mountain bikers. The trails are, however, open to hikers, and because there are more than 10 miles of trails, it does not feel overwhelmingly crowded (though you certainly won't feel lonely). The trails are arranged in numbered loops; the higher the number, the more difficult the trail for a biker. What makes this trail particularly appealing is that almost all of it is shaded, making for an ideal summer hike.

ⓘ KEY AT-A-GLANCE INFORMATION

LENGTH: 4 miles
CONFIGURATION: Double loop
DIFFICULTY: Moderate
SCENERY: Woodland, creek
EXPOSURE: Shady with a section of sun
TRAIL TRAFFIC: Heavy
TRAIL SURFACE: Packed dirt
HIKING TIME: 1.5 hours
ACCESS: Free; open daily
FACILITIES: Portable toilets, water fountain, picnic tables
WHEELCHAIR TRAVERSABLE: No
SPECIAL COMMENTS: Keep an eye out for snakes sunning on the trail.

Directions ──────────→

Take the President George Bush Turnpike (TX 190) to the end, to TX 78 north. Turn right onto 78 north (Lavon Drive), heading toward Garland. Go about 2 miles and turn left onto Castle Drive to Rowlett Creek Preserve. The parking lot is about 1.7 miles down, at the intersection of Castle Drive and East Centerville Road.

GPS Trailhead Coordinates

UTM Zone (WGS84) 14S
Easting 724835
Northing 3644995
Latitude N 32° 55' 12"
Longitude W 96° 35' 44"

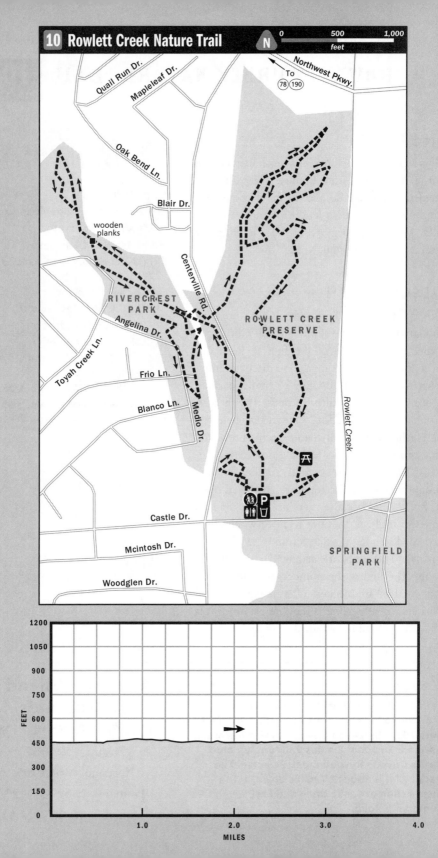

The shady trail passes through dense woodlands.

The hike starts with the Loop 1 trail. You'll find the trailhead on the north side of the parking lot, to the left of a gazebo and just behind a kiosk displaying a map of the preserve. The narrow dirt path disappears north into the woods and curls lazily in a half loop through the trees until you reach a turnoff at 0.57 miles for the Loop 7 trail. Turn left onto the trail, and at about 0.63 miles, the path crosses under the bridge for Centerville Road then emerges into more woods. The trail then follows a narrow creek north toward the northern edge of the preserve. Dense wood in this section casts the trail into a deep shade, providing welcome relief during a sunny day. To the right, the wood ends at the backyards of private homes, which abut the opposite side of the creek.

As you continue on the trail, you'll reach a fence and a small sign at the edge of the preserve; the trail winds along the fence before reaching a junction at 1 mile. Take the trail to the left, which heads downhill. The trails that cut through this section are close enough together that you are likely to glimpse bikers or hikers winding through the woods on trails completely obscured by the dense trees. This gives the confusing illusion that a person might be heading toward you, or coming up from behind you, when in fact they are on a completely different part of the trail. Be sure to remain alert because, when a rider is on the same trail, the path's twists and turns prevent you from knowing it until they are right in front of you, leaving little time to step aside.

You'll reach the next junction at 1.1 miles, where trails head off to the left and to the right while one continues straight ahead; head down the middle path to avoid the steep hills intended for mountain bikers. At 1.23 miles, go right and follow a long wooden boardwalk overlaying the trail. You'll dodge a couple of low-hanging limbs, then reach the end of the boardwalk's wooden planks. At 1.4

miles there is yet another junction, where you should head right. At this point, the trail climbs out of the woods and onto a small, sun-drenched ridge, where you'll see Centerville Road in front of you. Bear right, heading downhill; the path curls in a short loop through another section of woods, then at 1.8 miles comes back up onto the sunny, treeless ridge. Follow the trail straight back into the woods; the trees lean together, forming a cave-like entry into the inviting relief of the deep shade.

A couple hundred feet farther and you'll be back at the bridge. Just after the overhang, stay to the right to pick up a trail that will bring you back to the Loop 7 turnoff. At about 1.9 miles, you'll reach the split, where you should bear left. At about 2 miles, bear left, following the Loop 1a sign. You'll cross a small brook; follow it until you reach 2.25 miles, where you'll bear right, continuing on Loop 1a. The trail is level for the rest of the hike, making for easy walking. Keep an eye out for snakes; we spotted a 3-foot one curled up in the middle of the trail, just barely slithering out of the way as bikers whizzed past.

At 2.9 miles, join Loop 1. The trail passes straight through a wide field, the only sunny portion of the trail. At 3.88 miles you'll reach a picnic table set conveniently in the shade of a huge lone tree, a nice spot to stop and eat lunch before heading home. From the picnic table, the trail merges onto a paved pathway that ends at the parking lot.

NEARBY ACTIVITIES

Just a couple miles away, the Firewheel Town Center—an open-air complex of department stores, retail shops, and restaurants—is a good spot to grab a bite to eat and do some shopping. It's about 2 miles northwest, at the intersection of TX 78 north and the President George Bush Turnpike (TX 190).

SPRING CREEK PARK NATURE TRAIL 11

IN BRIEF

This well-maintained, flat, forest trail follows a creek toward a bench nestled in the shade beneath the trees. With a keen eye, you can catch sight of the variety of resident and migrant birds that make this a popular spot with birders. Bear in mind that neither Spring Creek Forest nor Spring Creek Park have restroom or drinking facilities, so be sure to come prepared.

DESCRIPTION

The Spring Creek Forest Preserve and the Spring Creek Park Preserve, which straddle Holford Road in North Garland within about 500 feet of each, offer hikers quiet patches of forest wilderness remarkably preserved less than a mile from the George Bush Highway. The Spring Creek Forest Preserve, which is popular with naturalists and plant enthusiasts, boasts a unique occurrence of bur, chinquapin, shumard, and Texas red oaks growing in community with various types of elm, ash, and hackberry. More than 150 different species of birds have been identified here. A short, paved path to a bench overlooking the creek makes for a pleasant stroll. Across the street, the Spring Creek Park Preserve offers similar plant

KEY AT-A-GLANCE INFORMATION

LENGTH: 1.02 miles
CONFIGURATION: Loop
DIFFICULTY: Easy
SCENERY: Woodland forest, birds, creek
EXPOSURE: Shady to sunny
TRAIL TRAFFIC: Light
TRAIL SURFACE: Packed dirt
HIKING TIME: 30 minutes
ACCESS: Free; open daily
FACILITIES: None; bring water.
WHEELCHAIR TRAVERSABLE: No
SPECIAL COMMENTS: For additional information, go to www.springcreekforest.org.

Directions

From Dallas, take TX 75 north to Garland, and take Exit 24 toward Belt Line Road. Turn right on Belt Line Road and go 1 mile, then make a left onto North Grove Road, then a right onto Arapaho Road. Go about 3 miles, and turn left onto Holford Road. The Spring Creek Park Preserve is about 0.5 miles down on the left. Spring Creek Forest Preserve is 0.1 mile farther on the right. Park in Spring Creek Park Preserve.

GPS Trailhead Coordinates

UTM Zone (WGS84) 14S
Easting 718986
Northing 3649777
Latitude N 32° 57' 52"
Longitude W 96° 39' 25"

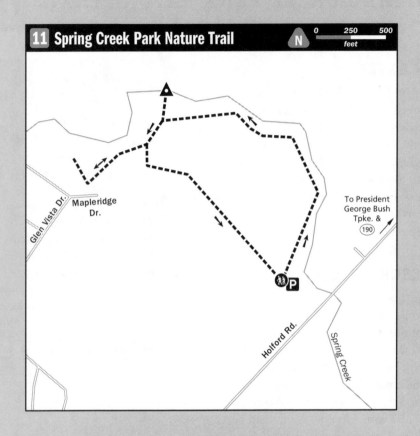

11 **Spring Creek Park Nature Trail**

N

0   250   500
feet

Glen Vista Dr.

Mapleridge
Dr.

To President
George Bush
Tpke. &
(190)

Holford Rd.

Spring Creek

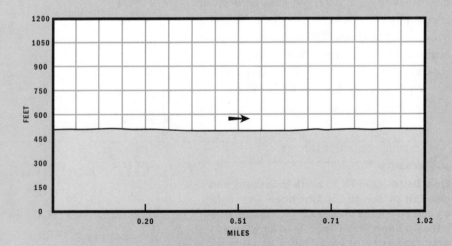

FEET

1200
1050
900
750
600
450
300
150
0

0.20   0.51   0.71   1.02

MILES

and animal life, along with an inviting, unpaved, shady trail looping along the creek through the woods.

The trailhead is located in Spring Creek Park Preserve, which is on the northwest side of the road (Spring Creek Forest Preserve is only slightly farther down, on the southeast side of the road.) The huge parking lot can easily accommodate a crowd of hikers, although on the gorgeous day that we hit the trail, there was only one other car in the lot. The hiker, who was there with his two dogs, was just getting off the trail and gave us a friendly nod before heading for a picnic table.

The trail starts just off the parking lot. Follow the wide, gravel path that heads north. Within a few dozen feet, it becomes a narrow, hard-packed dirt trail and enters a riparian forest. The chirping and buzzing of birds and insects perfects the illusion that you're miles away from civilization.

The well maintained trail curls in a half loop through the trees, following the creek, and remains fairly level throughout. Except for a short section at the end of the hike, you'll find that the trail is shaded, making this an excellent hike for a hot, sunny day.

As you walk, you'll catch glimpses through the trees off to the right of some ragged, sand-colored bluffs, which give way to a long ravine through which a creek gurgles. If you've brought younger hikers with you, caution them to stay on the main trail; they may find some of the short side trails that branch off through the brush toward the ravine's edge tempting. Innocent curiosity can be dangerous for children, who may step too far and slide over the edge. In many cases, logs and branches block these trails, discouraging their use, and barbed wire along the edge serves as an extra deterrent. A couple of nice lookout spots farther down the trail provide for easy, safe viewing.

At about 0.5 miles you'll reach a clearing. The trail splits, with a path leading toward Spring Creek Trail Loop. A convenient bench in the shade of the thick grove of trees towering overhead is a nice spot to enjoy the scenery. Take the short trail on the right that passes in front of the bench and heads north a few dozen feet through the woods to a nice overlook of the creek. The various summer, winter, and migrating winged residents help make this one of the more popular birding spots in the metroplex. Keep an eye out for these short- and long-term residents, which include bluebirds, woodpeckers, finches, warblers, owls, sparrows, and kinglets. The most common wildlife you're likely to see, aside from birds, are a few squirrels scurrying beneath the trees.

Retrace your steps to the bench and take the opposite trail, following the signs for Spring Creek Trail Loop. The path heads away from the creek, and a couple of hundred feet farther reaches a fork. Take the trail to the left, which finishes the loop back toward the trailhead. (The trail to the right passes through a small grassland and after 0.2 miles reaches the edge of the preserve and an alternate exit.) As you continue, the path quickly leaves the tree covering and

> The well-maintained trail is clearly marked.

emerges into the sun, heading in a straight line southeast through a small meadow. On a spring or summer day, you're likely to see butterflies fluttering out of your path as you make your way down the narrow trail. After 0.3 miles, you'll see the picnic table and the parking lot from which you started.

The Preservation Society for Spring Creek Forest (**www.springcreekforest .org**) has a wealth of information on the plant and animal habitat of the area (including logs of the various bird species sighted), and information on nature walks and talks.

NEARBY ACTIVITIES

Just a couple miles to the southeast, the Firewheel Town Center, an open-air complex of department stores, retail shops, and restaurants, is a good spot to grab a bite to eat and do some shopping. To get there, head northeast on Holford Road, and turn south onto President George Bush Turnpike, traveling about 1.3 miles. Take the TX 78 north exit toward Sachse/Wylie and turn right onto Lavon Drive.

TURTLE CREEK LEISURE TRAIL 12

IN BRIEF

This scenic trail winds alongside Turtle Creek and Turtle Creek Boulevard, heading northeast through a greenbelt that passes through a couple parks. In several sections, the trail runs atop wooden bridges. Hike this trail in the fall for brilliant displays of fall foliage.

DESCRIPTION

Named after the renowned French botanist Julien Reverchon, Reverchon Park in Dallas serves as the trailhead for this hike. The park was originally modeled to be the "Central Park" of Dallas. In its 46 acres of open space, you'll find tennis and basketball courts, a recreation facility, and picturesque narrow staircases that wind up small landscaped hills to stone-bench seating areas. You'll also find access to the nearby Katy Trail. On the trail, traffic is light; most of the people there are joggers who live in the nearby condos and couples strolling along the creek. The path, which in some sections is built onto wooden trestle bridges suspended above the water, is slightly below street level and hidden from view in a few sections. As you would in any large city park, hike this trail with a pal.

The trailhead is located to the south of the rec center, adjacent to a smaller parking

KEY AT-A-GLANCE INFORMATION

LENGTH: 3 miles
CONFIGURATION: Out-and-back
DIFFICULTY: Easy
SCENERY: Fall foliage, creek, turtles
EXPOSURE: Partly sunny
TRAIL TRAFFIC: Light
TRAIL SURFACE: Paved path
HIKING TIME: 1.5 hours
ACCESS: Free; daily
FACILITIES: Restrooms, water fountains
WHEELCHAIR TRAVERSABLE: No
SPECIAL COMMENTS: Avoid this trail after heavy rains—the creek can be flooded, resulting in trail closures. Some sections of trail are secluded; hike with a pal.

Directions

Take I-35 to Oak Lawn Avenue and turn right. Turn right onto Maple Avenue. Reverchon Park is 0.25 miles down on the right. Park in the lot in front of the main entrance and recreation center.

GPS Trailhead Coordinates

UTM Zone (WGS84) 14S
Easting 704926
Northing 3631259
Latitude N 32° 48' 1"
Longitude W 96° 48' 41"

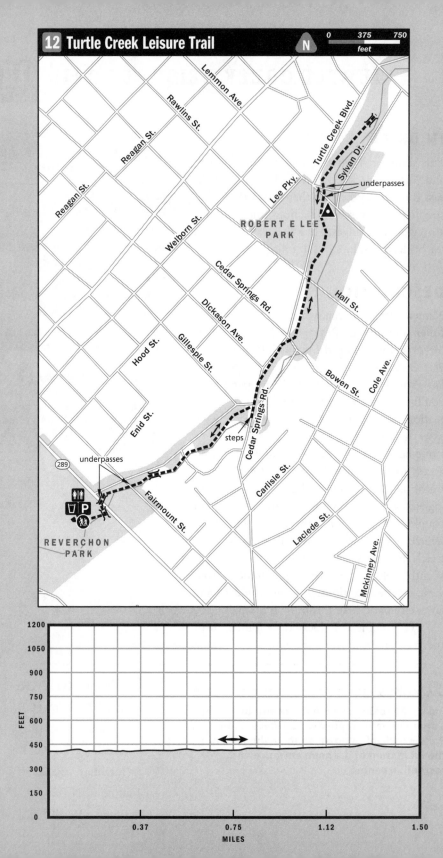

lot. Cross the short bridge and turn left. The paved path heads onto a long wooden bridge with wooden trestles suspended a few feet above Turtle Creek then rounds a curve and goes under an overpass. The trail continues northeast at creek level and crosses another bridge at 0.15 miles, staying on the western bank of the creek.

A few hundred feet farther, you'll bear right to reach another underpass at 0.23 miles. The trail continues, rising to street level then winding atop another long trestle bridge. On your left is Turtle Creek Boulevard, lined with condos and apartments. On your right the creek, which is actually a tributary of Trinity River, is still within view.

At 0.38 miles, you'll cross Park Bridge Court and follow the sidewalk past a wide grassy field, on the far side of which is the creek. The sidewalk curls to the right, approaching the creek, then goes over another wooden bridge. The trail then splits to the right and left. To the right, the trail winds downhill to go below street level and under an overpass. The city has closed off this section, so you should stay to the left, and cross over Cedar Springs Road at the crosswalk. Across the street, head about 400 feet to the right and you'll find an entrance through the railing with steps leading back below street level down to the creek, where you can pick the trail back up. A wooden walkway suspended above the water continues for several hundred feet alongside the creek. To your right, the far side of the creek's shores are densely covered with trees. As you walk along, it quickly becomes apparent why the creek was named after turtles; you can often spot their heads or shells popping out of the clear water as they laze along. In the afternoon, shade from the wall to your left shields you from the blazing sun on a hot day.

The trail ascends to street level at 0.88 miles and continues alongside the boulevard. Cross North Hall Street and enter a park. A plaque posted alongside the trail confirms that you're still on Turtle Creek Leisure Trail. To your right, a dam built into the creek helps pool its waters. The creek is wide enough here that it almost forms a pond—a perfect backdrop for the beautifully manicured park grounds. The surroundings are so attractive and distracting that you'll hardly notice the slow-moving cars on the boulevard to your left. A circular fountain has been placed in the creek's center, and the gentle sound of falling water drowns out the sounds of city life. Dozens of ducks can often be seen circling the waters or nestled along the green bank. On the far side of the creek, the bank slopes gently to the water's edge. Narrow stairs at intervals along the banks provide nature-goers easy access to the water. Stone benches on the water's edge complete the tranquil scene. In the fall, the leaves of the trees along both sides of the creek turn to brilliant colors of yellow, red, orange, and gold. As you walk along, you'll feel as though you've entered a painting and find it impossible not to let the beauty of your surroundings lift your spirits.

Before long, you'll leave the park, still continuing along the creek. You'll go through two underpasses then pass through William B. Dean Park. A bridge at the

One of the many wooden walkways suspended above the creek.

far end of the park is a congregating place for ducks and a good place to stop and check the creek for turtles before turning around and retracing your steps to the trailhead.

NEARBY ACTIVITIES

Head over to Uptown's West Village for some shopping. Uptown is an upscale neighborhood known for its boutiques and restaurants. To get there, head southeast down Maple Avenue 0.8 miles and turn left onto McKinney Avenue.

WHITE ROCK LAKE TRAIL 13

IN BRIEF

A popular spot with joggers, bikers, walkers, and hikers, this lengthy trail runs along White Rock Lake. The hike starts just past the waterfall-like spillway and hugs the shoreline, offering constant views of the water as it winds past the Dallas Arboretum.

DESCRIPTION

White Rock Lake is one of the most well-known outdoor spots among Dallasites. It has a 9-mile trail that circumnavigates the lake and attracts joggers, walkers, hikers, bikers, and skaters. One of its draws is that it's only 6 miles northeast of Dallas, in a populated area just 4 miles east of Highland Park.

The lake was completed in 1911 and was originally intended to be a primary reservoir for the city of Dallas. The city quickly outgrew the lake, however, and eventually the larger Lake Dallas was created to supply water. In its early days, the lake was also a popular swimming hole among locals; I even ran into an older gentleman by the trailhead reminiscing about the days he spent as a child with his father playing in the waters. Swimming there was banned in the early 1950s and has not been permitted since. The lake is also widely

KEY AT-A-GLANCE INFORMATION

LENGTH: 4.66 miles

CONFIGURATION: Out-and-back

DIFFICULTY: Easy

SCENERY: Lake, spillway

EXPOSURE: Sunny

TRAIL TRAFFIC: Heavy

TRAIL SURFACE: Paved

HIKING TIME: 1.75 hours

ACCESS: Daily; free

FACILITIES: Water fountains, benches

WHEELCHAIR TRAVERSABLE: Yes

SPECIAL COMMENTS: Bring a windbreaker if it's a windy day—the wind can really pick up over the water.

Directions

Follow I-30 east toward I-45 south, and take Exit 488 (Barry Avenue) onto E. R. L. Thornton Freeway toward East Grand Avenue. Turn left on East Grand Avenue and drive 2 miles. East Grand Avenue will become Garland Road. Turn left onto Winsted Drive. You'll see a sign for White Rock Park. Park in the lot on the right.

GPS Trailhead Coordinates

UTM Zone (WGS84) 14S

Easting 712780

Northing 3632974

Latitude N 32° 48' 51"

Longitude W 96° 43' 38"

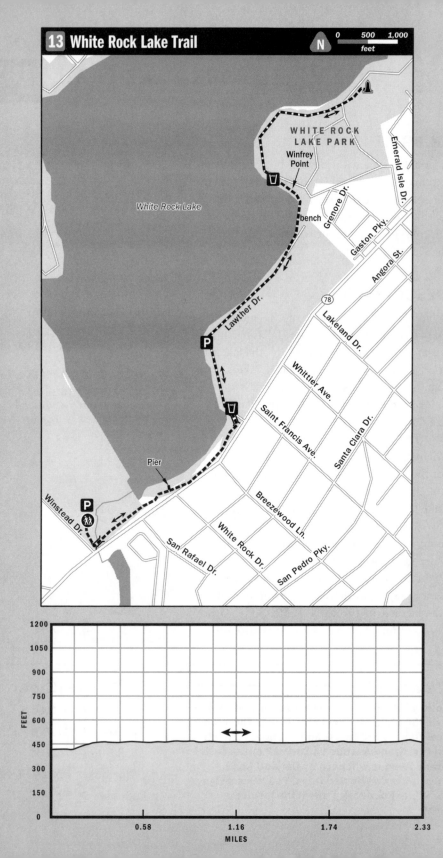

known for the annual White Rock Marathon, which started in 1971. Its route runs a loop from downtown to the lake and back.

Unfortunately, because of the lake's urban location, it has something of a reputation for being unsafe. Occasionally, you'll hear of assaults or thefts in the lake area—and for this reason, although I've lived very close to the lake for much of my life, I'd never been there. If, like me, you have preconceived notions of what the lake is like, you'll be thoroughly surprised at what you find. A volunteer group known as For the Love of the Lake (FTLOTL) has worked to clean and renovate the park, and their efforts show. The lake is very well kept, feels safe, and is surprisingly scenic. Also contributing to the feeling of safety is the fact that this section of the trail is exposed. During the day, you'll find it very busy—there are folks with baby strollers, dogs, and kids. Although I didn't spot a single vagrant or suspicious person on the trail, there are signs by the parking lot advising you to keep your valuables in your trunk. It's also a good idea for women and kids to bring a buddy along.

All the land surrounding the lake is part of White Rock Park, which has a several entrances. This hike starts from the southern end of the lake, at an entrance near the spillway. The small parking lot stays fairly full on weekends, although you can almost always manage to find at least one spot to squeeze your car into. The path is within view off to the left, running just in front of the spillway. Head onto the trail, and turn right, heading away from the parking lot toward Garland Road. The trail immediately curves left, heads over a concrete bridge, which bounces as folks jog by, and takes you directly alongside the massive, tiered spillway. Water cascades down its huge steps, which creates a thunderous noise. Ducks can often be spotted paddling on the top level, ignoring the nearby waterfall. Just across the bridge, the trail, which once wound very close to the edge of the lake, has been rerouted along Garland Road. This is the loudest and least pleasant section of the trail because, for a few hundred feet, you'll find yourself essentially on the sidewalk of a busy road. The trail soon curves downhill, away from the road and back toward and alongside the shoreline to your left. You'll have a good view of the path curving out before you, following the shoreline until it disappears around a bend in the shore. Expect the path to be busy. Bikers and joggers are constantly coming and going, and if you stop for a minute or two, expect to be overtaken by other hikers or dog-walkers.

At 0.4 miles, you'll pass a pier; walk out to the water and you might see ducks just around the shore here. Thanks in part to the Adopt-a-Shoreline program, you'll find the shore well kept. Through the program, various groups agree to be caretakers of certain sections of the lake's trail. You'll see wooden signs along the shore as you hike, identifying the group—such as Boy Scout troops or REI—whose section you're in. Trash receptacles along the trail also help keep the area clean.

As you continue on, you'll catch sight of a few very nice residences bordering Garland Road on your right before the trail curves northwest away from the

A view of the spillway adjacent to the trailhead.

street and over a bridge at 0.78 miles. Take a moment to glance over your shoulder for a nice view of the Dallas skyline. A couple hundred feet farther, you'll reach a water fountain where you can refresh yourself and read a nearby historical marker.

Continue down the trail, following the shoreline. Off to your right a fence runs behind the Dallas Arboretum. To your left, you'll have a complete view of the lake's grassy, tree-dotted shoreline. The trail is mostly sunny and exposed, allowing great visibility wherever you are on the trail; however, at 1.55 miles you'll reach one of the few sections with a small grouping of trees providing much-needed shade.

At 1.63 miles, you'll see a parking lot to your right and kids playing on the shoreline to your left. This lake entrance is known as Winfrey Point. Joggers joining the trail here are likely to merge and pass you on their quest for fitness. The trail then turns into a wide path painted with double lanes on each side. Continue north, and you'll soon round another curve and see a densely wooded section up ahead. A playground on your right marks yet another entrance. To your left, a shallow inlet attracts wading and shorebirds. A short dock extends into the waters, offering a good spot from which to view the birdlife. Here you'll also find a statue honoring the Civilian Conservation Corps, which worked at White Rock Lake from 1935 to 1942. Take a few minutes to rest before turning and retracing your steps to the trailhead. If you wanted to extend the hike, the trail continues another 6.5 miles, looping the rest of the way around the lake before returning you to the trailhead.

A stone marker memorializing the
Central National Highway of the
Republic of Texas

NEARBY ACTIVITIES

Head into downtown Dallas and explore the Arts District. You can visit the Dallas Museum of Art, which has a great collection of European paintings. Their Web site, **dallasmuseumofart.org**, lists the current exhibitions. Other nearby museums include the Nasher Sculpture Center, which houses pieces by Matisse, de Kooning, Picasso, and Rodin, and also the Crow Collection of Asian Art. From White Rock, take I-30 west about 2 miles, then exit onto I-45 south/US 75 north onto to reach Elm Street. Turn right on North Central Expressway; you'll soon turn left onto North Pearl Street.

Drive approximately 0.5 miles. Turn left on Flora Street, and left again on North Harwood; the Dallas Museum of Art is at 1717 North Harwood.

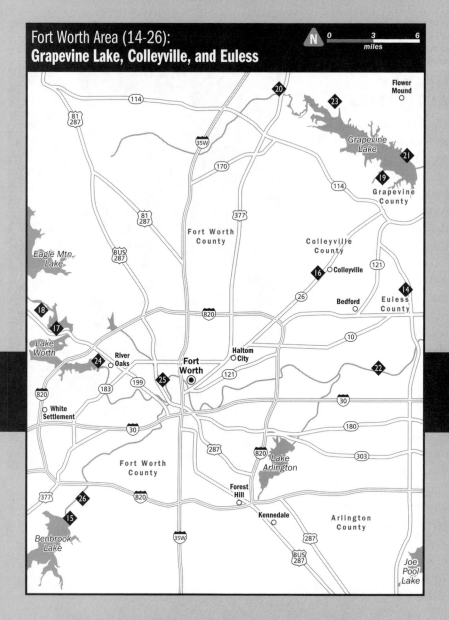

Fort Worth Area (14-26):
Grapevine Lake, Colleyville, and Euless

N   0   3   6
miles

ORT WORTH AREA (INCLUDING GRAPEVINE LAKE, COLLEYVILLE, AND EULESS)

14 BEAR CREEK-BOB EDEN TRAIL

KEY AT-A-GLANCE INFORMATION

LENGTH: 5.88 miles

CONFIGURATION: Out-and-back

DIFFICULTY: Easy

SCENERY: Creek, pond; woodland mixture of elms, oaks, and pecans; greenbelt

EXPOSURE: Partially sunny

TRAIL TRAFFIC: Heavy

TRAIL SURFACE: Paved

HIKING TIME: 2 hours

ACCESS: Daily, 7 a.m.–11 p.m.; free

FACILITIES: Restrooms, water fountains, picnic tables

WHEELCHAIR TRAVERSABLE: Yes

SPECIAL COMMENTS: For a shorter hike, turn around at McCormick Park.

IN BRIEF

Leave your plant-identification guidebook at home on this scenic trail along Bear Creek that winds through an undeveloped corridor linking three city parks. Plant markers, a bird-watching area, and nicely maintained park areas make this an enjoyable year-round hike.

DESCRIPTION

As far as greenbelts go, this linear trail connecting Bear Creek Park with Bob Eden Park is one of the prettier ones in the metroplex. It's a wild green oasis designed so that you'll hardly notice the urban setting it slices through. The community surrounding the trailhead consists mostly of quiet, well-kept apartment complexes inhabited by young professionals. You're likely to encounter many of these folks on the trail, walking their dogs or jogging along with iPod buds in their ears. Midway along the trail, a small pond attracts parents looking to laze away the afternoon fishing with their kids.

One of the things I love most about this trail are the dozens of markers labeling the various plants, trees, and shrubs along its route. If you're like me, you enjoy examining the leaves, bark, and fruit of trees you're unfamiliar with; this trail will deliver on helping

GPS Trailhead Coordinates

UTM Zone (WGS84) 14S

Easting   680874

Northing 3637607

Latitude N 32° 51' 42"

Longitude W 97° 4' 1"

Directions

Take TX 183 (Airport Freeway) into Euless and turn north onto TX 360. Go approximately 0.7 miles, then turn left onto Harwood Road. Drive about 0.8 miles, and the first right onto Bear Creek Parkway. Park in the lot on your right in Bear Creek Park.

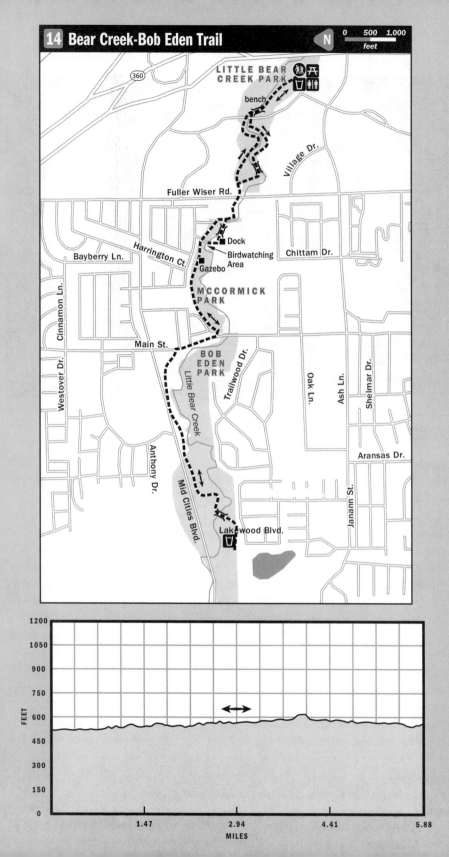

Markers identify trees and plants along the trail.

you identify them. If you've paid attention, after a few visits here, you'll be able to pick out trees such as chittamwood, cedar elm, and box elder on any trail. The trail has even fittingly been labeled a "Texas Outdoor Education Trail."

The trailhead is in 40-acre Bear Creek Park, adjacent to the parking lot. Wear a comfortable pair of walking shoes because the trail, which starts as fine gravel, later becomes a hard, paved path. This is also a great trail for dogs. Not only do fellow hikers welcome them readily, but the dogs themselves seem to love the shade-covered path—a few that I passed even held firmly to souvenir sticks they'd picked up along the way. Waste bags are available at the trailhead so you can clean up after your pet.

As you start down the trail, you'll see the waters of Bear Creek just off to your right. The trail is shaded by a mixture of slippery elm, ash, Indian currant, eastern red cedar, box elder, black walnut, and cedar elm—each painstakingly marked. Occasionally, you'll find signs marking "Bear Crossing," usually in spots where the trees part, allowing you to look out over the creek.

You'll pass a bench in the shade of a Shumard red oak (a tree known for its beautiful fall foliage) before the trail curves left and crosses the parkway. For those hiking with younger kids, it's good to know that this is not a busy street; motorists only occasionally pass by, and at very slow speeds. The road also has a clearly marked crosswalk. The trail winds through a nicely manicured park-like setting dotted with deciduous trees such as pecans and hackberries. Benches, a little plaza, and shaded picnic tables atop of a small rise make this a pretty spot for picnickers. Bear right and cross the wooden footbridge, bypassing the park, and continue along the creek. In the summer, the unmistakable song of cicadas fills the air.

The well-manicured path continues heading purposefully northwest, staying close to the creek. Every now and then, narrow dirt trails branch off to the right, heading a couple of dozen feet to the creek's edge, where you can get a better look at the brownish-green water. A mixture of elms and pecans close in on the trail, providing shade and obscuring the quiet apartments off to your left. You'll soon pass the first of several signposts for the "Advanced Timber Challenge Course." These exercise stations, a few of which you'll find in this section, instruct trail users on how to perform an exercise, such as the alternate-toe touch or horizontal ladder. As you continue, the vegetation becomes thicker and wilder, and you'll soon find yourself walking through a lush green understory thriving in the shade of the surrounding tall trees.

At 1.2 miles, you'll reach a junction, where you should bear left. You'll skirt the edges of a small sports field then reach another junction a few hundred feet down, where you'll again bear left. You'll then pass under a low overpass. When you emerge into the sun on the other side, you'll find the path has changed, becoming more like a greenbelt, with neatly maintained grassy slopes bordering the paved, sunny path. In the spring, small clusters of bluebonnets and Indian paintbrush bloom in rich displays of color just off the trail.

The trail winds through a field dotted with trees then reaches a junction where there is a bridge off to your left. The path continues straight; however, for a pleasant detour, cross the bridge. On the other side, you'll find a little pond typically full of kids and parents fishing from a short dock. Just beyond the dock, turn right to find a designated bird-watching area with a small wooden arbor amid a thick canopy of foliage adjacent to the creek. From here, retrace your steps across the bridge to the detour turnoff and continue on the trail, heading west. At the next turnoff, bear left onto Species Trail—a pretty section of shady, gravel trail through a wooded mixture of seep-willow, cedar elm, and bur oak. Severe erosion is deteriorating this section of the creek's banks.

You'll soon reach a parking lot; at this point, you've entered McCormick Park, which was named after the McCormick family who, in the early 1900s, used the area as a 130-acre farm. From here, the trail reenters a manicured park-like setting, passing a playground on the left and a pretty gazebo on the right. Just beyond the park, the trail returns to greenbelt; you'll see little besides cactus and wildflowers along this long, sunny stretch of trail. A striped yellow line divides the trail in half here, hinting that bikers use this flat section; on my hike I saw only a few dog-walkers. You'll briefly hike parallel to Mid Cities Boulevard before turning back south, crossing the creek, and reaching a sports field at Bob Eden Park. A few picnic tables provide a nice spot for you to lunch before you retrace your steps to the trailhead.

Bluebonnets grow in colorful clumps alongside the trail in the springtime.

NEARBY ACTIVITIES

Baseball fans will enjoy a visit to Ameriquest Field in Arlington, home of the Texas Rangers. Check their Web site **texas.rangers.mlb.com** for ticket information during baseball season. Year-round you can visit the Legends of the Game Museum, also at the stadium; it has a huge collection from the National Baseball Hall of Fame. The ballpark is only about 9 miles away. To get to there, go 6 miles south on TX 360, and exit at Lamar Boulevard. Bear right onto Lamar and take a left onto Ballpark Way.

BENBROOK DAM TRAIL 15

IN BRIEF

This trail runs along a grassy strip atop the Benbrook Dam and ends at the dam's spillway. Appealing for its unobstructed views of the lake and surrounding area, its flat, straight path makes it ideal for walkers and joggers.

DESCRIPTION

Located in southwest Fort Worth, Benbrook Lake is a 3,770-acre reservoir on Clear Fork of the Trinity River. It was dammed in 1952 and has contributed significantly to preventing flooding of the surrounding area. The Army Corps of Engineers' Web site describes severe flooding in the early '90s that might have led to more than a billion dollars in flood damage had the reservoir not been there. The corps manages the lake and surrounding lands, including a number of parks along its shorelines offering all types of recreation, including camping, fishing, swimming, boating, and hiking.

The trailhead is located a short walk east of the roundabout, at the gated road. As you drive in, you'll pass the gated road just off to the right before you reach the parking lot. A tall locked metal gate deliberately blocks the road to car traffic; however, foot traffic is permitted. Although foot traffic was light on my visit due to overcast weather, the path is

KEY AT-A-GLANCE INFORMATION

LENGTH: 3.1 miles
CONFIGURATION: Out-and-back
DIFFICULTY: Easy
SCENERY: Lake
EXPOSURE: Sunny
TRAIL TRAFFIC: Light
TRAIL SURFACE: Paved/grassy
HIKING TIME: 1.5 hours
ACCESS: Daily; free
FACILITIES: Restrooms (not open during this visit), picnic tables
WHEELCHAIR TRAVERSABLE: No
SPECIAL COMMENTS: After the hike, walk or drive south down the park road to the boat ramp for a nice, up-close view of the water.

Directions ⟶

Follow I-20 west toward Abilene and take Exit 434A toward Granbury Road/South Drive. Turn left onto Granbury and go approximately 3 miles, then turn right onto Dirks Road and travel 2 miles. Bear right onto Lakeside Drive and go 0.5 miles. The parking lot will be on the left, just past the lake office. Park near the roundabout off to the right.

GPS Trailhead Coordinates

UTM Zone (WGS84) 14S
Easting   645762
Northing 3613585
Latitude   N 32° 39' 1"
Longitude   W 97° 26' 45"

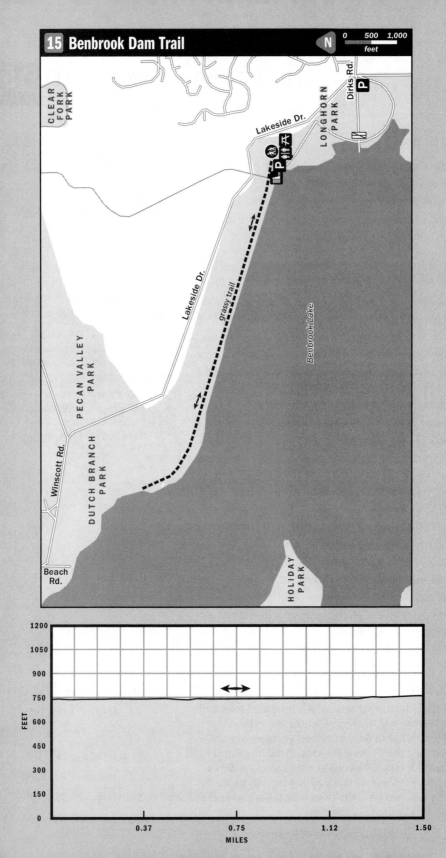

said to be especially popular with joggers. To access the area, you'll need to step over the low barrier adjacent to the gate. From here, just head down the road toward the lake.

Yucca sprout alongside the road, drinking in the sun on this exposed section of path. Continue heading west, following the road until you reach the lake. The trail surface then changes from paved to partial grass as it continues west atop the crest of the dam, an earth-fill embankment that stretches 1.5 miles across the north end of the lake to a spillway at the western end. Steep grassy slopes lead down to the lake level; you'll hike along the flat top. Be aware, however, that even though there is no fence restricting access to the dam's steep slopes, walking down or on them is strictly prohibited.

Because it was overcast the day I hiked this trail, I was concerned that the hike might not be enjoyable. To my surprise, the weather proved to be ideal. The cloud cover kept the temperature cool, allowing me to maintain a fast clip on the ridge's flat, even, exposed surface without even breaking a sweat. The lack of wind caused the lake to be ripple-free and eerily still. The lake reflected the gray sky perfectly, making it impossible to discern where sky ended and water began. Overall, it ended up being perfect weather. If you come on a sunny day, be sure to bring a hat and sunscreen because there is no shade on this trail.

Regardless of the weather, your hike across the dam will afford fantastic views of the lake spreading below and off to the left. Looking to the right, you'll have a bird's-eye view of encroaching development to the north. You'll also be able to spot golf carts roaming the nearby Pecan Valley Municipal Golf Course, and you'll hear the rumble of cars as they barrel down Lakeside Drive.

As you hike along, keep an eye out for birds flying low over the lake or standing along the shoreline. You're most likely to see wading birds and shorebirds such as herons, grebes, cormorants, ducks, and egrets. Birders have spotted more than 269 species of birds in the area, so be sure to bring some binoculars.

As you approach the western side of the dam, you'll see a narrow road that runs down along the shoreline to your left and curls out to a small inlet. Unfortunately, the road actually starts on the opposite side of the lake and is not accessible from this side of the dam.

A short walk farther and you'll have reached the spillway, where the path ends at a locked gate. Although the gate prohibits you from crossing to the other side of the lake, there is a nice overlook with views of the spillway. From here, just retrace your steps across the dam to the trailhead.

NEARBY ACTIVITIES

The nearby Fort Worth Botanic Gardens, at 3220 Botanic Garden Boulevard, offers 109 acres with more than 2,500 species of plant life and includes a Japanese garden, rose garden, and fragrance garden. The grounds are open 8 a.m. to dusk; visit their Web site at **www.fwbg.org** for specifics on fees and the

A windless day creates a mirror-like surface on Benbrook Lake.

restaurant's hours. Near the botanical gardens, Forest Park offers a few acres with a historic log cabin village, which includes interpreters and demonstrators. Information on the small admittance fee and access hours can be found at their Web site **www.logcabinvillage.org**. To get to Forest Park from the trail, head down Dirks Road and turn left onto Bryant Irvin Boulevard. Continue 6 miles. Turn right onto Camp Bowie Boulevard. After 0.5 miles, bear right onto I-30 east; go 2 miles then take Exit 12A onto West Rosedale Street toward University Drive. Bear right, heading south onto South University Drive; the Log Cabin Village is about 1 mile down on the right. To get to the botanical gardens from the intersection of I-30 and University Drive, head north on University Drive. The garden entrance is on the left.

COLLEYVILLE NATURE TRAIL 16

IN BRIEF

This hike starts on a paved trail through the woods then heads off onto a dirt path that winds around some picturesque ponds, where you'll find ducks, geese, and folks fishing.

DESCRIPTION

Though small, the 46-acre Colleyville Nature Center is remarkably picturesque, boasting pretty nature trails that wind around nine different ponds. It's popular with both adults and kids, many drawn in by the charm of resident ducks and geese that move from pond to pond in a never-ending quest for food. Fishing is allowed, and on a sunny day you're likely to see parents with their kids on the banks of the ponds, casting lines and hoping for nibbles. Pets are also allowed, though they must be leashed.

The trailhead is the paved path adjacent to the parking lot. Turn right, following the wide path toward the tree line. To your left you'll see a short trail leading to a small pond where a wooden pier overlooks the water. You can sometimes spot ducks huddled on the bank in the shadow of the pier's wooden decking. To the left of the pond is a small pavilion with a picnic table, where I spotted a gaggle of geese congregating—likely hoping to get food left by a fellow hiker finishing his lunch.

KEY AT-A-GLANCE INFORMATION

LENGTH: 1.38 miles
CONFIGURATION: Loop
DIFFICULTY: Easy
SCENERY: Multiple ponds, ducks, geese
EXPOSURE: Sunny to shady
TRAIL TRAFFIC: Moderate
TRAIL SURFACE: Packed dirt, paved path
HIKING TIME: 35 minutes
ACCESS: Free; daily 30 minutes before sunrise to 30 minutes after sunset
FACILITIES: Playground, picnic table
WHEELCHAIR TRAVERSABLE: No
SPECIAL COMMENTS: Identified by the Fort Worth Audubon Society as a great spot for birding; they suggest looking for warblers during the winter months.

Directions

Take TX 114 west toward Grapevine and exit onto TX 26 west/Ira E. Woods Avenue and travel 5 miles. Turn right onto Glade Road and go 0.5 miles, then turn left onto Mill Creek Drive. Continue 0.3 miles to the Colleyville Nature Center's entrance.

GPS Trailhead Coordinates

UTM Zone (WGS84) 14S
Easting 671565
Northing 3639074
Latitude N 32° 52' 35"
Longitude W 97° 9' 58"

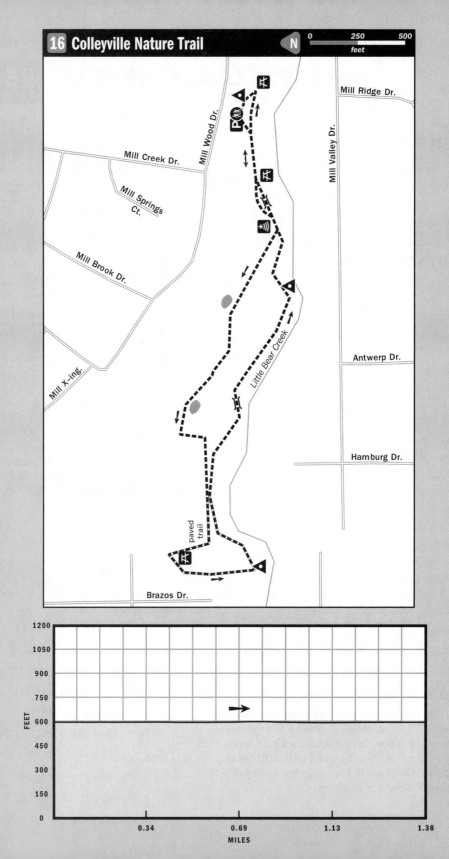

N

0   250   500
feet

Mill Ridge Dr.

Mill Valley Dr.

Mill Wood Dr.

Mill Creek Dr.

Mill Springs Ct.

Mill Brook Dr.

Mill X-ing.

Little Bear Creek

Antwerp Dr.

Hamburg Dr.

paved trail

Brazos Dr.

1200

1050

900

750

600

450

300

150

0

FEET

MILES

0.34   0.69   1.13   1.38

The trail winds beneath some towering trees then, at 0.13 miles, reaches a split where you'll see a bridge heading into the woods to the left. Stay right. The trail curls through a wooded area where vines encircle tall trees that lean into the trail, shrouding it in shade. In the fall, the woods echo with the sounds of squirrels loosening nuts from the trees and tossing them to the ground for storage.

The next trail junction, at 0.2 miles, has some picnic tables and a sign describing the history of the nature center. This is the where the nature trail starts. Turn left, leaving the paved path to turn onto the nature trail. About 150 feet down, you'll cross a bridge then reach the amphitheater, an open area with log benches. A couple of hundred feet past the amphitheater, you'll reach another junction. Turn right, following the wide dirt trail northwest through the forest. Listen for the cheery trills of warblers (small songbirds you may spot here).

There are a couple of interpretive signs placed on the trails. The first one you'll come across is at 0.3 miles, at a turnoff to the right; it discusses the inhabitants of the surrounding forest. Continue straight west, bypassing the junction. The trail leaves the shelter of the trees and emerges onto a sunny, grassy lawn that abuts a small pond. Yellow wildflowers, berry-bearing bushes, and small bird boxes make for a cheery scene. At 0.4 miles, another interpretive sign describes aerial residents you may spot here, including great blue herons and the smaller green herons, kingfishers, and flycatchers.

At 0.53 miles, you'll reach another pond; two more are within sight to the west. The trail curves along the pond's edge, and at 0.65 miles connects with a paved path that runs along a narrow bank between the ponds, where you should turn left. You can sometimes catch sight of ducks happily waddling in straight lines out of one pond and into another. Keep an eye out for turtles, whose heads you'll catch popping in and out of the water if you look carefully, and small frogs, which quickly hop off the trail as you pass by.

A few hundred feet farther, the paved path ends, becoming gravel; take a right at the trail split. You'll be able to see a pond off to the right for a few more minutes before you're back in the shade of the forest. This section is fairly close to the nature center's boundaries. Though you'll briefly glimpse some houses to the right, the trail veers away from them and they're quickly hidden from view.

Continue on the gravel trail, bypassing any smaller turnoffs you see. At 0.85 miles, you'll reach an overlook with a view of a small babbling creek; shortly thereafter, you'll bear right, off the gravel trail and back onto the paved path.

You'll soon find yourself back in the familiar territory near the ponds. Bear right to rejoin the dirt trail along the lake, then make another right to reenter the forest. Next, take the right-hand trail as it curves south around a large pit of dirt mounds.

The distinctive cacophony of cicadas drowns out the gurgling of the creek to your right as you continue through the forest. At 1 mile, you'll cross a bridge. Continue another 0.1 mile to the next junction, where you'll turn right. You'll soon reach a sign mounted on a stone pillar overlooking the water and identifying

Ducks rest along the banks of one of nature center's many ponds.

this as Little Bear Creek. Keep an eye out for turtles lazing on its banks, and small birds flitting through the trees along its shore. Head right at the next split, at 1.2 miles. You'll pass some cedar trees and find yourself back at the amphitheater. From here, retrace your steps to the trailhead.

NEARBY ACTIVITIES

The popular North East Mall, which has department stores such as Macy's, Nordstrom, and Sears and dozens of smaller specialty shops, is only 5 miles southwest of the Colleyville Nature Center. There is a wide selection of restaurants in and around the mall. To get there, head south down Colleyville Boulevard. Turn left onto Precinct Line Road and go 1.5 miles, then make a right onto West Bedford and travel 0.6 miles before turning left onto Melbourne Road.

FORT WORTH NATURE CENTER:
Canyon Ridge Trail

IN BRIEF

This rigorous trail climbs into the hills, winds through massive patches of yuccas, and provides scenic overlooks with views of Lake Worth before descending back down to lake level. Deer are abundant on this trail.

DESCRIPTION

The Fort Worth Nature Center's sprawling 3,600 acres is one of the largest city-owned nature centers in the country and has miles of hiking trails covering a range of habitats, including woodlands, grasslands, and wetlands. There's enough variety in the center's trails to appeal to anyone, with hikes that reward you with pretty views as they climb up through the hillsides, and flat trails that meander lazily along the river bottom.

The area is also surprisingly full of wildlife. I counted nearly a dozen white-tailed deer on a recent hike and glimpsed (before they jumped off into the woods) two coyotes running down the nature center's narrow road. And you're almost certain to catch sight of something in the enclosed buffalo range, in the field housing the well-established prairie dog population, or on the boardwalk. Of the many available, I've selected two hikes, which

KEY AT-A-GLANCE INFORMATION

LENGTH: 4.71 miles
CONFIGURATION: Loop
DIFFICULTY: Difficult
SCENERY: Woodlands, canyon views, yucca
EXPOSURE: Partly sunny to sunny
TRAIL TRAFFIC: Light
TRAIL SURFACE: Dirt
HIKING TIME: 2.5 hours
ACCESS: $4 adults, children $2; summer: weekdays 8 a.m.–8 p.m.; weekends 7 a.m.–8 p.m.; winter: 7 days a week, 8 a.m.–5 p.m.
FACILITIES: Restrooms, water fountains, picnic tables
WHEELCHAIR TRAVERSABLE: No
SPECIAL COMMENTS: Bring repellent for spiders, gnats, and other flying insects. Pets are allowed but must be leashed. Bicycles are not allowed on trails, so many folks take advantage of the slow and sparse traffic on the nature center's roads to ride around.

Directions

Take Loop I-820 to Jacksboro Highway (TX 199). Go 4 miles west and exit at Confederate Park Road. Go about 0.5 miles and turn right onto Buffalo Road to reach the entrance to the Fort Worth Nature Center. From the entrance, take a right at the first two forks to get to the trailhead. The road ends at the trailhead parking lot.

GPS Trailhead Coordinates

UTM Zone (WGS84) 14S
Easting   644187
Northing   3632866
Latitude   N 32° 49' 28"
Longitude   W 97° 27' 35"

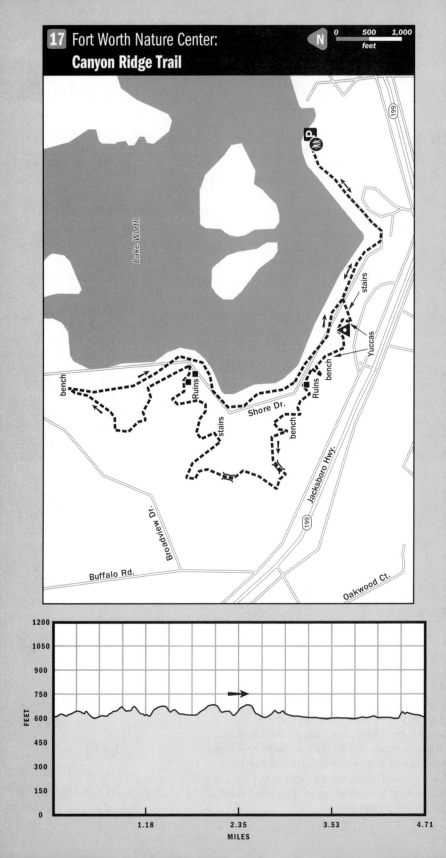

will give you a good introduction to the center. To explore the entire nature center, you'll need more than one visit.

Until 2006, the nature center was free; however, it now charges a small entrance fee, which will go toward improvements. In exchange for your fee, you'll receive a map of the park, which is worth a review, especially if you plan on visiting the Hardwicke Interpretive Center (located in the center of the nature center) or driving by the buffalo range. Water fountains, picnic areas, and restrooms can be found ata the Hardwicke Interpretive Center.

To get to the trailhead from the entrance booth, take a right at the first intersection, and a right at the next intersection. The road ends 1 mile down, at a small parking area—the trailhead is on the southwest side of the lot. The trail heads steeply uphill and is marked with the Canyon Ridge Trail sign, a picture of a flowering yucca. Your map has a key to help you identify the other trail signs.

The first part of this hike takes you gradually uphill. Stairs worked into the hillside at the steep points make this a fairly easy climb. The trail continues up wooded hillsides and over some wooden bridges. As you gain altitude, look to your right for views of Lake Worth, which the nature center abuts. The trail runs fairly parallel to the road in this section, and you'll catch glimpses of it to your right before the path veers away from the road and enters a section of towering trees. At 0.73 miles you'll reach a long staircase built into a towering hill. From here, the trail winds through the hilltops after circumventing a couple of fields overtaken by hundreds of yucca. Overlooks at 0.83 and 0.98 miles offer pretty views of Lake Worth and Greer Island below.

At 1.08 miles, the trail splits. To your left, you'll see the dilapidated remnants of an old bathroom. If you decide to explore, look out for spiders hanging from its entryway and corners. Ruins such as these, left over from the Civilian Conservation Corps' initial work in the area, can be found all along the trail.

The rocky trail climbs a little more through the wooded hillside and at 1.4 miles reaches a bench positioned to overlook the canyon—a nice spot to take a break. If you like to hike early in the day, be aware that the webs of orb-weaving spiders sometimes span the trail in this section. The large spiders sitting in the center of the webs can be intimidating to arachnophobes. Carry a walking stick to clear the path. Alternatively, consider hiking later in the day after other hikers have cleared the trail!

Continuing on, the trail passes through a couple of pretty fields filled with purple wildflowers, an excellent spot to sight some of the many white-tailed deer that live here. I came upon a couple groups of them that I was able to admire before they saw me and hopped out of sight. On my way out of the nature center, I spoke with a visitor who was equally impressed by the deer he had seen, having spotted both a ten-point stag and an eight-point stag hopping into the woods elsewhere in the park.

A staircase built into the hillside leads you to views of Lake Worth.

The trail continues past a couple bridges and starts a gradual descent, passing more old, building remnants, including one at 2.61 miles, which affords a beautiful view of Lake Worth. Just after the ruins, there are stairs built into the hillside. Descend here and you'll quickly spot the park road through the woods. At 3.11 miles, the trail intersects the road then picks back up across the street, continuing as Riverbottom Trail. For this hike, you'll turn right onto the road, following it back to the trailhead.

NEARBY ACTIVITIES

The nature center offers monthly canoe tours down the West Fork of the Trinity River, and a monthly canoe fest where, for a small fee, you're provided with canoes, paddles, and lifejackets, and can float around Greer Island. Check their Web site **www.fwnaturecenter.org** for a calendar events and fees.

Year-round, stop by downtown Fort Worth to visit Sundance Square, the city's entertainment and shopping district, which has restored buildings housing museums, galleries, gift shops, and a diverse selection of restaurants covering everything from sandwiches to sushi to steaks.

FORT WORTH NATURE CENTER: 18
Prairie Trail

IN BRIEF

Children especially will love this flat trail that winds alongside a buffalo range and Prairie Dog Town, then through a wide prairie that offers excellent wildlife viewing.

DESCRIPTION

From the entrance, get to the trailhead by turning left at the first fork in the road. About 1 mile down, you'll see a small parking lot on the right with a huge "Buffalo Range" sign; a smaller sign next to it announces "Prairie Dog Town." The trailhead is just to the right of the sign. A huge fenced-in prairie adjacent to the trailhead keeps the aforementioned buffaloes and prairie dogs separated from hikers so that they can be viewed from a safe distance.

If you look closely at the prairie, you'll spot dozens of dirt mounds throughout it, marking prairie dog burrows. The small squirrel-like rodents can at first be difficult to spot because their fur is so close to the color of the dirt. Look for the prairie dogs by their burrows; you'll see them bobbing up and down—and it is difficult to miss their high-pitched barks. Prairie dogs bark to alert the colony to predators.

You may or may not see the other prairie resident—the buffalo—in this area; the Buffalo

KEY AT-A-GLANCE INFORMATION

LENGTH: 1 mile
CONFIGURATION: Loop
DIFFICULTY: Easy
SCENERY: Prairies
EXPOSURE: Sunny
TRAIL TRAFFIC: Moderate
TRAIL SURFACE: Packed dirt
HIKING TIME: 25 minutes
ACCESS: $4 adults, children $2; summer: weekdays 8 a.m.–8 p.m.; weekends 7 a.m.–8 p.m.; winter: 7 days a week, 8 a.m.–5 p.m.
FACILITIES: Restrooms, water fountains, picnic tables
WHEELCHAIR TRAVERSABLE: No
SPECIAL COMMENTS: This is a sun-drenched trail. Bring sunscreen and water. Binoculars are also useful—the prairie dogs are small and stay a few hundred feet behind a fence. Pets are allowed but must be leashed. Bicycles are not allowed on trails, so many cyclists take advantage of the slow and sparse traffic on the nature center's roads.

Directions

Take Loop I-820 to Jacksboro Highway (TX 199). Go 4 miles west and exit at Confederate Park Road. Go about 0.5 miles and turn right onto Buffalo Road to the entrance of the Fort Worth Nature Center. From the entrance, bear left at the fork in the road to get to the trailhead; you'll see a parking area about 1 mile down on the right.

GPS Trailhead Coordinates

UTM Zone (WGS84) 14S
Easting 642408
Northing 3634760
Latitude N 32° 50' 30"
Longitude W 97° 28' 42"

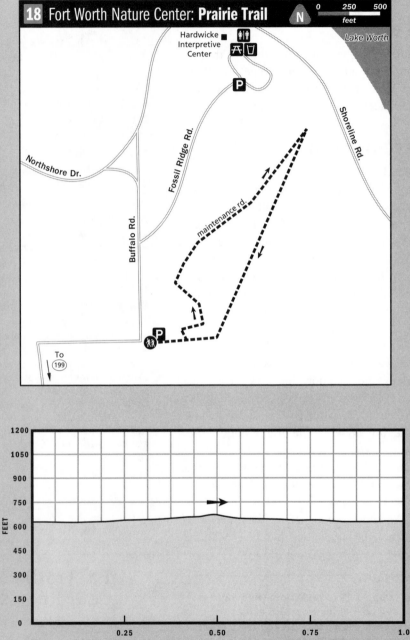

A glimpse of a buffalo in the Buffalo Range.

Range is actually quite large, and the animals have a lot of space in which to roam. Benches along the trail face the fence, offering a nice spot to linger while looking for wildlife. I stopped at various points along the fence, waiting with high hopes for even a single sighting, but the prairie dogs seemed to have taken over the entire prairie and there was not a single buffalo to be seen. I did not, however, leave the park disappointed—as we drove away from the trailhead, I spotted a whole herd roaming another section of their range, within a dozen feet of a fenced enclosure alongside the park road. Park staff at the interpretive center or the gate entrance can often tell you where the herd is.

The trail follows the fence east. At about 400 feet, you'll bear left, heading north away from the Buffalo Range and through some brush. Keep an eye out for the variety of birds that migrate through the refuge. The Fort Worth Audubon Society lists the refuge as good for bird-watching and notes that in the summer you'll find a variety of hummingbirds, whereas, in winter, sightings include the yellow-bellied sapsucker, purple finch, and blue warbler.

At 0.25 miles, the trail crosses a grassy maintenance road and continues northeast into a huge, sunny prairie filled with tall grasses and small red and purple flowers, a good spot for sighting some of the many white-tailed deer that live here. The prairie buzzes with the pleasant hum of grasshoppers, crickets, and the occasional flying insect, so it's a good idea to apply insect repellent before your hike.

A hilltop overtaken by yucca

You'll reach a split at 0.45 miles. You should bear right to loop back south through the prairie. Heading left would take you to the Hardwick Interpretive Center, which has refuge information and exhibits, including a reclusive bobcat that can sometimes be seen in his outdoor enclosure. The center is also adjacent to an interesting short trail along a fossil-shell outcrop.

Continue straight, following the trail until you reach the Buffalo Range again at 0.7 miles, where you should turn left. The trail will split again at 0.9 miles. Following the left trail takes you alongside the Buffalo Range another 500 feet until you're back at the trailhead. On my visit, I noticed at least one trail in this area had been blocked off and marked with an "Earth Healing" sign; encourage children to stay on the trails to minimize visitor impact to the refuge.

NEARBY ACTIVITIES

The nature center offers monthly canoe tours down the West Fork of the Trinity River, and a monthly canoe fest where, for a small fee, you're provided with canoes, paddles, and lifejackets, and can float around Greer Island. Check their Web site **www.fwnaturecenter.org** for a calendar events and fees.

Year-round, stop by downtown Fort Worth to visit Sundance Square, the city's entertainment and shopping district, which has restored buildings housing museums, galleries, gift shops, and a diverse selection of restaurants covering everything from sandwiches to sushi to steaks.

HORSESHOE TRAIL 19

IN BRIEF

A very popular spot with locals, Horseshoe Trail offers a lively hike along a paved path circling the a small section of Lake Grapevine's southern edge. Dog-walkers, hikers, joggers, and bikers abound along this cheery trail. There is also the opportunity to hike along some dirt paths if you're so inclined.

DESCRIPTION

Horseshoe Trail is inside Oak Grove Park, which sits on the southern shoreline of Grapevine Lake, very close to downtown Grapevine. When you enter the park, turn left at the park sign and park in the parking area by the restrooms, a short drive down on the right.

The trailhead is on the pathway across the road from the restrooms. To your left, the paved pathway has a yellow stripe down its center; to your right, you'll see an old park road just beyond a gate blocking auto traffic. A marker adjacent to the gate identifies the road as Horseshoe Trail. Take a right here. Small brush and trees adjacent to the trail conceal the lake (which is off to the right) as you make your way southwest. Keep an eye out for the brilliant red cardinals flitting through the trees.

KEY AT-A-GLANCE INFORMATION

LENGTH: 4.08 miles
CONFIGURATION: Out-and-back
DIFFICULTY: Easy
SCENERY: Lake, woods
EXPOSURE: Sunny
TRAIL TRAFFIC: Heavy
TRAIL SURFACE: Paved
HIKING TIME: 1.5 hours
ACCESS: Daily; free
FACILITIES: Restrooms, picnic tables, benches
WHEELCHAIR TRAVERSABLE: Yes
SPECIAL COMMENTS: Dogs are welcome on this lively trail.

Directions

From Dallas, take TX 114 west toward Grapevine and exit at TX 26/TX 114 –BUS, turning right onto Texan Trail. From here, turn left onto Northwest Highway, pass Main Street, and turn right onto North Dove Road (which becomes Dove Loop Road), heading North into Oak Grove Park.

GPS Trailhead Coordinates

UTM Zone (WGS84) 14S
Easting 678121
Northing 3648865
Latitude N 32° 57' 49"
Longitude W 97° 5' 39"

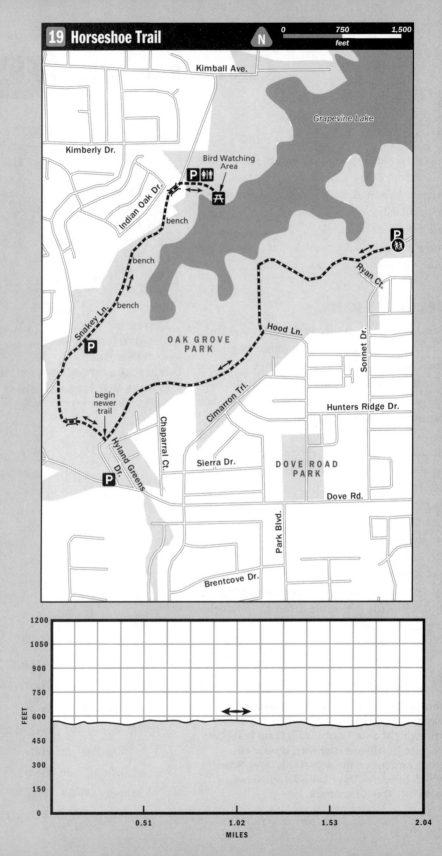

This is not a trail for those looking to be alone with their thoughts—it is almost always teeming with the infectious cheer of fellow outdoor-goers. Folks are friendly and wave or smile as they pass by, giving you a few minutes alone before another group passes by. Trail users include everyone from inline skaters and bikers to dog-walkers and joggers to those just looking to get outside. Unlike other trails, which can become popular with a certain niche, folks on this trail seem to include every age group. I spotted every demographic, from young families out for the day to older couples out for a stroll to teenagers and 20-somethings out for some sun. I even spotted a group of Boy Scouts marching happily along an adjacent path following their scout master.

At regular intervals along the path, you'll see single-track dirt trails veering off the road and disappearing beneath the trees to the right. These trails loop out to the lake, providing a nice detour for those looking to explore the woods. If you miss one, just keep walking and another path will appear soon enough. Many of the dirt trails you'll see off to the left lead only to the back porches of local residents' houses.

The road continues curling southwest past more thickets and scrubby trees. At 0.55 miles you'll reach a junction with another park road, which is gated and inaccessible; continue straight. You'll come upon the intersection of Horseshoe Trail and Colt Road 0.1 mile later. A solitary bench sits near the intersection. The bench may have served a purpose at some time, but it now sits almost inaccessible amid a small patch of grassland at the junction of two roads open only to foot traffic. Continue straight on Horseshoe Trail. A short trek later, you'll reach a junction with Bronco Drive. Again, continue straight along the trail.

On the left, the backyards and back porches of houses abutting the trail spring into view. A short distance farther, you'll reach another junction. At this point, the trail changes from old, paved road to a narrower paved path with a yellow dividing line down its center. Off to the left, you'll see an alternate trailhead and parking lot with a plastic bag dispenser for cleaning up after your dog. This is a busy access point, and the parking lot is often quite full. To the right, the trail continues northwest. Bear right and follow the trail downhill past much of the same scenery: trees and underbrush. The trail follows the shoreline, making its way around the end of the lake.

As you round a bend of the lake, the foliage clears and you find yourself sandwiched between a road to the left, and the lake to your right. Thankfully, the roadway is slightly raised above the trail and mostly blocked from view, so you will not find the car traffic distracting. At 1.23 miles, you'll cross a bridge. Just 0.25 miles farther, a parking lot on the left marks another trail entrance. Off to the right, you'll have a clear view of the end of the lake—a barren expanse of marshland. A sign adjacent to the trail indicates that this section is part of a Blue Bonnet Naturalization Eagle Scout Project.

At 1.93 miles, you'll cross another bridge before reaching yet another parking area at 2 miles. Just beyond the lot and off to the right, you'll find a

> When the lake levels are low, you may only catch brief glimpses of the water from the trail.

bird-watching area dotted with a few picnic tables. My favorite spot is at the back of the picnic area, where one table has been placed on the edge of the outcrop to overlook the lake. This is the perfect spot to have lunch and scan for herons and egrets in the shallow waters and along the sandy shore below. From here, just turn back and retrace your steps to the trailhead.

NEARBY ACTIVITIES

Head into downtown Grapevine and take a ride on the Grapevine Vintage Railroad. The steam locomotive and open-air coaches head down the Cotton Belt Route into Stockyards Station in Fort Worth. The train runs only on the weekends; for schedules and fees visit their Web site at **www.grapevinesteamrailroad.com.** The depot is at 707 South Main Street in Grapevine, just off Northwest Highway.

KNOB HILL TRAIL

IN BRIEF

Located west of Grapevine Lake, this trail roughly follows Denton Creek on a pleasant trek through impressive stands of cactus and wildflowers. A bench atop a wildflower-covered hill awaits you at its end.

DESCRIPTION

This unexpectedly scenic trail is just west of Grapevine Lake. From the trailhead, the path makes a roundabout loop toward the lake. In the spring, when the cactus flowers are blooming and the hills are green and dotted with wildflowers, the trail inspires a sense of renewal.

Maintained by the Dallas Off Road Bicycle Association (DORBA), this trail sees its fair share of mountain bikers, who love it for its initial steep winding sections. Though bike traffic can be moderate on the weekends, bikers quickly pass by, intent on doing the full 9-mile-plus round-trip in an hour, which makes traffic feel much lighter. Since the trail is winding, and some parts are also narrow, allowing for only single-file walking, you'll

KEY AT-A-GLANCE INFORMATION

LENGTH: 6.96 miles
CONFIGURATION: Out-and-back
DIFFICULTY: Moderate with some strenuous sections
SCENERY: Cactus, wildflowers, woods, hilly meadow
EXPOSURE: Mix of sunny and shady
TRAIL TRAFFIC: Moderate
TRAIL SURFACE: Packed dirt
HIKING TIME: 3 hours
ACCESS: Free; closed when muddy
FACILITIES: There are no restrooms or water.
WHEELCHAIR TRAVERSABLE: No
SPECIAL COMMENTS: The trail has a couple of steep, slippery sections and is also exceptionally hard packed, which can be tough on the feet. Wear comfortable shoes with a good tread.

Directions

Take TX 114 West to Farm to 377 north. About 1.3 miles down, just after you cross over Denton Creek, you'll see the trailhead and a small dirt parking lot just off FM 377 on the right. Don't let the trailhead's highway-adjacent location scare you. This is a secondary rural highway, and the parking area is sufficiently large and acceptably safe. When visiting for the first time, just be sure to keep an eye out for the dirt parking lot, which often has at least a few cars in it—if you whiz down FM 377 too fast, you may miss it.

GPS Trailhead Coordinates

UTM Zone (WGS84)   14S
Easting   667409
Northing   3657669
Latitude   N 33° 02' 41"
Longitude   W 97° 12' 26"

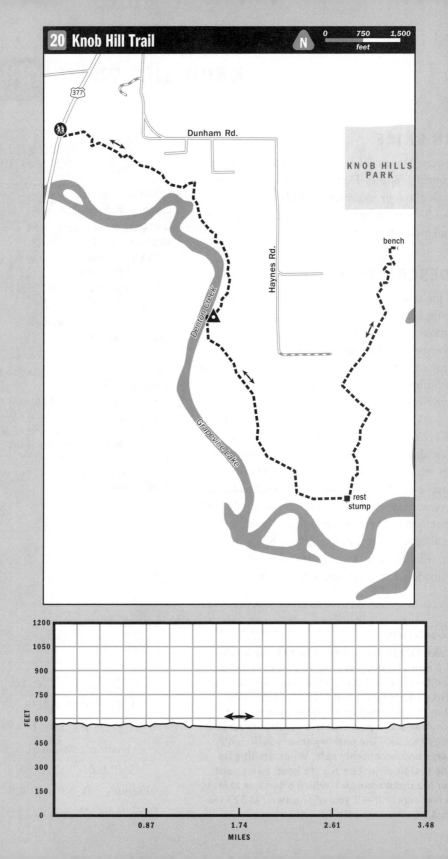

need to let others know bikers are approaching, especially if you're bringing kids. Yelling "Bike!" as a signal for everyone to step off to the same side of the trail works best. The trail is closed when muddy, so if it's just rained, you'll have to pick another hike.

Although the trailhead is almost adjacent to the highway, within a couple hundred feet, the sounds of cars are replaced by the chirping of birds as the trail curls away from the road and around some small hills. The hillsides on the first half of this trail are blanketed with hundreds of prickly pear cacti. In the spring, they bloom with beautiful large yellow flowers, creating an impressive display. Even the remnants of an old, abandoned road have been taken over by the wild cactus garden.

The trail winds gently downhill into a small section of woods, where the path has a few short, steep drops—a favorite section of mountain bikers. On my hike, evidence of helmet fragments littered a portion of the trail, where some unfortunate person had misjudged the roughness of this section. Although there are a couple of steep, slick spots, hikers will find these sections of path wide and easily maneuvered if they are careful. The most difficult spot, a neck-breaking cliff-like drop of about 12 feet, has a gentle sloping footpath encircling it. The trail soon crosses a small creek littered with horse apples (also known as hedge apples) from a nearby Osage orange tree. The path soon reaches a small opening in the brush overlooking the muddy, slow-moving waters of Denton Creek. Although the trail loosely follows the creek, this is the only glimpse of it you'll find on the hike.

From here, the trail's terrain quickly changes as you leave the woods and head into a sunny, flat section that leads through a large field of tall reeds. A little farther down the trail and just past the billowing fluffy seed clouds of a cottonwood tree, look for a large log, which marks the outbound midpoint and serves as an excellent spot for a break.

From here, the surrounding terrain changes yet again as the trail turns north and heads through dense green foliage where hundreds of delicate purple wildflowers do their best to flourish in patches of sun. If you listen beyond the cicadas, crickets, and birds, you're likely to hear the moos of nearby cows. As you emerge into an area open to the sky, the path soon changes from hard-packed brown dirt to packed red clay. Ahead, the trail curls through a rolling meadow dotted with Indian paintbrush and other wildflowers. The nearby mooing perfects the restful country feeling. Although I did not see any cattle, there were a couple of cow patties in the trail, indicating you may spot one or two roaming the area.

Where the path forks, choose the left branch for a longer walk; this spur winds around the hill before rejoining the main path. At the next fork, turn right to find a lonely bench surrounded by wildflowers atop a small hill. Take in the view before turning around and heading back. If you want to extend the hike, turn left at the previous fork. The trail winds downhill, continuing on toward the

In the spring, cactus and wildflowers bloom in force alongside the trail.

lake for another couple miles. The path eventually reaches a fork that leads to Dunham Trail. Staying on the main trail, you'll reach a bridge and eventually the end of the trail at Pocahontas Road, near Grapevine Lake.

NEARBY ACTIVITIES

If you're a NASCAR fan, just 6 miles away, is the Texas Motor Speedway. For a schedule of race events, visit their Web site **www.texasmotorspeedway.com.** To get to the speedway, go south on FM 377 for about 1.2 miles, and turn right onto TX 144 west. Go 3.8 miles and turn right on Allison Avenue.

NORTH SHORE TRAIL 21

IN BRIEF

Nice views from the bluffs overlooking the lake dominate the first half of this very popular trail. The second half is less busy because it twists and turns through the hardwood forest just out of view of the lake.

DESCRIPTION

Dammed in the 1950s, Grapevine Lake is a very popular reservoir just north of Dallas Fort Worth International Airport. The lake gets very busy on weekends with families who come to enjoy camping, boating, fishing, and picnicking, and the miles of multiuse trails. North Shore Trail, certified as a National Recreation Trail in 1991, is by far the most popular trail on the lake and arguably the most popular in the area. A deserved favorite thanks to its accessibility, length, and scenic lake views, the trail sees a high volume of hikers, joggers, and bikers.

The trail is on the north side of the lake in Rockledge Park. On nice weekends, the parking lot here quickly fills with picnickers who come to enjoy the excellent lake views from the cliff-top picnic tables adjacent to the lot. To ensure a parking space and avoid the lunchtime crowds, you'd be wise to arrive earlier in the day or come on a weekday.

KEY AT-A-GLANCE INFORMATION

LENGTH: 8.96 miles
CONFIGURATION: Out-and-back
DIFFICULTY: Easy to moderate
SCENERY: Lake views from bluffs, hardwood forest, birds
EXPOSURE: Mix of sunny and shady
TRAIL TRAFFIC: Heavy
TRAIL SURFACE: Packed dirt
HIKING TIME: 4.5 hours
ACCESS: Free; 6 a.m.–9 p.m.
FACILITIES: Restrooms, picnic area
SPECIAL COMMENTS: This trail is very popular with mountain bikers and joggers, in addition to hikers, and is especially busy on weekends.

Directions

From I-635 west, take Exit 36B, Bass Pro Drive. Go 0.5 miles and turn left on Bass Pro, then go about 0.6 miles and turn left onto TX 26. Continue about 0.5 miles and turn right on FM 2499 (AKA Fairway Drive). You'll cross over the dam, then turn left into Rockledge Park. Stay to the right, the road dead-ends at the parking lot.

GPS Trailhead Coordinates

UTM Zone (WGS84) 14S
Easting 680541
Northing 3651043
Latitude N 32° 58' 58"
Longitude W 97° 4' 4"

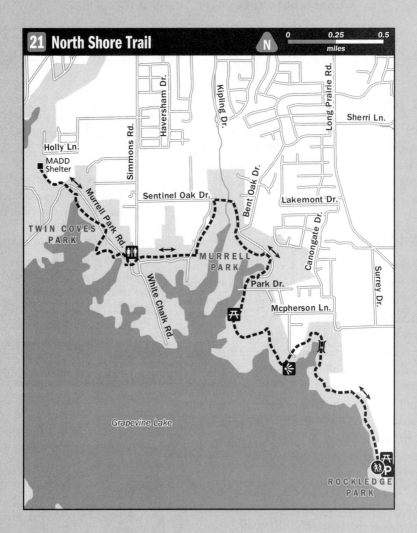

0   0.25   0.5
miles

N

Holly Ln.

MADD Shelter

Simmons Rd.

Haversham Dr.

Kipling Dr.

Long Prairie Rd.

Sherri Ln.

Murrell Park Rd.

Sentinel Oak Dr.

Bent Oak Dr.

Lakemont Dr.

TWIN COVES PARK

Canongate Dr.

MURRELL PARK

White Chalk Rd.

Park Dr.

Surrey Dr.

Mcpherson Ln.

Grapevine Lake

ROCKLEDGE PARK

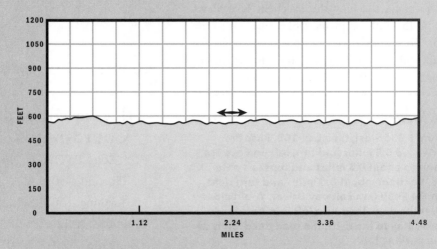

The trailhead is tucked away in the back corner of the parking lot. It can sometimes be crammed with people, especially mountain bikers, getting on and off the path. As you get farther down the trail, however, the traffic thins quite a bit as folks spread out more evenly over its length. You'll immediately pass a small rock-strewn beach that dog owners and amateur fishermen scramble down to access the lake. Continue following the trail as it winds along the top of some small rocky cliffs that follow the shoreline. On sunny days, watch for sailboats gliding past as they circle around the lake.

The path then climbs uphill and meanders around some of the large rocks (which help give the park its name) before flattening and heading slightly away from the shoreline and among tall trees with an understory of dense brush. The path runs parallel to the water slightly inland, offering occasional glimpses of the lake.

At the first two forks you encounter, go right. At the next fork, continue straight on the main trail. As you near the 1-mile mark, you'll reach a long wooden bridge then another junction, where you'll head right onto a wider trail. About 1.2 miles into the hike, gaze over the lake below at a scenic overlook at the top of a bluff. This spot is a good place to orient yourself. Off to the left, you'll see the 1,500-plus-room Gaylord Texan, a resort and convention center that opened in 2004. The airport is also nearby and though, for the most part, air traffic is not overly noticeable, you'll probably have already seen an airplane or two making its approach.

More interesting than airplanes, fossils have also been found nearby. Recent record heat has left the lake level substantially below normal, exposing million-year-old dinosaur tracks embedded in sandstone along the shoreline on this side of the lake. Unfortunately, the tracks are not open for viewing because vandals destroyed a couple of the tracks, prompting the lake's controlling authority, the Army Corps of Engineers, to block access and cover the tracks until the water levels rise enough to again hide them.

Continuing along the trail, head through grasslands and, at 1.6 miles, you'll come to an old road. Cross the road and pick up the trail on the far side, continuing until you reach a clearing at about 1.8 miles. This area, which is virtually always empty, has about a half dozen old picnic tables tucked under the trees and a vacant parking lot. Probably attracted by the solitude, the birds here are loud and abundant, flitting through the trees. On my hike, I was able to spot only the most obvious—cardinals, whose telltale bright-red plumage makes them easy to pick out, and a vulture that slowly circled nearby. If you want to shorten this hike, this is a good spot to turn around. Continue by picking up the trail as it enters a patch of forest on the opposite side of the parking lot. At 2.2 miles, you'll reach a small bridge and shortly thereafter cross an old gravel road. At 2.5 miles, you'll reach another road, where you'll hang a left, following the road until it deteriorates into a dirt path and then rejoins a paved road. When you reach a spot where the road forks, turn left at the fork and, at the next fork at 3.1 miles, bear

A couple enjoys a view of the lake on a rocky outcrop.

right. You'll eventually reach another road where you'll cross and pick up the trail on the opposite side. For the next mile, the trail twists and turns through the trees, more of a thrill for mountain bikers. The trail comes out at the trailhead by the MADD Shelter at Murrell Park.

NEARBY ACTIVITIES

After the first half of your hike, while you're still at the Murrell Park trailhead, walk over to the marina for a bite to eat at Little Pete's, where you can sit on the patio overlooking the water and the boats and munch on comfort food such as burgers or chicken-fried steak. In the evenings, they typically have entertainment, which might include karaoke or poker night. Visit their Web site at **www.littlepeteslakegrapevine.com** for more information. The Gaylord Texan, which sits on Grapevine Lake, is also a fun place to stop after your hike. The huge resort has a 4.5-acre atrium, each section of which represents a different part of Texas. A short stroll takes you to the Hill Country, Palo Duro Canyon, and the San Antonio Riverwalk, where there are plenty of restaurants where you can grab a cold drink and some hot food. Their Web site, **www.gaylordhotels.com/ gaylordtexan,** has more information on special events and entertainment.

RIVER LEGACY TRAIL

IN BRIEF

This lengthy paved trail stretches alongside the river, offering a few good overlooks for bird-watching.

DESCRIPTION

River Legacy Parks' 1,300 acres and 8 miles of trails are a popular attraction in Arlington, drawing hikers, bikers, joggers, and dog-walkers. A few different access points to the park's recreational trails help spread the visitors throughout. The park's name originates from the River Legacy Foundation's vision of preserving a "living legacy for future generations."

Trail maps and park information can be picked up a short drive from the trailhead at the River Legacy Living Science Center. The center's unique design was inspired by a children's fort built of sticks and leaves, a picture of which can be found on the center's Web site. According to the Web site, not only is the center designed to be part of its natural surroundings, but its construction included trees salvaged from a city project, and its maintenance relies on recycled gray water for landscaping. Another reason to stop by the center is to enjoy its large exhibit hall and pretty observation decks. A short trail winds through the grounds surrounding the center.

KEY AT-A-GLANCE INFORMATION

LENGTH: 5.46 miles
CONFIGURATION: Out-and-back
DIFFICULTY: Easy
SCENERY: Woods, river
EXPOSURE: Shady
TRAIL TRAFFIC: Moderate to heavy
TRAIL SURFACE: Paved path
HIKING TIME: 1.5 hours
ACCESS: Free; daily, 5 a.m.–10 p.m.
FACILITIES: Water fountain
WHEELCHAIR TRAVERSABLE: Yes
SPECIAL COMMENTS: Presentations and festivals are among the events at the Living Science Center; check their calendar at www.riverlegacy .org.

Directions

Follow I-30 toward Arlington, take Exit 28 and turn left onto FM 157. The entrance to River Legacy Parks is 0.6 miles down Collins on the left, at 3020 North Collins Street. Park in the first parking area.

GPS Trailhead Coordinates

UTM Zone (WGS84) 14S
Easting   678017
Northing 3629488
Latitude   N 32° 47' 20"
Longitude   W 97° 5' 56"

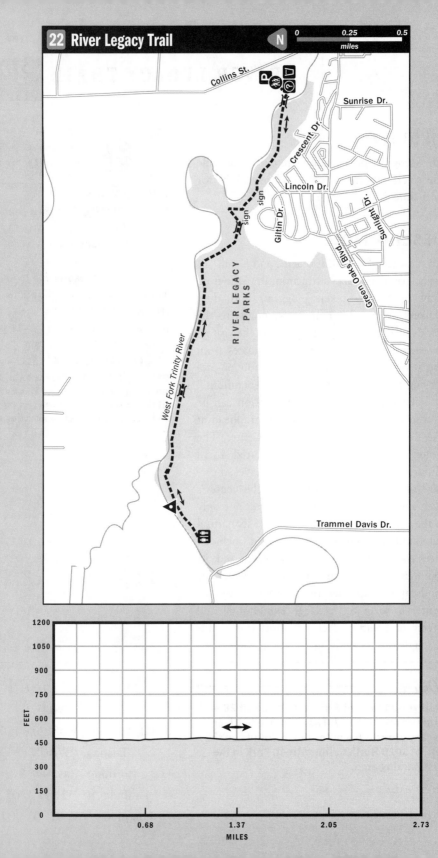

N

| 0 | 0.25 | 0.5 |

miles

Collins St.

P

Sunrise Dr.

Crescent Dr.

Lincoln Dr.

sign

sign

Giltin Dr.

Sunlight Dr.

Green Oaks Blvd.

RIVER LEGACY PARKS

West Fork Trinity River

Trammel Davis Dr.

| 1200 |
| 1050 |
| 900 |
| 750 |
| 600 |
| FEET 450 |
| 300 |
| 150 |
| 0 |

| 0.68 | 1.37 | 2.05 | 2.73 |

MILES

A bench provides a respite from the trail.

To get to the trailhead for the described hike; however, you'll have to drive a few blocks to the lengthier paved sections of the parks.

The trailhead is adjacent to the parking lot. Head down the paved path toward the kiosk, which is adjacent to a water fountain and displays a huge aerial photo of the area. After getting oriented, head straight past the kiosk and turn right at the first junction onto the path that has a dotted line down its center. You'll immediately come upon a wide bridge spanning the West Fork of the Trinity River. You're likely to find folks at its railings enjoying the pretty views of its green, slow-moving waters.

The trail continues through the woods along the river. The route is mostly shaded, making it a good hike for a hot day. At 0.17 miles, take a right at the junction onto the path with a red-dotted stripe down the center.

A couple of interpretive signs along the trail provide information on local wildlife. You'll pass one of these signs on the left; it tells about raccoons: the small masked animal, commonly associated with trashcans and late-night raids, is a nocturnal animal that can often be found in hollowed-out tree trunks.

As you continue, you'll see some smaller dirt trails heading off to the left toward the river. Some of these overlooks offer nice views of the river. Just be careful not to step too close to the edge, which is slightly raised above the river. The banks easily erode and can cause you to slide into the river. Farther down the trail, structured overlooks complete with benches offer safer viewing.

At 0.6 miles, you'll reach another display on the left, describing an insect commonly found here—the wolf spider. These large brown spiders can grow to more than an inch long and are typically spotted scurrying along the ground, as opposed to hanging in webs.

At 0.88 miles, you'll reach a long wooden bridge across a narrow river. The path continues with woods on both sides until it reaches a split at 0.92 miles, where you'll bear right onto a path with a blue line. In another couple hundred feet, you'll reach another trail split. To the right, the trail terminates at a bench set alongside the river—a good spot for a quick break. The initials of two lovers are carved into a tall tree at this pretty spot. When you're rested, continue on the path, staying to the right. The trail reaches a break in the trees, where, to the left, you'll see a large pavilion across a field. From here you'll pass a few more overlooks providing opportunities to scan for turtles and birds, before reaching 1.34 miles, where you'll head right, following the yellow-striped path. The trail straightens here; among the few distractions are folks jogging with their dogs and others cruising along on their bikes heading toward the end of the trail. I was even passed by a fellow in his wheelchair, sailing along toward the turnaround just a little more than a mile down.

You'll pass a circular stone bench at 1.82 miles, off to the right, before reaching a wooden deck overlooking the river at 2.47 miles. The deck has high wooden railings, providing adequate cover for bird-watchers discreetly scanning the river. The trail continues another 0.26 miles to the end, where you'll find trees and a ring of seats at this dead end. From here, retrace your steps to the trailhead.

NEARBY ACTIVITIES

Baseball fans will enjoy a visit to Ameriquest Field in Arlington, home of the Texas Rangers. Check their Web site **texas.rangers.mlb.com** for ticket information during baseball season. Year-round you can visit the Legends of the Game Museum, which is on the same site and has a huge collection from the National Baseball Hall of Fame. To get to the ballpark, go south on North Collins Street and turn left onto Northeast Green Oaks Boulevard. Continue 1.4 miles, then turn right onto Ballpark Way. The baseball stadium is 2 miles down.

ROCKY POINT TRAIL 23

IN BRIEF

This is a peaceful trek down a rocky hill and alongside a wooded creek toward Grapevine Lake. When you near the lake, the path changes from dirt to soft sand as it leads onto the lake's beach.

DESCRIPTION

This rocky trail is one of Grapevine Lake's less frequented paths, often overlooked in favor of other more popular trails such as Northshore Trail. Its small parking area—which holds maybe half a dozen cars—is just off the shoulder of a secondary residential road and marked by nothing more than a small trail sign. If you're not paying attention, you're likely to drive past before you realize it's actually a trail. You will therefore be fairly surprised when you step onto the trail and discover a lovely tree-covered path following a creek. It's a great choice if you're looking for a winter hike; the cooler weather will allow you to spend as much time as you want beachcombing the long, sandy lakeshore at its end.

The trail starts out heading east into a narrow, grassy, tree-covered strip of land sandwiched between private residences. The path parallels the boundary fence of a private driveway. After a few hundred feet, it starts

KEY AT-A-GLANCE INFORMATION

LENGTH: 3.84 miles
CONFIGURATION: Out-and-back
DIFFICULTY: A couple of difficult patches in the beginning
SCENERY: Creek, woods, lake beach
EXPOSURE: Partly shady to sunny
TRAIL TRAFFIC: Light
TRAIL SURFACE: Dirt, sand
HIKING TIME: 1.75 hours
ACCESS: Daily; free
FACILITIES: None
WHEELCHAIR TRAVERSABLE: No
SPECIAL COMMENTS: Bring a bag to carry the goodies you collect while beachcombing.

Directions

Take FM 1171 (Cross Timbers Road) west from I-35E, in Lewisville, or east from I-35W in Justin. Turn south onto High Road. There is a small parking area on the left, about 0.5 miles down, between Stallion Circle and Sunnyview Lane.

GPS Trailhead Coordinates

UTM Zone (WGS84) 14S
Easting 672767
Northing 3656549
Latitude N 33° 2' 1"
Longitude W 97° 9' 0"

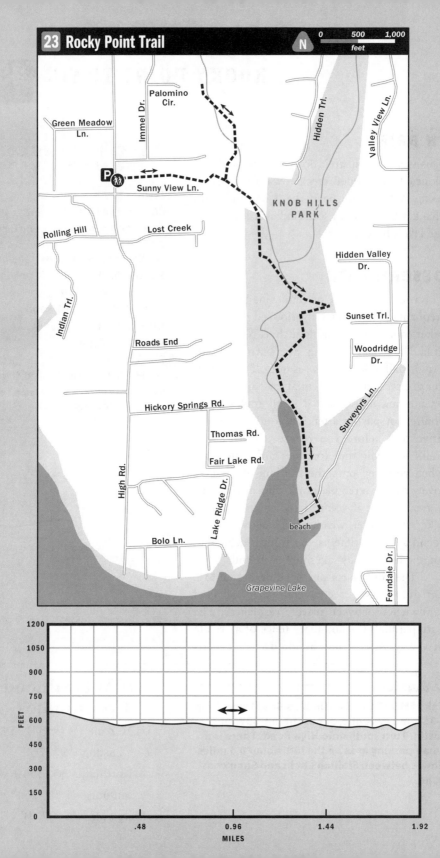

to head downhill, becoming steep and rocky as it makes its way to a creek. If you have a hiking stick, bring it along—although most of the trail is only slightly hilly, you'll find the extra support useful for navigating the descent of this section, which, though short, is fairly steep, with rocks and roots making for uneven footing.

At 0.33 miles, you'll reach the creek. Here the path splits, heading north toward FM 1171 and south toward the lake. Turn right toward the lake. Lush green vegetation grows richly along the creek's banks, and, unlike many creeks, which stagnate in murky puddles, here the waters flow briskly over the rocks, providing a pleasant gurgling backdrop for your hike. After a brief flat stretch, you'll head gently uphill through wooded terrain, away from the creek. Bear right at the junction at 0.73 miles and round a small pond decorated with bird boxes.

If you could see an aerial view of the trail, you'd see you're actually winding around the outskirts of a residential neighborhood on a small point that juts into the lake. Just after you pass the pond, you'll start to notice the backyards of some of these residences. They are, however, set amid wooded hilly lots and widely spaced; as a result, they don't feel overly obtrusive and are easily ignored. The trail curls back toward the creek—which by now has widened to the width of a river. It peeks in and out of view to your right and will stay within sight the rest of the way to the lake.

You'll soon see Grapevine Lake ahead of you in the distance. The lake is popular, and if it's a nice day you're likely to spot motorboats chugging to and from the more than half a dozen boat ramps along its shores. The trail heads steadily toward the water, passing through a small stand of eastern red cedars, before emerging into the sun. To your left, huge houses sit atop a small hill, their backyards overlooking the lake.

With the lake only a short distance away, the trail becomes sandy and the trees fall back, leaving you in full sun. To your right, the river, which had been gradually widening, is now a couple hundred feet across. During droughts, the part nearest the lake dries out, forming a long, brown beach where the water should be. During my visit, the waters were so low that an entire dock had been stranded on the banks where there should have been water.

You'll soon reach a trail split where you should continue straight, heading up a short, rocky hill. A few hundred feet farther, you'll reach a detour; going left will take you out to Rocky Point, whereas if you go right, you'll reach the beach, where you can spend some time walking the soft, sandy lakeshore. When the lake is low and the water has receded, shells, old driftwood, and all sorts of other interesting artifacts are exposed, making it a fun spot to explore. If it's a sunny day, you're likely to spot kids playing in the water, and folks with towels and beach chairs soaking up the rays. It's easy to lose track of time lazing around the shore, making this a good spot to have a picnic lunch on the beach before retracing your steps to the trailhead. If you'd like to continue, just go back to the turnoff and bear left; the trail continues around Rocky Point.

The trail follows the creek as it heads towards Grapevine Lake.

NEARBY ACTIVITIES

The huge Grapevine Mills Mall—an outlet mall with more than 190 shops and a 30-screen AMC movie theater—is only a short drive away. You'll also find a selection of restaurants both within and around the mall. To get there, turn right onto FM 1171 (Cross Timbers Road) and go approximately 5 miles. Turn right onto FM 2499 south (Long Prairie Road) and drive 5.6 miles. The Grapevine Mills Mall is on your left.

SANSOM PARK TRAIL   24

IN BRIEF

Rough, rocky trail dominates the first half of this hike, which winds down a bluff and along the southeastern edge of Lake Worth before circling back on a flatter route. Fossils can easily be spotted in the path's rocky sediment.

DESCRIPTION

Thanks to the efforts of the Fort Worth Mountain Bikers' Association (FWMBA), Marion Sansom Park offers good hiking on hike-and-bike trails built along Lake Worth's shoreline. Although it looks fairly small from the park, which is on the lake's southeastern tip, the lake does continue around to the north. An impoundment of the West Fork of the Trinity River, the lake was created in 1914. Parks, including the huge Fort Worth Nature Center and Refuge, abound along the lake's shoreline, offering plenty of recreation for locals. Fishing is a popular activity, and you're likely to see anglers searching for white crappie, large mouth bass, and catfish.

This city park has little by way of amenities, except for a couple of picnic tables and the trails; however, this doesn't deter visitors, and you'll often find at least a few cars in the large parking lot. Most of the visitors are bikers drawn in by FWMBA's efforts to build

KEY AT-A-GLANCE INFORMATION

LENGTH: 2.24 miles
CONFIGURATION: Loop
DIFFICULTY: Difficult
SCENERY: Lake
EXPOSURE: Partly sunny to sunny
TRAIL TRAFFIC: Heavy on weekends
TRAIL SURFACE: Dirt
HIKING TIME: 55 minutes
ACCESS: Daily; free
FACILITIES: Picnic table
WHEELCHAIR TRAVERSABLE: No
SPECIAL COMMENTS: A lot of winding and twisting back and forth, but rugged and fun

Directions ⟶

Take Jacksboro Highway /TX 199 west. Turn left onto Biway Street then right onto Roberts Cut Off Road and into Marion Sansom Park.

GPS Trailhead Coordinates

UTM Zone (WGS84) 14S
Easting   648595
Northing   3629737
Latitude   N 32° 47' 44"
Longitude   W 97° 24' 47"

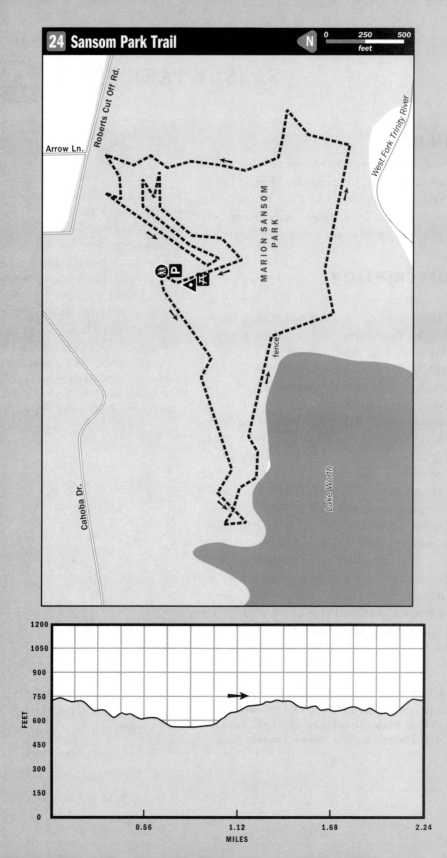

the trails, but the 5 or so miles of trails accommodate both hikers and bikers, so you won't feel overrun. Sections of the trail are fairly rugged, so go prepared with sturdy hiking shoes and a walking stick.

Just to the south of the parking lot, you'll find a scenic overlook for viewing the southeastern end of the lake. A table here is an ideal spot to have lunch after the hike. Continue to the trailhead by walking down the wide, rutted, dirt path off to the right of the overlook. At 0.2 miles, bear left, continuing steeply downhill. Ignore any smaller side trails and stay on the wide, dirt lane, following it downhill toward the lake. Off to the left, you'll glimpse a rolled-earth dam abutting the southeastern edge of the lake. Cacti and small shrubs dot the trailside.

The trail winds parallel to the lake, continuing west through steep, rocky terrain. Stay to the left at the junction at 0.3 miles, then follow the path as it swings left onto a narrow, single-track trail heading back southeast. (If you were to continue heading straight downhill toward the lake, the path would loop back to your present location after a few hundred feet.)

The trail winds uphill through scrubby trees and follows the shoreline, below and to your right. As you hike along, keep an eye to the ground for fossils from millions of years ago when this area was underwater. Without much effort, it's easy to find aged shells and imprints from ancient ammonites—an extinct type of mollusk distinguishable by its spiral shape—in the trail's rocky sediment.

Yucca and junipers encroach upon the trail as you continue making your way east. The lake stays almost constantly within view off to your right. The gentle lapping of its waters on the shoreline below remind you it's there even when it briefly disappears from sight. The trail starts a brief, rocky descent as it continues winding through the brush before climbing up the rise of a small hill and exposing the rocky wall of the outcrop from which you've just descended. Just beyond, you'll pass the dam, which is surrounded by a chain-link fence with a "No Trespassing" sign. The narrow dirt path winds around the fence and continues briefly through the woods before merging with an old road. Follow the road past an overlook with a view of the blue-green waters of an inlet of the lake on the right. The Fort Worth Fish Hatchery is just to the south. Continuing down the trail, at 0.95 miles, you'll bear left back onto a narrow dirt path that heads steeply up an uneven, rocky hillside. When you reach the summit, enjoy the bird's-eye view of the lake down below, then bear left to return.

At the next two junctions, bear left. Compared to what you've done already, this last half of the trail is relatively flat. Wind over a hill to make your way back to the trailhead. At 1.13, miles you'll reach a junction, with another trail to your right; just continue following your trail to the left. You'll wind through more wooded terrain and bear left yet again, a few hundred feet down (following the green arrow on the rock). The green trail is the easy trail for mountain bikers, so here is where you're likely to encounter a little traffic. Continue, staying to the left at the next junction. Finally, at 1.33 miles, you'll bear right, following the blue arrow. Take a right at the next junction, at 2 miles. At this point, you're in

The rocky trail offers some nice viewpoints of the lake.

the homestretch. Continue straight through the next junction and finish the final uphill stretch back to the overlook and parking area.

NEARBY ACTIVITIES

Head over to Exchange Avenue to see cowboys and cowgirls drive the Fort Worth Texas longhorn steers down Exchange Avenue through Stockyard Station. The cattle drive happens twice daily at 11:30 a.m. and 4:00 p.m. To get there from Sansom Park, turn right onto Jacksboro Highway (TX 199) and go about 1.5 miles, then turn left onto TX 183 north. Go 2 miles, turn right onto Main Street, then turn left onto Exchange Avenue.

TRINITY RIVER TRAIL (NORTHSIDE) **25**

IN BRIEF

Views of the skyscrapers in downtown Fort Worth dominate the skyline of this flat, sunny trail that winds alongside the West Fork of the Trinity River.

DESCRIPTION

Fort Worth's Trinity Trail system comprises approximately 40 miles of hike-and-bike trails along the Trinity River. It is readily accessible and is bordered by a number of city parks, including downtown Fort Worth's Heritage Park. The trail has a few different legs, which all meet in or around Heritage Park, making the park a popular starting point for newcomers to the trail system. Bikers, inline skaters, joggers, and walkers all frequent the trail, attracted by the paved surface. Trinity Park, the Fort Worth Zoo, and the Fort Worth Botanic Garden also border sections of the trail.

This trail covers a short section of one of the northern legs of the trail network. Although the Northside and Heritage Park trailheads

KEY AT-A-GLANCE INFORMATION

LENGTH: 3.9 miles
CONFIGURATION: Out-and-back
DIFFICULTY: Easy
SCENERY: River
EXPOSURE: Sunny
TRAIL TRAFFIC: Light
TRAIL SURFACE: Paved
HIKING TIME: 1.5 hours
ACCESS: Daily; free
FACILITIES: Benches
WHEELCHAIR TRAVERSABLE: Yes
SPECIAL COMMENTS: The entire Trinity River Trail network is extensive and will take you many days to thoroughly explore; visit www.trinitytrails.org for a complete map of the system.

Directions

Start this trail at the Northside Drive trailhead of the Trinity River Trails at 600 East Northside. To get there, follow I-35W north and take Exit 53 onto Northside Drive, then turn left onto East Northside and go 1.5 miles. The trailhead is below the bridge. Alternatively, you can start the hike from the other end, at Heritage Park, located on Congress Street, on the northeast side of downtown Fort Worth. To get there, follow I-30W toward Abilene and take Exit 13B. Turn right on Hendersen Street and then right again on Congress to reach the parking lot. Feed the meters weekdays 8 a.m.–6 p.m.

GPS Trailhead Coordinates

UTM Zone (WGS84) 14S
Easting 655388
Northing 3627931
Latitude N 32° 46' 42"
Longitude W 97° 20' 27"

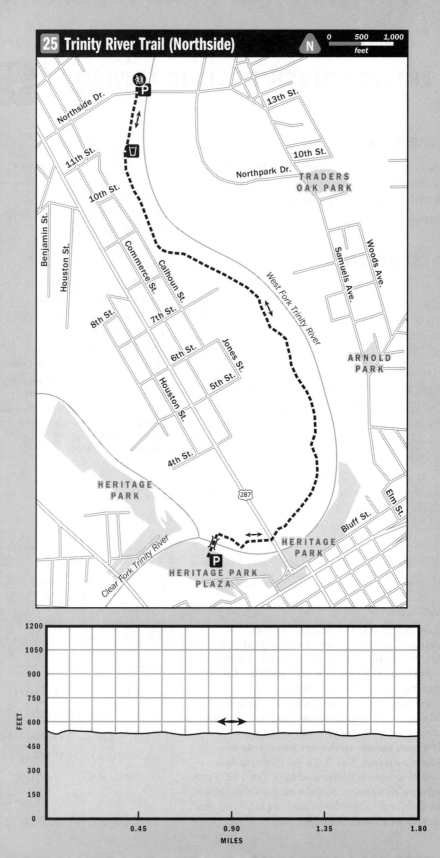

allow you to start from either direction, I found the trail is best started from Northside Trailhead, heading south toward downtown Fort Worth. Starting at this end, you'll have a fantastic view of the Fort Worth skyline to motivate you throughout the hike. The skyscrapers—which are just a small grouping on the horizon at the start of the hike—will loom larger and more massive with your every step, until you finally reach Heritage Park, which sits just in their shadow.

Be sure you've brought a water bottle with you, and applied plenty of sun-screen—this hike is completely exposed. There is a water fountain just beyond the trailhead, but on my visit it was not working.

Northside Trailhead is at a small parking area with a kiosk and benches just at the base of the Northside Drive Bridge. The trail itself is very clean and well maintained. You'll also find the parking lots on both ends of the trail feel safe and secure. If you are interested in seeing a good map of the entire Trinity Trail network, be sure to visit the Trinity Trails Web site before you leave home.

You'll see the trail curling away both to the north and to the south, follow-ing the curve of the Trinity River. Turn right onto the trail, passing under the bridge and down the paved path. The downtown skyline is on the horizon ahead and to the left; this small clustering of shiny skyscrapers is your ultimate destination.

The flat, smooth trail runs inside a greenbelt bordered by small earth embank-ments on the west and east. The embankments block the surrounding city and neighborhoods from view, isolating you from the stresses of urban life. Within the embankments is the Trinity River, just to your left. A neatly mowed strip of grass reaches toward the embankment to the right. Trees and benches, carefully placed at regular intervals along the trail, complete the park-like setting.

At 0.6 miles, you'll reach a junction where the main path continues straight and a spur splinters left, crosses the river, and continues along the opposite bank. Continue straight along the main trail, bypassing the river crossing. As you hike on, you'll pass a few rocks with plaques describing the history and significance of portions of the trail.

With little to block the scenery ahead, you'll have charming views of the upcoming sections of trail snaking off into the distance before disappearing around the bends of the river. Downtown is always within tantalizing view. Although the embankment to your right blocks almost everything in that direction, you'll soon start to see houses and businesses sitting atop the embankment on the opposite side of the river to your left, signaling that you're approaching downtown. Soon, you'll find yourself within the shadows of the buildings you had admired from afar. You'll cross under a bridge where ducks and geese can regularly be sighted resting in the shade. Finally, following a last sharp curve, you'll find yourself at a bridge spanning the river. The path crosses the bridge, delivering you into Heritage Park. From here, the trail branches in several directions, allowing you to continue the hike if you're not yet ready to turn back. Ducks and geese are likely to come up to

A peaceful day in Heritage Park.

greet you in their never-ending quest for food. Take some time to explore and to greet the winged residents before retracing your steps to the trailhead.

NEARBY ACTIVITIES

Only 8 miles away, the Fort Worth Zoo is a great spot to explore; its residents include raptors, primates, cheetahs, and Komodo dragons. The zoo also has a petting corral and a rock-climbing wall. Visit their Web site **www.fortworthzoo .com** for information on entrance fees and hours. To get there, take I-35W south to I-30 west toward Abilene. Take the University Drive exit and head south on University Drive 1 mile, then turn left onto Colonial Parkway.

TRINITY RIVER TRAIL (OAKMONT PARK) 26

IN BRIEF

A paved section of the Trinity River Trail system, this pleasant trail is popular with bicyclists and dog-walkers. The trail winds through the woods between two parks. A turnoff near the park at the other end will take you down a dirt trail to the huge Texas State Champion bur oak tree.

DESCRIPTION

Part of the Trinity River Trail system, a network that spiders for a total of 30 miles through Fort Worth, this paved trail follows the Clear Fork River (a branch of the Trinity River) southwest from Oakmont Park to Pecan Valley Park. The trail is popular with bikers, joggers, and walkers because it is level, with only gentle turns. Hikers will find the trail, which curls through the woods, a nice escape from the bustle of the nearby city. The Texas Parks and Wildlife Department recently listed Oakmont Park among its suggested routes for hikes in the Prairies and Pineywoods areas.

The small parking area at the trailhead fills up quickly on pretty days; arrive early to ensure a spot. If the parking lot is full, you can do the hike in reverse, starting from Pecan Valley Park, which has much more parking.

At the trailhead, you'll find a couple of

KEY AT-A-GLANCE INFORMATION

LENGTH: 3.36 miles
CONFIGURATION: Out-and-back
DIFFICULTY: Easy
SCENERY: Woods, champion oak tree
EXPOSURE: Partly shady
TRAIL TRAFFIC: Light to moderate
TRAIL SURFACE: Paved path and short, dirt trail
HIKING TIME: 1.25 hours
ACCESS: Free; daily
FACILITIES: Picnic tables
WHEELCHAIR TRAVERSABLE: On the paved portion
SPECIAL COMMENTS: The trail does not have many river overlooks, but the few it has are great for birders. Bring binoculars for an up-close look.

Directions

Take I-20 west toward Abilene to Exit 431, and turn left onto Bryant Irving Boulevard heading southwest. Turn right onto Oakmont Boulevard and go about 0.5 miles to Bellaire Drive South, then turn right again to Oakmont Park. Parking is on the left.

GPS Trailhead Coordinates

UTM Zone (WGS84) 14S
Easting 647120
Northing 3615814
Latitude N 32° 40' 13"
Longitude W 97° 25' 52"

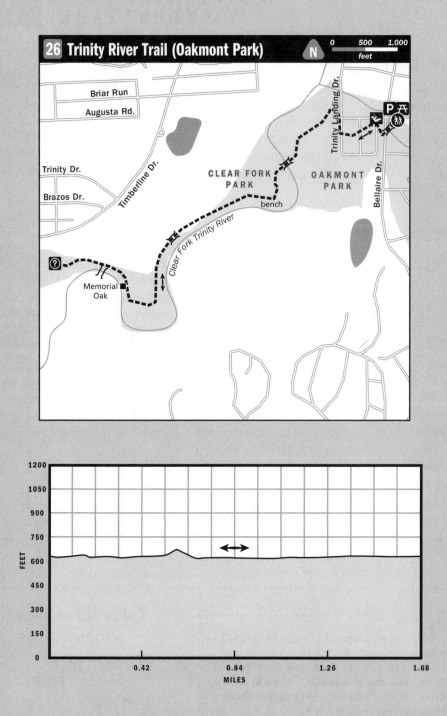

The path winds through a grove of trees straight to the Memorial Oak Tree.

picnic tables at the start of this paved trail. Follow the trail over a bridge spanning a small creek. You'll pass the park's playground and then hike through a wide field dotted with trees. The trail then curls downhill, goes through a dried-up gully, and passes another field, this one dotted with purple wildflowers, bright yellow sunflowers, and trees such as mesquite and oak.

Turn left at the junction at 0.28 miles. Continue until you reach a bridge spanning a wide river at 0.63 miles. Enjoy the view, but be careful not to lean too far into the railing—the posts often have large webs with huge spiders in them awaiting prey. Signs just across the bridge mark this spot as the entrance to Clear Fork Park. Continue heading southwest. Native trees line both sides of the trail, keeping the path in partial shade for most of the hike. Sunflowers bloom alongside the trail, and butterflies flutter across the path. Trail traffic is light, although cyclists will occasionally pass. Many are kids accompanied by parents, and all respect the signs and cruise at low speeds. Once they've disappeared around the bend, you may find yourself completely alone again, with only the chirping of birds for company. Just when you've begun to wonder where the trail is going, you'll pass a sign indicating a rest area is 1 mile farther up the trail. The trail winds slowly there, passing more oak trees and wildflowers.

At 0.63 miles, you'll cross a bridge. Continuing straight, the trail passes a ranch on the right, where donkeys and horses sometimes linger by the fence. At 1.58 miles, you'll see a footbridge off to the left. Turn left, crossing the bridge. (If you were to continue straight, you'd reach the Pecan Valley Park parking, just 0.1 mile farther down the trail. In front of the parking lot there, you'll find a kiosk with a detailed map of the entire trail network.)

The small bridge spans a wide creek with pretty green waters. As I crossed the bridge, I spotted a beautiful great blue heron perched on a log downstream stalking fish. Wishing I had brought my binoculars, I watched him for a few minutes, until the huge bird spread his wings and took off with a few elegant strokes. I later found out from the Texas Parks and Wildlife Web site that several herons nest in the area, and it is not unusual to see them.

Across the bridge, you'll find a few narrow posts and a gate. Head through the gate and onto the dirt trail. Within a few steps, you'll reach a junction; take the trail to your left, which runs closest to the creek. Ahead, you'll see a lovely grove of tall trees, so unexpectedly picturesque that you'll feel as though you've just crossed a bridge into another world. After passing through the grove you'll see a small fence off to the right marking the boundary of a golf course. About 300 feet down the dirt trail you'll find the Memorial Oak, a huge bur oak tree. This tree is listed on the Texas Big Tree Registry, sponsored by the Texas Forest Service, which reports the tree is 81 feet tall and 18 feet around. After you're done admiring the tree, have lunch at the picnic tables a couple hundred feet farther up the trail, behind the grove. From here, just retrace your steps to the trailhead.

NEARBY ACTIVITIES

The Fort Worth Zoo, which is home to primates, cheetahs, and the Komodo dragon, among others, is only 8 miles away. Check the zoo's Web site for special events and hours—**www.fortworthzoo.com**. To get there, take Oakmont Boulevard east 2 miles then turn left onto South Hulen Street and drive 3 miles. Turn right onto Bellaire Drive South, which becomes West Berry Street. Turn left onto South University Drive and bear right onto Colonial Parkway.

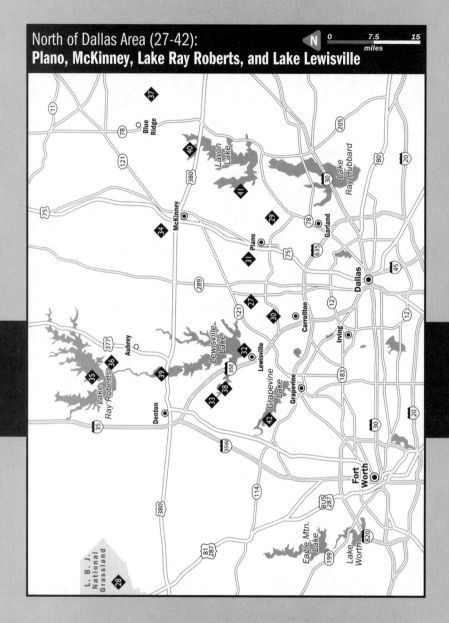

NORTH OF DALLAS/FORT WORTH (INCLUDING PLANO, MCKINNEY, LAKE RAY ROBERTS, AND LAKE LEWISVILLE)

27 ARBOR HILLS LOOP

**KEY AT-A-GLANCE
INFORMATION**

LENGTH: 2.3 miles
CONFIGURATION: Loop
DIFFICULTY: Easy to moderate
SCENERY: Blackland prairie, riparian forest, upland forest
EXPOSURE: Partly shady
TRAIL TRAFFIC: Heavy
TRAIL SURFACE: Paved path
HIKING TIME: 55 minutes
ACCESS: Free; daily, 5 a.m.–11 p.m.
FACILITIES: Restrooms, water fountains, picnic tables, playground
WHEELCHAIR TRAVERSABLE: Yes
SPECIAL COMMENTS: Dogs are allowed but must be leashed.

IN BRIEF

Popular with young families, this trail winds its way slowly uphill, moving from wetland to prairie to forest before looping back to the beginning. On any sunny weekend day, you'll find the trails bustling with families.

DESCRIPTION

Located in West Plano, the 200-acre Arbor Hills Nature Preserve is nicely laid out into three sections: the Blackland Prairie, the Upland Forest, and the Riparian Wetland. On any given weekend, you can find the parking busy. Most of the folks—young parents strapping their kids into strollers and young professionals leashing their dogs—are regulars who live in the area, already have their favorite routes in mind, and disappear down the trail within seconds. For newcomers, a map at the trailhead describes the three zones, offering a wealth of information for the naturalist, including the types of trees and animals you can find in each zone, and displays a map of the entire trail network. In addition to the paved trail, Arbor Hills boasts some primitive nature trails. These dirt trails are unstructured and their access points are not marked, disappearing into the woods at various spots along the main paved trail.

GPS Trailhead Coordinates

UTM Zone (WGS84) 14S
Easting   700896
Northing   3658617
Latitude   N 33° 2' 51"
Longitude   W 96° 50' 55"

Directions

Take the Dallas Tollway north to the Parker Road exit. Turn left onto West Parker. Arbor Hill Nature Preserve is a mile down on the right, just past Midway Road.

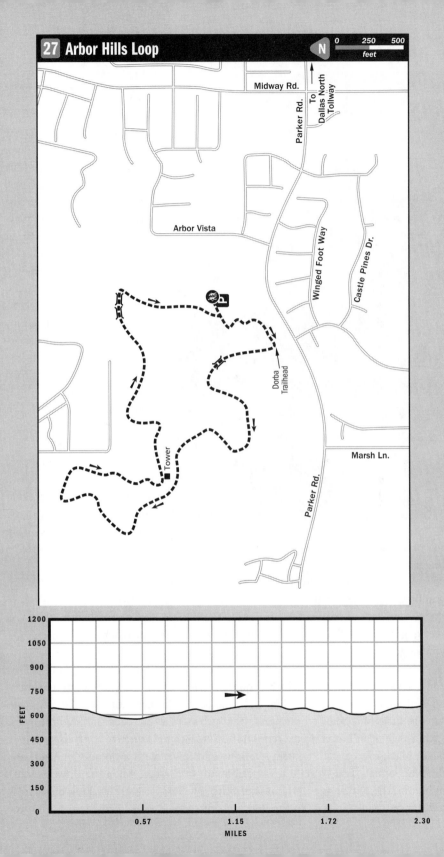

N

0   250   500
feet

Midway Rd.

Parker Rd.

To Dallas North Tollway

Arbor Vista

Winged Foot Way

Castle Pines Dr.

Dorba Trailhead

Tower

Marsh Ln.

Parker Rd.

1200
1050
900
750
600
450
300
150
0

FEET

0.57   1.15   1.72   2.30

MILES

View of the lookout tower from the trail

The trailhead is inside the pavilion and picnic shelter adjacent to the parking lot. Follow the paved trail heading south through the pavilion and past the playground toward West Parker Road. The trail will quickly loop back north, heading into the riparian wetland habitat. Mountain bikers are welcome here, but they do not pose a nuisance—most head straight for the DORBA (Dallas Off Road Bicycle Association) trail. At about 0.2 miles, you'll pass that trailhead diverging into the brush to the left.

As you continue down the trail, you'll reach a bridge crossing a creek at about 0.35 miles. The dense trees here, which make up the riparian forest, form a relaxing canopy of shade and make this a nice spot to linger and try to identify some of the area's avian inhabitants.

A little farther down the trail, just before the tree cover gives way to sky, you'll pass a huge bur oak tree nestled among other hardwoods. Keep an eye to the ground on the right side of the trail. You'll know you've reached it when you see its golf-ball-sized acorns littering the ground; if you reach the stone bench, you've gone too far.

As you continue, the trees thin and the trail winds into the blackland prairie zone. This type of prairie, which is quickly disappearing because of urbanization, takes its name from its rich black clay soils. The prairie consists of tall grasses such as little bluestem, a bunchgrass that grows to 2- to 4-feet tall. Wildflowers, such as Mexican hat, a pretty red wildflower with a distinctive long cone-shaped head; black-eyed Susan, a cheery yellow wildflower with a dome-like head; and the bluebonnet, Texas's state flower, abound. In the fall, when the flowers aren't in bloom, the prairie is a dark mass of brittle, yellow grasses that look black from a distance, thanks in part to the hundreds of spent flower heads. Folks can often be seen here wandering the trails, entranced by the mesmerizing rippling of the tall grasses in the wind. The sun in this exposed area can be brutal in the summer, but you soon reenter forest just up the trail.

At 0.68 miles, you'll reach a junction where you should turn left, heading uphill alongside the prairie. Another junction, at 0.83 miles, leads to a tower overlooking the preserve; the trail you're on climbs up to the tower the back way, so continue on this path, bypassing the turnoff. The trail continues, leaving the prairie behind as it heads slightly uphill, past wildflowers and into a forest of tall trees. Off to the right in the distance you'll see apartment complexes abutting the edge of the preserve.

At 1.5 miles, you'll reach the lookout tower. You'll usually find a few people at its railings enjoying the breeze and the views of the landscape. You'll also have a bird's-eye view of the trail you just came up.

Back on the trail, you'll head through the forest, following the path as it slowly winds downhill. The trail easily accommodates wheelchairs, and alongside the hikers, dog-walkers, and joggers, I encountered a couple of folks in wheelchairs, happily enjoying the outdoors. I also couldn't help but notice that the preserve's smooth, gentle slopes lured a surprising number of new and young parents, who were enjoying a nature walk and a workout as they pulled toddlers in little red wagons uphill, or pushed strollers and baby carriages downhill.

At 1.63 miles, you'll find a wheelchair access point. Head left, following the trail another 100 feet to a turnoff where you should again head left. You'll cross a couple of bridges then, at 1.98 miles, you'll reach a trail split where you'll bear right. Heading south now, you reach the parking lot and trailhead from the other end.

NEARBY ACTIVITIES

Southfork Ranch, the famous home of the fictional Ewing family on the old TV show *Dallas,* lies just to the west of Plano. Its magnificent white mansion served as the home of the show's infamous J. R. Ewing from 1978 to 1991. It was opened to the public in 1985 and continues to offer daily tours of the mansion and ranch grounds. Visit **www.southfork.com** for more information. To get there from Arbor Hills, go east 15 miles down Parker Road toward Lavon Lake. Turn right onto Hogge Road.

28 BLACK CREEK-COTTONWOOD HIKING TRAIL

(i) KEY AT-A-GLANCE INFORMATION

LENGTH: 9.58 miles

CONFIGURATION: Out-and-back

DIFFICULTY: Moderate

SCENERY: Grasslands, woodlands, small lakes

EXPOSURE: Partly sunny

TRAIL TRAFFIC: Light

TRAIL SURFACE: Dirt

HIKING TIME: 4.5 hours

ACCESS: Daily, $2 day-use fee

FACILITIES: Pit toilet, picnic tables

WHEELCHAIR TRAVERSABLE: No

SPECIAL COMMENTS: There is no water at either recreation area! Pack a lunch, water bottle, and insect repellent.

IN BRIEF

This long day hike explores the wild, grassy woodlands between the small Black Creek and Cottonwood lakes of the LBJ National Grasslands. Although the bulk of the trail is open woodland, you will pass through many small pockets of sunny grassland as you make your way north.

DESCRIPTION

One of only 20 national grasslands in the country managed by the USDA Forest Service, the Caddo–Lyndon B. Johnson (LBJ) National Grasslands consists of close to 40,000 acres of land. The grasslands are actually divided into two sections—the Caddo section, which is located northeast of the metroplex, and the LBJ section, located northwest of the metroplex.

The Caddo is slightly smaller than the LBJ and consists of a few recreational areas at Lake Coffee Mill and Lake Davy Crockett— small lakes built in the 1930s when the land for the preserve was acquired. Its trails are popular with equestrians. The second section—the LBJ—is a hiking hub. Not only does it have a 75-mile multiuse trail system accessible from

GPS Trailhead Coordinates

UTM Zone (WGS84) 14S

Easting 630741

Northing 3690416

Latitude N 33° 20' 42"

Longitude W 97° 35' 42"

Directions

From Decatur, take US 287/TX 81 north and turn right at the rest area onto County Road 2175, heading east. Cross the railroad tracks and turn left, heading north on Old Decatur Road. After about 4 miles, turn right onto CR 2372, heading east. Turn left, heading north on CR 2461, then make another left onto Forest Service Road 902, following it to the entrance of the Black Creek Recreational area. Parking is on the left, adjacent to the lake.

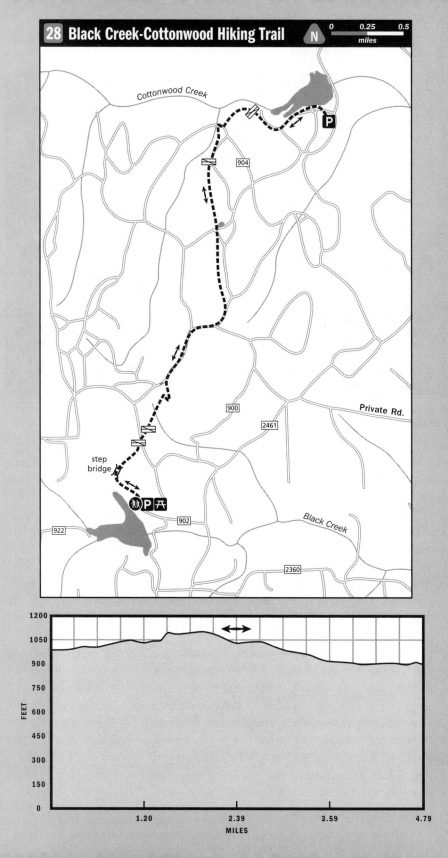

N

0   0.25   0.5
miles

Cottonwood Creek

P

904

Private Rd.

900

2461

step
bridge

P

922

902

Black Creek

2360

1200
1050
900
750
600
FEET
450
300
150
0

1.20   2.39   3.59   4.79
MILES

The top of a small hillside provides wide views of the surrounding countryside.

its main campsite—TADRA Point, but it also has a 4-mile hiking trail connecting two of its small lakes—Black Creek Lake and Cottonwood Lake—the hike outlined here.

You should be aware that there are designated hunting seasons in the grasslands. The trail, however, receives enough visitors that, as long as you stay on the designated trails and aren't rooting through the underbrush, you're unlikely to encounter any problems. The USDA Forest Service recommends that if you're hiking during hunting season, you should wear colorful clothing as an extra safety precaution. Be sure to check out the Texas Parks and Wildlife Web site (**www.tpwd.state.tx.us**) for specific information on hunting season dates, which vary by animal.

It's a long drive down a remote, primarily gravel, road to the trailhead, which is located in the Black Creek Recreational Area. Although you'll feel like you're driving to a secluded, little-visited place, if you visit on a weekend, you'll be surprised to find a fair number of folks at the rec area, which attracts a lively mixture of hikers, equestrians, hunters, and campers. I also noticed quite a few local teenagers who drove up for the day to splash around the 30-acre Black Creek Lake. There is a small day-use fee; drop your money in a box by the parking lot. There is no visitor center, office, or even park ranger on site, so be sure you've come with exact change.

You'll find the trailhead at the entrance to the rec area on the right side of the entrance road, just behind a large wooden sign with faded lettering that identifies this as Black Creek—Cottonwood Hiking Trail 901. The trail is hidden in the shrubbery behind the sign and is marked with a smaller "901" signpost. There are markers at regular intervals along the trail, so if you're ever in doubt at a junction, look for that number to get you back on the right track.

The trail starts by heading northwest through thickets and shrubbery occasionally interspersed with small, sunny clearings filled with prairie grasses. On this hike, you won't find the expansive grasslands you might envision when you hear the term "national grassland." Instead, this trail traverses a number of small grassland clearings with tall grasses that harbor butterflies, crickets, and dragonflies, all of which emerge to greet you as you pass.

At 0.35 miles, you'll reach a split where you'll bear right. The trail then becomes rough, with a couple of short, steep, rocky grades before it reaches another junction. Bear right and cross the barbed-wire fence by going over the small step bridge intended to keep horseback riders out of the developed recreational area. At 0.75 miles, you'll bear left. The trail becomes wider, following an old, partially overgrown park road enclosed by light woodlands. You'll pass through a few small patches of grassland that are quietly being overtaken by shrubs and small trees. White-tailed deer, cottontail rabbits, wild turkeys, and coyotes are all commonly found here. If you're not lucky enough to catch sight of any, you're likely to spot their tracks in the loose dirt of the trail.

As you hike, you'll find a series of metal gates along the trail, these separate tracts of land. You'll pass the first of these at 0.95 miles, where you should bear right to head north just after you pass through the gate. Bypass the next gate, continuing straight. At 1.35 miles, bear right and climb the steep grade to the top of the hill; the trail here has been severely eroded, and a hiking stick would be useful. This is one of the highest points on the trail, and at the top you'll find a pleasant breeze and a nice view. The path rounds the ridge then emerges onto the hilltop—a grassy plain with a dirt park road passing through it. The road is used but not busy; this is the route you'd take if you were to drive to Cottonwood Lake. It's also the hiking route, and as you walk along you'll see the 901 trail markers.

Head straight (north) on the dirt road, then turn right onto the gravel road at 1.55 miles. It's sunny and hot in this section, but a cool breeze and the flat road make for easy, fast hiking. You'll bypass a small half-loop in the road where you may see campers or RVers; turn left at 2.3 miles. A few trails join in this section, and it can be hard to figure out which one you should take—the easiest way is to just stay on the road until you see the dirt trail just off the road to the left at 2.45 miles; the 901 signpost marks it. Turn onto the dirt path and then bear right at the next junction.

At 3 miles, turn left onto a wide, flat trail. TADRA Point, which has a huge multiuse trail system popular with equestrians, is located just off to your right. Its trails are color-coded, and as you hike along, you'll see signs pointing the way to

A visitor enjoying a sunny day at Black Creek Lake

the Blue, Yellow, and Red trails. Bypass all turnoffs, cross the road, and go through another metal gate at 3.45 miles. Bear right, heading downhill through cactus and shrubs, then turn left through a wide grassland. At the next junction, bear right. You'll pass through another gate at 4.1 miles. Here the trail winds through a thicker mixture of trees and underbrush before finally emerging at Cottonwood Lake. Although the lake is only 40 acres, you'll still see a fair amount of activity, including ducks and egrets along its marshy edges, fishermen settled onto its sandy banks, and possibly a boat or two sitting quietly on the lake's edge. You can walk along the shoreline until you reach the shady parking area. If you're planning to eat lunch here, be sure to bring a picnic blanket to lay out on the grassy banks of the lake. Besides the boat launch and parking area, you won't find any picnic tables or other facilities at this end of the trail. From here, retrace your steps to the trailhead.

NEARBY ACTIVITIES

Head 10 miles south to Decatur for a burger at the Whistle Stop Café, a lunchroom dating to 1929. It is part of the Texas Tourist Camp Complex, designated a Texas Historical Landmark in 1995. The complex also includes the Petrified Wood Gas Station and some cabins that, until the 1960s, were popular among travelers. There are even unsubstantiated rumors that Bonnie and Clyde may have stayed here. To reach the complex, take US 287/81 south back into Decatur and turn left on US Business 380. The café is about 0.5 miles down on the right.

BRECKENRIDGE PARK TRAIL

IN BRIEF

This scenic trail winds through a beautiful city park and offers excellent birding, a picturesque lake, and innumerable scenic spots to stop and have a picnic lunch.

DESCRIPTION

As far as paved trails go, this one, located at Breckenridge Park in Richardson, is one of my favorites. It's never boring (offering something new around every turn), has tons of birdlife, and has surprisingly scenic paths. The trails are meticulously maintained and landscaped to preserve a wild and natural feel. For example, instead of planting one small tree for shade, the park plants many trees in natural clusters and groves. In the springtime, instead of putting in rows of planted flowers, sections of grass alongside the trail are left unmowed to allow colorful wildflowers to sprout. The cumulative result is that when you hike here you feel one step removed from the stresses of urban life—and yet not so removed that you'll have to do anything other than slip on a pair of tennis shoes.

KEY AT-A-GLANCE INFORMATION

LENGTH: 3.27 miles

CONFIGURATION: Loop

DIFFICULTY: Easy

SCENERY: Creek, lawns, lake, woodlands, birds

EXPOSURE: Partly sunny, sunny

TRAIL TRAFFIC: Moderate

TRAIL SURFACE: Paved

HIKING TIME: 1.5 hours

ACCESS: Free

FACILITIES: Toilets, picnic tables, water fountains, playground

WHEELCHAIR TRAVERSABLE: Yes

SPECIAL COMMENTS: Great option for those with younger kids

Directions

The park is located at 3300 Brand Road in Richardson. To get there, follow US75 north and take Exit 28B (President George Bush Turnpike). Go 1.8 miles to the Renner Road exit, and turn left onto East Renner. Go 3 miles, then turn right onto Brand Road. Follow the signs to the Breckenridge Park parking lot A. Park on the northern side of the soccer fields, in the lot adjacent to the toilets. (The entrance to the soccer field is down a one-way road; you'll see the parking area and toilets just in front of it, on your left).

GPS Trailhead Coordinates

UTM Zone (WGS84)   14S

Easting   721531

Northing   365307

Latitude   N 32° 59' 51"

Longitude   W 96° 37' 44"

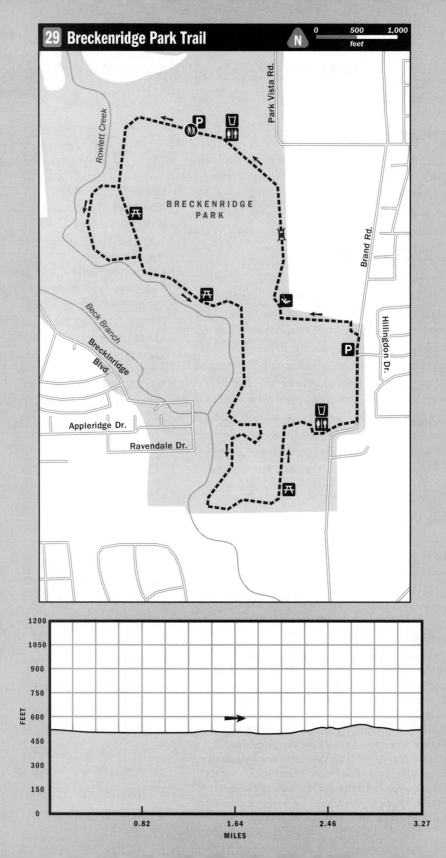

Rowlett Creek rushes past a rocky bank.

The 417-acre park includes a small lake, pavilions, a playground, and 12 (yes 12!) soccer fields—although you won't see much of them, except at the very beginning and end of the hike. The trails are popular with bikers, hikers, and explorers of all ages. The park is also well known throughout the city as the site of its annual Fourth of July celebration.

Pick up the trail just across the road from the toilet and parking area. The trail heads gently downhill just low enough that the soccer fields to your left are blocked by a grassy hillside. Bypass the first turnoff, where you'll see a bridge to your right, and continue straight until you reach the turnoff at 0.33 miles. Turn right at this junction and follow the trail as it makes a half-loop detour into the woodlands bordering Rowlett Creek. When you turn down the path, you'll see the creek just off to your right, its waters rushing and gurgling loudly as it cuts a wide swath through a pretty rock bank. The dense foliage in this loop keeps the temperature a few degrees cooler than the rest of the trail and attracts not only hikers but also birds, who chirp and whistle loudly in the surrounding trees. As you near the end of the half loop, you'll pass a picturesque picnic area beneath a grove of tall trees on your left.

Back on the trail, turn right, heading southeast. The open path winds ahead of you, offering a clear view straight ahead to the central part of the park, where you'll see crisp, green, neatly mowed lawns punctuated by clumps of trees. To your right is the thick woodlands surrounding the creek that abuts the western edge of the park; it has been left undeveloped and wild, and you can see a lot of birds along this stretch. Bring binoculars so you'll have an easier time identifying them when they fly across the trail and disappear into the wood's depths.

To your left is the mowed, grassy slope that hides the soccer fields above. As you pass the southern edge of the soccer fields, the park's small lake comes into view ahead of you. A green expanse of lawn leads down to its grassy shore—an ideal spot for laying out a blanket for a picnic lunch. Across the water are a pavilion, a small bridge, and a thick grove of trees. Benches along the trail allow you to relax and enjoy the beauty of this scenic spot.

The path turns slightly southeast. Stay to the right at each trail junction you pass in order to get into the very southern portion of the park. On your way, you'll curl lazily through a beautiful, open, park-like setting. When you enter a huge grove of tall trees dotted with picnic tables and benches, you'll know you're nearing the park's southern boundary. The trail then loops back east and north alongside the grove. Again, stay to the right at any trail junctions you pass.

The path will then take you uphill and past a pavilion and parking area. Follow the route past the restrooms and you'll soon find yourself atop a rise overlooking the park. For the first time on the hike, you'll have a glimpse of the soccer fields as the trail traverses the eastern edge of the southern field grouping before cutting west past another parking area and heading back downhill toward the lake and playground. Stay to the right at each junction, passing the pavilion and crossing the bridge. On the other side, bear right; the trail winds around a final curve then presents you with the northern section of soccer fields where you started the hike. Just follow the trail to the 3-mile point and turn left onto the red-brick path, which will take you back to the parking area.

NEARBY ACTIVITIES

If you feel like shopping, don't miss the popular Allen Premium Outlet Mall—a collection of about 100 upscale retail outlet stores, including Eddie Bauer, Kenneth Cole, Anne Klein, DKNY, and Tommy Hilfiger. The mall is only 13 miles away in nearby Allen. To get there, head north on 75, and take Exit 37 toward Stacy Road, where you'll turn left and see the outlet mall.

CARROLLTON GREENBELT 30

IN BRIEF

This flat, greenbelt path through green, mowed fields is best for a quick midday or after-work break. Mostly grassy, with a few sparse trees, the trail is better suited for folks wanting to get outside and stretch their legs than for those looking for inspiring scenery.

DESCRIPTION

In a city having well over 100,000 residents and teeming with highways, office buildings, and retail businesses, the importance of a little stretch of greenspace cannot be underestimated. Although the Carrollton Greenbelt is not the most scenic, the most educational, or the most unforgettable spot, it is certainly one of the most valuable spots in this rapidly expanding city. It's the larger of the city's two greenbelts and encompasses 177.8 acres of linear park. A typical greenbelt, it cuts a band of green through the city to provide a recreational spot for urban dwellers. It is fairly wide and completely sun-drenched. Although it offers little more than a creek and an expansive lawn by way of scenery, it is centrally and conveniently located near a main road, making it an ideal spot for folks who live or work nearby and are looking for a place to walk at lunch or before and after work. Its smooth,

KEY AT-A-GLANCE INFORMATION

LENGTH: 2.34 miles
CONFIGURATION: Out-and-back
DIFFICULTY: Easy
SCENERY: Creek, grassy lawns
EXPOSURE: Sunny
TRAIL TRAFFIC: Light
TRAIL SURFACE: Paved
HIKING TIME: 40 minutes
ACCESS: Daily, sunrise–10:30 p.m.; free
FACILITIES: Picnic tables, water fountain, benches
WHEELCHAIR TRAVERSABLE: No
SPECIAL COMMENTS: Bring a Frisbee.

Directions

Take the President George Bush Turnpike northeast into Carrollton, and exit at Josey Lane. Turn left onto North Josey Lane, and go north 0.7 miles. An entrance to the greenbelt is on your right at the intersection of Josey Lane and Southern Oaks. Park at the far eastern end of the drive, next to the picnic area.

GPS Trailhead Coordinates

UTM Zone (WGS84) 14S
Easting   697530
Northing   3652730
Latitude   N 32° 59' 42"
Longitude   W 96° 53' 9"

30 Carrollton Greenbelt

0   250   500
feet

N

Winterberry Dr.

Frankford Rd.

bench

Yewpon Dr.

Furneaux Ln.

bench

Mill Trl.

Scott Mill Rd.

Lockwood Dr.

GREENBELT PARK

P

Southern Oaks

Greenvalley Dr.

bench

Stonebrook Dr.

Glenbrook Dr.

Scott Mill Rd.

Statler Dr.

To 190

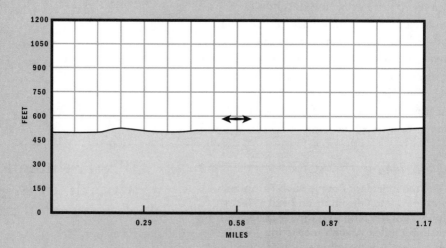

flat surface and accessibility make it great for folks who don't have the time to mess with gear such as hiking shoes, walking sticks, and maps. Just about the only things you'll need to remember to bring are a comfortable pair of sneakers and sunscreen—the entire trail is exposed.

The greenbelt is expansive and has several access points; I started this hike at one that has a large parking area and nearby picnic tables where you can enjoy lunch after your hike. Dragonflies, small gnats, and other flying insects are prevalent in the springtime, and you'll find insect repellent helpful.

To start the hike, cross through the picnic area and head over the small bridge that spans the narrow creek. Its waters are funneled through a narrow brick passage, which not only prevents erosion but also adds a pretty accent to the grassy field it passes through. If you've brought younger hikers with you, they'll delight in frolicking on the grassy banks and peering at the lily pads that grow profusely in the bridge's shadow.

Across the bridge, bear left, following the path east. The trail does follow the direction of the creek but does not run directly alongside it, instead curling away and up a gentle rise to follow it from atop a small hill. At 0.25 miles, a bench facing the greenbelt below offers a sunny overlook and resting spot. In the lush, green fields below, you're likely to spot folks playing Frisbee golf, families picnicking in sunny spots, and kids walking alongside the creek in search of bugs, frogs, and tadpoles. A thin sprinkling of wildflowers attracts a few butterflies in the spring, but for the most part, it is just a mowed lawn. Off to your right, a residential neighborhood abuts the greenbelt, offering a pleasant sense of community.

At 0.38 miles, you'll cross Scott Mill Road. Pick the trail up again across the street slightly to your right and follow it as it continues winding slowly east along the creek. You'll pass some tennis courts then near a residential neighborhood where the greenbelt reroutes itself, heading back west and away from the residences, over the creek, and back across Scott Mill Road. Once you've crossed the road, turn left onto the sidewalk and you'll see a refreshing expanse of green to your right. Turn right to rejoin the trail and reenter the greenbelt.

From here on, it's a quiet, peaceful walk through an expanse of grass. Ducks can regularly be spotted in the creek on your left, many congregating around a small bridge at 0.85 miles, which leads off to an apartment complex. At this point, not held in by the brickwork you saw earlier in the hike, the creek becomes a bit less manicured, its ragged banks strewn with rocks and twigs. A few trees alongside the creek provide much-needed shade, although none provide relief on the trail itself.

Many folks, attracted by the shaded grass in this area, bring their dogs to this section. Encouraged by the light trail traffic and absence of major roadways, many of them unleash their dogs, letting them romp freely through the grass next to them as they play Frisbee or explore the creek. Most of the animals are well behaved and will ignore you as you walk by, but be prepared for at least a couple of curious sniffs and wagging tails from excited pets.

Manicured lawns adjacent to the trail soak in the sun.

As you continue through the grassy field, you'll pass a couple benches before eventually reaching Frankford Road. This is a good place to turn around. If you're interested in continuing, however, the greenbelt does extend farther; cross Frankford Road and turn left to rejoin it.

NEARBY ACTIVITIES

Addison's high concentration of restaurants makes it a great post-hike lunch or dinner destination. You can find just about everything here, including Indian, Japanese, Mexican, Mediterranean, and even Mongolian food. There are more than 170 restaurants to choose from, so be sure to visit Addison's Web site (www.addisontexas.net) to help you decide where you might like to go. Many of the eateries are on Belt Line Road between Marsh Lane and Preston Road. To get there, head south on North Josey Lane 3 miles, then turn left onto East Beltline Road; the intersection of Marsh and Beltline is 2 miles down.

CHISHOLM TRAIL 31

IN BRIEF

This trail, located in a linear park, follows Spring Creek and serves as a pleasant commuting and exercise route for local residents. Designated as a National Recreational Trail, this strip of flat, sunny greenbelt is sandwiched between neighborhoods and eventually joins a second greenbelt—Bluebonnet Trail—just to the northwest.

DESCRIPTION

Chances are that if you've lived in the metroplex for any length of time, you've heard of Chisholm Trail. There are museums, districts, businesses, murals, schools—and even a country song—named after it. An important part Texas's heritage, it was a route used to drive cattle north to market in the mid- to late 19th century. It was eventually made obsolete by the railway's expansion. Plano's Chisholm Trail is a well-used route down a linear park funneling local residents northwest and southeast through a long greenbelt connecting a chain of neighborhoods, parks, and schools. Just to the northwest, it connects with Bluebonnet Trail—another section of greenbelt, which runs west to east. Chisholm is the more pleasant trail, however; Bluebonnet follows a mainly sunny, flat route along power lines.

KEY AT-A-GLANCE INFORMATION

LENGTH: 3.09 miles
CONFIGURATION: Balloon
DIFFICULTY: Easy
SCENERY: Greenbelt, parks, creek, bluebonnets in spring
EXPOSURE: Sunny
TRAIL TRAFFIC: Moderate
TRAIL SURFACE: Paved
HIKING TIME: 1 hour
ACCESS: Free
FACILITIES: Picnic tables, water fountains, playground, dog park
WHEELCHAIR TRAVERSABLE: No
SPECIAL COMMENTS: Hike this trail in April to get that treasured springtime photo of yourself amid the bluebonnets.

Directions ⟶

Park in the lot next to Schimelpfenig Library (5024 Custer Road) in Plano. To get there, take US 75 to Exit 31 and turn west onto Spring Creek Parkway. Go approximately 2.5 miles down to Custer Road, then turn left.

GPS Trailhead Coordinates

UTM Zone (WGS84) 14S
Easting 711728
Northing 3659740
Latitude N 33° 3' 20"
Longitude W 96° 43' 56"

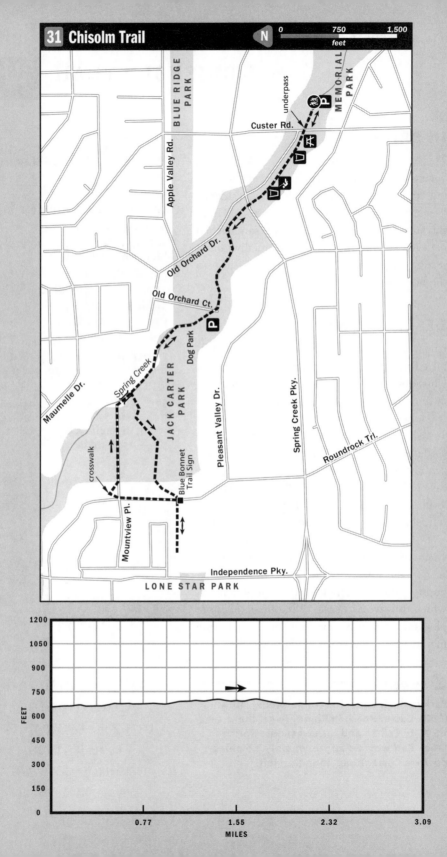

The Chisholm–Bluebonnet Trail, as it is sometimes called, was certified as a National Recreational Trail in 1981. It's open to everyone, and you'll find a broad mix of road bikers, dog-walkers, and joggers here. It's also on the regular roster of outings with the local walking, in-line skating, and running clubs. Nevertheless, it is actually not that busy because folks come and go quickly.

One of the most convenient spots from which to access the trail is the Schimelpfenig Library, where I started my hike. From here, the wide trail goes both northwest and southeast. Start the hike by turning left, heading northwest toward Custer Road and Spring Creek Parkway. The trail stays in the middle of the greenbelt, so although you'll see residences and roads around you, you're separated from them by a sea of grass. The trail is not compellingly landscaped but rather simple, offering just the sunny path and occasional tree. The creek, which has a smattering of tree growth along its banks, follows a few dozen feet off to the right alongside the trail. The path itself is sunny and treeless though nicely manicured and neatly mowed. A picnic area and playground to the left at 0.23 miles encourage a sense of community and help present the trail as family-friendly.

A couple of bridge underpasses prevent your having to cross major roadways and provide a haven for ducks, who like to congregate there. Be advised that because the trail winds downhill and follows the creek under the bridges, the path is prone to flooding, in particular at the underpass for Spring Creek Parkway at 0.3 miles. When I hiked, it had been a few days since the last rainfall, but I found a mud pit beneath one of the bridges, along with the footprints of folks who slipped and slid through. You can usually navigate wet areas by stepping around the edges or slightly up the underpass's sloping sides. If it has rained heavily, however, you may find some places impassable.

You'll wind along behind some office buildings then reach the Dog Park at Jack Carter Park, which abuts the trail at 0.7 miles. A bridge crosses the creek off to the right, leading into the 2-acre off-leash dog area popular with residents. Continue straight, bypassing a bridge turnoff on your right and a sports field on your left. When there is no activity in the fields, there is good birding in this area. On the spring morning that I visited, the grasses here were filled with robins— I counted more than 40 of the charming, small, orange-chested birds pecking at the ground in search of worms.

Just a few hundred feet farther, you'll reach a road junction for Roundrock Trail, where the path picks back up on the other side of the street. A large sign marks the greenbelt as Bluebonnet Trail. If you visit during the spring, you will indeed see a lovely mass of bluebonnets growing just beneath the sign. Cross the bridge and hike down the trail to the first road junction, and you'll find even more displays of the pretty wildflowers forming puddles of color in the grassy strip to the left of the trail. When you're done exploring, retrace your steps back to the Bluebonnet Trail sign, and turn left, following the sidewalk toward Jack Carter Park.

A bridge spans a small creek on the latter part of the trail.

It's a 0.2-mile walk to the park, which will be on the right. Cross the street when you reach Mountview Place and rejoin the paved path next to the "Jack Carter Maint Shop" sign. The trail heads east past an often-busy sports field then reaches a bridge at 1.88 miles. Stay straight, bypassing this bridge to continue to a second bridge a few hundred feet beyond. When you cross the bridge, turn left and you'll find yourself back on the trail you came in on. From here, just retrace your steps to the trailhead.

NEARBY ACTIVITIES

Switching gears from urban to rural, visit the Heritage Farmstead Museum, where you can take a guided or self-guided tour of the house and grounds of a restored Victorian farmhouse. To get there, just take Custer Road south 2.5 miles, then turn left onto West 15th Street. The museum is about 0.3 miles down at 1900 West 15th Street. There is a small admittance fee. Visit the museum's Web site at **heritagefarmstead.org** for information on hours and cost.

CICADA-COTTONWOOD LOOP **32**

IN BRIEF

You'll hike through the woods to an overlook with a view of the wetlands, where a camouflaged blind allows for bird-watching. The trail's highlight is a restored pioneer cabin from the 1850s, complete with period furnishings.

DESCRIPTION

The 2,000-acre Lewisville Lake Environmental Learning Area (LLELA) is adjacent to the southern shore of Lewisville Lake, opposite the lake's dam. It is a Federal Wildlife Management Area and offers a variety of activities, including primitive camping, canoeing, kayaking, fishing, and hiking. LLELA also offers tours of its bison herd on the last Sunday of the month for an additional $2. If you're interested in the tour, be sure to call ahead to confirm tour times. The bison are in a separate enclosure, so there is no worry of being confronted by an errant bull on the hike.

LLELA is operated by a consortium of local universities, the city of Lewisville, and the Lewisville Independent School District and is involved in ongoing research and education programs, including prairie restoration, wetland research, and water retention. A number of graduate theses and dissertations have also focused on the habitat and ecology of LLELA and the surrounding lake area.

KEY AT-A-GLANCE INFORMATION

LENGTH: 1.7 miles

CONFIGURATION: Loop

DIFFICULTY: Easy

SCENERY: Woods, wetlands, interpretive signs, pioneer log cabin

EXPOSURE: Shady to sunny

TRAIL TRAFFIC: Light

TRAIL SURFACE: Packed dirt

HIKING TIME: 45 minutes

ACCESS: $3 per person, children under age 5 free; winter: Friday–Sunday, 7 a.m.–5 p.m.; summer: Friday–Sunday, 7 a.m.–7 p.m.

FACILITIES: Toilet, picnic tables, benches

WHEELCHAIR TRAVERSABLE: No

SPECIAL COMMENTS: Bring binoculars and spend some time scoping the wetlands.

Directions

Follow I-35E north toward Denton and take Exit 454A toward 407/Justin. Turn right onto East Jones Street. The LLELA entrance is at the end of Jones at the intersection of North Kealy Street and Jones. To get to the trailhead, follow the road from the entrance booth to the first parking area on your right.

GPS Trailhead Coordinates

UTM Zone (WGS84) 14S

Easting   689017

Northing   3660377

Latitude   N 33° 3' 56"

Longitude W 96° 58' 31"

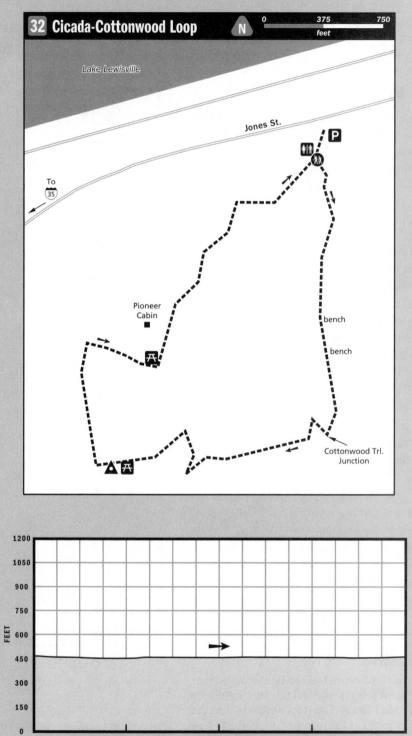

At the LLELA entrance, someone in the small booth will collect your admission fee and give you a pamphlet that includes a small map of the grounds. The hike starts on Cicada Trail, just to the south of the parking area and behind the Cicada Pavilion picnic tables. A small sign marks the trailhead.

Cicada Trail is a self-guided nature trail meandering south through the woods and past signs describing the foliage, including cedar elm, coralberry, elderberry, and bois d'arc. The signs are actually quite descriptive, so plan on taking more time along this section if you intend to read each marker.

Go left at the trail junction at 0.33 miles. To the left you'll catch glimpses through the trees of a river that helps make the path a good place to spot birds. Year-round birds such as the red-winged blackbird, the northern cardinal, and the Carolina chickadee can regularly be spotted in the area.

At 0.4 miles, bear right at the split. You'll pass another interpretive sign; just beyond, the trail splits. To the left, the trail ends at a lookout over a gully. Bear right and follow the trail downhill. It emerges from woods then joins the wide Cottonwood Trail. Head right to take Cottonwood Trail, following the road as it heads west.

You'll pass a group of picnic tables abutting a narrow creek at 0.83 miles. Snakes such as the southern copperhead and the western cottonmouth are commonly spotted in the surrounding habitat. Although I did not see any, remind younger hikers to be cautious when traipsing off the trail through tall grass or dense underbrush.

Continuing down the road, you'll reach a camouflaged lookout over the surrounding wetlands. The pavilion is nicely shielded, allowing you to view the wetland wildlife unnoticed. A peek through the netting on my hike revealed dozens of ducks resting peacefully on the calm waters. Keep an eye out for other common birds, including the great blue heron, the great egret, and the smaller snowy egret.

Heading back down the trail, the marsh stays within sight to the left, with small trees and shrubs to the right. You're likely to spot gulls, turkey vultures, and red-tailed hawks circling overhead. Power lines briefly cross the path, reminding you of civilization. Just a few feet past the towers, however, the present is forgotten and you're instantly transported into the past as an old log cabin amid woods comes into view on your right. The cabin is surrounded by a few other log buildings and suggests what life must have been like on the North Texas prairie in the pioneer days. A log fence encloses the complex.

The cabin, built in the 1850s, originally belonged to a local resident. It was donated and transported to LLELA, where it has since been carefully restored to create a pioneer setting. The house sports original period furnishings and has a separate garden and smokehouse out back. The buildings are all made of logs and insulated with packed mud. As you explore, don't be surprised if you see the remnants of ashes in the pit of the smokehouse—it has even been put to use to roast a pig at a recent LLELA event! From here, head 0.3 miles back down the road to finish the trail loop and reach the trailhead.

A restored pioneer cabin from the 1850s abuts the trail.

NEARBY ACTIVITIES

If you're looking for a change of pace after the hike, you can stop by the nearby Vista Ridge Mall, only 6 miles away. It has a few large department stores, such as Macy's, Sears, Dillard's, JCPenney, and dozens of smaller gift shops and boutiques. There are also a number of eateries in and around the mall. To get there, follow I-35E south 3.5 miles, and take Exit 448B. Turn left onto East Round Grove Road.

ELM FORK TRAIL 33

IN BRIEF

Explore a historic bridge associated with tales of spooky hauntings, then hike through the woods and out to the tip of Lake Lewisville, where you can scope for shorebirds.

DESCRIPTION

The trailhead for this hike is located in Old Alton Bridge Park just outside Denton near the town of Copper Canyon. The park houses the historic Old Alton Bridge—not only well known for its historical importance but also notorious for its much-researched paranormal activity. In fact, the Denton County Paranormal Investigators have adopted a section of road adjacent to the park, and the bright-blue sign acknowledging their support is one of the first things you see as you enter.

The bridge is just west of the parking lot. Built in 1884, it was added to the National Register of Historic Places in July 1988. Within more recent years, the city's population growth has prompted the creation of a new bridge for motor traffic; this new route bypasses the narrow, iron-truss, one-lane, wood-planked Old Alton Bridge, which is now open only to pedestrian and equestrian traffic.

From the parking lot, the trail splits, heading southeast (left) and southwest (right).

KEY AT-A-GLANCE INFORMATION

LENGTH: 3.8 miles
CONFIGURATION: Out-and-back
DIFFICULTY: Moderate
SCENERY: Historic bridge, marshy banks of lake, woods
EXPOSURE: Partly shady to sunny
TRAIL TRAFFIC: Moderate
TRAIL SURFACE: Dirt
HIKING TIME: 1.5 hours
ACCESS: Daily; free
FACILITIES: Picnic tables
WHEELCHAIR TRAVERSABLE: No
SPECIAL COMMENTS: Bring water; there are no water fountains.

Directions

From I-35E, exit onto Swisher Road, and head west approximately 3 miles. Just after Swisher Road becomes Teasley Road/FM 2181, you'll turn left onto Old Alton Road. The entrance to Old Alton Bridge Parkwill be down a steep driveway to your left, just before you cross the bridge.

GPS Trailhead Coordinates

UTM Zone (WGS84) 14S
Easting 676893
Northing 3667228
Latitude N 33° 7' 46"
Longitude W 97° 6' 14"

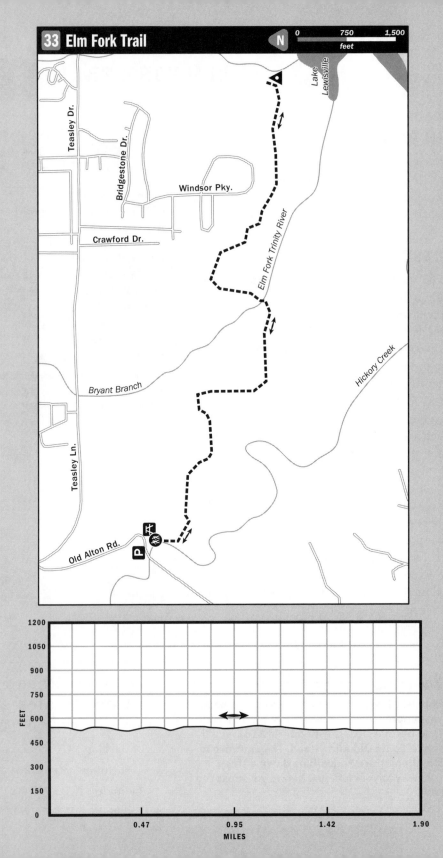

N

0   750   1,500
feet

Teasley Dr.

Bridgestone Dr.

Windsor Pky.

Crawford Dr.

Elm Fork Trinity River

Lake Lewisville

Hickory Creek

Bryant Branch

Teasley Ln.

Old Alton Rd.

P

1200
1050
900
750
600
450
300
150
0

FEET

0.47   0.95   1.42   1.90
MILES

The trail winds through thick woodlands as it winds towards the lake.

If you go right, you'll cross the bridge and head south, eventually joining Pilot Knoll Trail, which heads down toward Pilot Knoll Park. The hike described here does not cross the bridge in that direction, but rather follows the trail on the left. But before heading down the trail, take a detour to check out the bridge. Local legend holds that the bridge is haunted, and it has become a favorite spot for thrill-seekers, especially at Halloween. Those who know the legends will sometimes refer to it as Goatman's Bridge. There are several versions of the story, but essentially they all involve a man who was killed on the bridge and comes back as a creature that is half man and half goat. Some accounts say he was a goat herder; others say that the man lost his head and now uses a goat's head. Most accounts say that if you honk your horn two or three times (depending on the story), you'll see the goat-man in the distance. The legends attract not only local kids but also paranormal investigators, many of whom have posted photos and reports of their investigations online.

When you're done checking out the bridge, go back to the parking lot and head left down Elm Fork Trail. The wide path travels south through an open grassy plain toward a wood on the horizon, then turns east. Butterflies, dragonflies, and crickets buzz by, hopping and flying out of your path. A few narrow trails branch off the main trail to your right, leading to fishing spots at the creek's edge. Stay on the main trail, bypassing all turnoffs. The trail eventually reaches the trees and cuts a wide path through them, keeping you clear of any shade they might cast. To your left, a wire fence partially hidden beneath vines and mesquite trees marks the outer perimeter of a ranch where cows graze lazily in their sunny pasture, watching you as you pass. You'll traverse more grassland, which is punctuated by thin groves of short trees, before reaching a creek crossing. The trail stewards have layered blocks along the creek's banks here to prevent erosion and allow hikers to easily step across without getting their feet wet.

On the other side of the creek, you'll find less grass and more trees growing closer to the trail. A lush green understory provides dense pockets of shade. Birds are much more prevalent on this side of the creek as well, and you'll hear them whistling and chirping in the background, though spotting them in the trees is fairly difficult.

The flatness of the first half of the trail is soon replaced by slight hills, and the trees give way to shrubby grassland dotted with junipers before you finally reach another creek. Continue past it; at the next junction, bear right, heading southeast. A few houses off to the left hint that you're nearing the lake.

At the next junction, follow the trail right as it winds through the woods alongside the creek and past purple wildflowers, cacti, and small birds such as finches. Gentle hills give way to a couple of steep ones. After these, you'll spot a few houses built against the wooded hills, then you'll round a curve and finally get your first glimpse of Lewisville Lake. This is the northeastern tip, and you'll notice that the water is shallow and marshy. A lookout at 1.9 miles allows you to take a breather and scope for wading and shorebirds. Cardinals and woodpeckers can also be readily spotted in the surrounding trees. From here, turn and retrace your steps to the trailhead.

NEARBY ACTIVITIES

Visit Denton's historic town square, where you can often find musicians performing. The square's focal point is the old County Courthouse, which dates back to 1896. Restaurants, art galleries, boutiques, and other retail shops offer shopping and dining. To get there, head back onto I-35E south about 1.5 miles, take the exit for US 377/Fort Worth Drive, then make a right onto West Hickory Street.

ERWIN PARK LOOP 34

IN BRIEF

This easy trail leads you through open meadows as it loops in and out of the woods and through the preserve. Enjoy colorful wildflower displays in the spring and a variety of birdlife year-round.

DESCRIPTION

The 212-acre Erwin Park is a McKinney city park in a somewhat rural area surrounded by ranchlands, just north of Dallas/Fort Worth. Donated in 1971 to the Texas Conservation Foundation by the Erwin family, the land has belonged to the city of McKinney since 1973 and has been developed into a large park with much of its natural area preserved. It even offers overnight camping; visit the McKinney Parks and Recreation Department for details on making reservations (**www.mckinneytx.com/ parks.htm**).

The park's trails are maintained by the Dallas Off Road Bicycle Association (DORBA), and include about 8 miles of path through meadows and woodlands. The trails are narrow, and you will have to step aside to let bikers pass you; however, a lot of this hike is

KEY AT-A-GLANCE INFORMATION

LENGTH: 2.6 miles
CONFIGURATION: Loop
DIFFICULTY: Easy
SCENERY: Meadows, woodlands
EXPOSURE: Partly sunny to sunny
TRAIL TRAFFIC: Moderate
TRAIL SURFACE: Dirt
HIKING TIME: 1 hour
ACCESS: Daily, 8 a.m.–10 p.m.; free
FACILITIES: Toilet, picnic tables, water fountain
WHEELCHAIR TRAVERSABLE: No
SPECIAL COMMENTS: This hike can easily be extended with a second loop.

Directions

Follow US 75 north toward McKinney. Take Exit 41 toward US 380/Greenville/Denton. Turn left onto West University Drive/US 380E and go 2.5 miles, then turn right onto FM 1461 and travel 2 miles. Turn right onto CR164, go approximately 1 mile, then turn left onto CR 1006. The entrance to Erwin Park is on the right. Inside the park, turn left at the end of the road, and park in the second parking lot next to the pavilion and picnic area. The trailhead is on the right and is marked by a kiosk.

GPS Trailhead Coordinates

UTM Zone (WGS84) 14S
Easting 718452
Northing 3682040
Latitude N 33° 15' 19"
Longitude W 96° 39' 18"

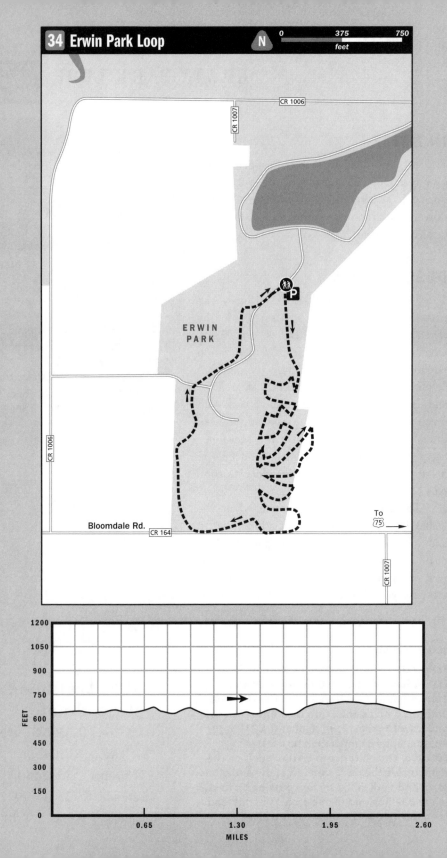

through open, tree-studded meadows, and you'll have no problem seeing the bikers as they approach. The trail traffic varies, and there are times that you can come here and find no one else on the trail at all. I visited on a slightly overcast weekend morning to find the pavilion and playground full of picnickers but the trail empty except for one other hiker. Prettier days will bring more bikers.

At the trailhead, you have two options: west (right) and south (left). The entire trail is actually one huge loop and, if you wanted to, you could start on one side and come out 8 miles later at the other. For those wanting something a bit more manageable, there are turnaround spots that make the trail shorter, and I took advantage of that on my visit. This hike covers the southeastern corner of the park; you'll loop back to the trailhead before the turnoff into the western and northern sides of the park. To start the hike, you'll therefore turn onto the trail on the left.

You'll immediately find yourself hiking through an expansive meadow, which in the spring is blanketed with tiny yellow wildflowers. The terrain is not completely flat but instead has gentle hills, expanding out to a tree line in the distance ahead of you. As you leave the vicinity of the picnic area, the sounds of folks laughing and kids playing will fade into the background and be replaced by other sounds echoing through the open clearing—woodpeckers pecking in the woodlands up ahead, and cows mooing somewhere nearby (don't worry, they're actually in an adjacent enclosed property, and you won't come face-to-face with any on the hike). Continue toward the woods in the distance, bypassing other trails that join the one you're on. At the tree line, the path dives into the woods—a shady mixture of old and young trees with thick vines climbing up their trunks and branches. Small dips and tight twists intended to spice up the biker's rides also add interest to your trek. You'll briefly emerge into another smaller meadow before you're again enclosed by woodland.

At 0.43 miles, you'll round a small pond hidden in the heart of the woods—one of two you'll discover along the hike. If it's recently rained, the shallow dips in the path just around it can sometimes pool with water, creating mud pockets, even though the rest of the trail might be dry. They're easy to navigate unless it's rained heavily recently—then you might emerge a bit messier than when you entered.

A few hundred feet farther, bear left and head down a short, steep slope, where you'll find yourself walking atop a ridge beside a creek along the eastern side of the park. Stay straight at the next two four-way junctions at 0.6 miles. The trail then briefly merges with the overgrown remains of an old gravel road that passes through another open, grassy clearing dotted with red, blue, yellow, and purple wildflowers. You'll head slightly downhill, winding through open grassland for quite a while before roots start breaking up the path and the woodlands once again enclose you. Just beyond the tree line, you'll find the second pond at 1 mile. From here, the trail heads northeast, meets back up with the creek, then heads south, following a high ridge. It then reaches a split at 1.28 miles. Bear right at the junction, bypassing a steep dip and climb intended for mountain bikers; a few of these bike dips punctuate the trail, but most have turnoffs just before them allowing hikers to circumvent them.

A hiker makes his way through a sunny meadow.

The trail then winds back east, passes the other side of the pond, and curls back out into an open, grassy field as it heads south. After some sun-drenched hiking through the grass, you'll spot the park road ahead of you. You'll meet the road at 2.3 miles and rejoin the trail just across it. Follow the trail as it heads north alongside the road. At 2.43 miles, stay to the left to enter a final bit of woods. Through the trees to your right, you'll spot the pavilion; a few hundred feet later, a narrow, dirt path bears right, leading you back out and up through the picnic area and back to your car.

NEARBY ACTIVITIES

The Heard Natural Science Museum and Wildlife Sanctuary is only 10 miles away, just to the southeast. It offers plant gardens, nature exhibits, and a wildlife sanctuary with hiking trails. The Heard is open Monday through Saturday from 9 a.m. to 5 p.m., and on Sunday from 1 p.m. to 5 p.m. Admission is $8 for adults and $5 for children ages 3 to 12. To get there, head south on 75. After 3.7 miles, take Exit 38A onto 121 south toward Fort Worth. Make a U-turn onto Spur 399 north toward McKinney, then turn right onto 5 south toward Fairview. Go approximately 0.7 miles, then turn left onto FM 1378, and pass the country club to reach the entrance.

LAVON LAKE: Trinity Trail **35**

IN BRIEF

This multiuse hiking and equestrian trail takes you out a couple miles through open woodlands and sunny grasslands adjacent to Lavon Lake before looping back along the sandy lakeshore, where you can beachcomb and search for shorebirds.

DESCRIPTION

This trail, already a favorite of many DFW hikers, is located on the 21,400-acre Lavon Lake, just east of Lucas in Collin County. It traverses a small portion of the lake's 83-mile shoreline and is an excellent choice for hikers wanting an invigorating lake hike. What I've mapped here is only a small portion of the 9 miles of trail. This is therefore an easy hike to extend and is ideal if you're not sure if you're in the mood for a long hike or a short trek.

The lake is on the East Fork of the Trinity River just south of McKinney. An Army Corps of Engineers lake, it was impounded in 1953 and built (as were most other North Texas lakes) for flood control and water conservation. It also accommodates a variety of recreational activities in its more than one dozen parks, which offer camping, boating, and swimming. It has a reputation among

KEY AT-A-GLANCE INFORMATION

LENGTH: 3.19 miles
CONFIGURATION: Loop
DIFFICULTY: Moderate
SCENERY: Lake, shorebirds, grasslands, open woodlands
EXPOSURE: Partly sunny to sunny
TRAIL TRAFFIC: Moderate
TRAIL SURFACE: Dirt
HIKING TIME: 1.5 hours
ACCESS: Daily; free
FACILITIES: None
WHEELCHAIR TRAVERSABLE: No
SPECIAL COMMENTS: Hike this sunny trail in spring or fall; it heats up quickly in the summer.

Directions

Take US 75 north and exit onto Bethany Drive in Allen. Turn right, heading east approximately 6 miles on Bethany (which becomes Lucas Road). At the stoplight next to Lucas Food Mart, turn left onto FM 3286. After 0.8 miles, you'll turn right onto Brockdale Park Road. The gravel parking lot is about a mile down on the right, just before the boat ramp.

GPS Trailhead Coordinates

UTM Zone (WGS84) 14S
Easting 728795
Northing 3662049
Latitude N 33° 4' 23"
Longitude W 96° 32' 57"

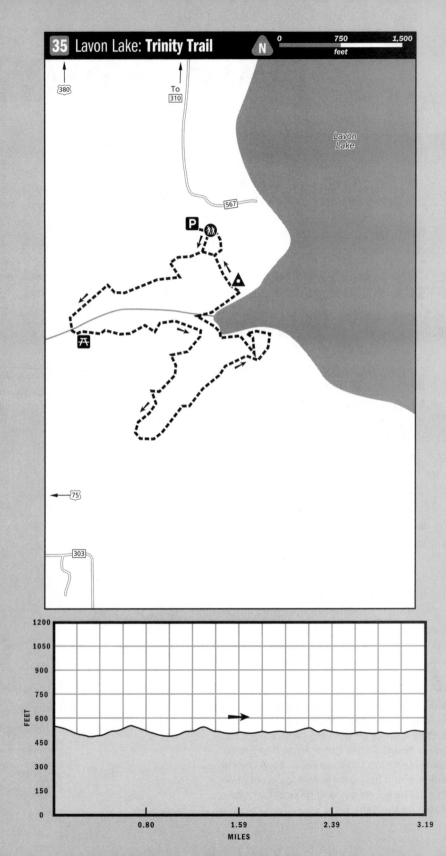

anglers for being an especially good spot for crappie fishing, and in the winter you'll see boats scoping the deeper waters for them.

Trinity Trail is on the western side of the lake. The Trinity Trail Preservation Association, a volunteer organization of horse owners, maintains this equestrian and hiking trail. You'll typically find at least one horse trailer in the trailhead's gravel parking lot. Hikers are welcome, too, and many come with daypacks and head out for several-hour hikes; bikes are not allowed on the trail. Don't hike this trail after it's rained because the loop back winds through soft sand and areas that can become marshy after a downpour.

The trailhead is in an open expanse of grassland atop a small hill overlooking the lake. It's on the eastern side of the parking lot; enter through a white pipe gate. You'll first trek down sunny, grassy slopes. Do not take the narrow branch that heads left down to the lake; instead, follow the wide trail that parallels the shore and heads southwest. Starting out as a sunny route through the open grassland, it soon curls west away from the lake and into the woodlands. The trees frame, but do not envelop, the trail, so it is only partially shaded. In the patches of sun that reach through and between the trees, clumps of grass grow freely, presenting you with a primarily open woodland free from dense underbrush and thickets. The scenery on the entire outbound route is similar to what you see here, and once you've walked through a mile of it, you won't find any major changes around the bend. There are a few landmarks that are worth noting, including a junction at 0.2 miles, which you'll reach just after crossing a creek. Stay to the left here. Bird boxes placed along the trail attract many colorful residents. Keep an eye out for small brown creepers camouflaged among the tree trunks and for other more colorful birds, such as bluebirds and common yellowthroats.

You'll cross another creek at 0.73 miles then reach a picnic area complete with picnic tables nestled in a grove of trees just off the path to your right. Continue heading straight, past the picnic area, and bypass the next left. At 2.3 miles, you'll finally reach another turnoff toward the lake, on the left. This is where you must decide if you'd like to continue hiking outbound, or complete the hike as I've outlined it here, which will loop you back to the trailhead along the sandy shoreline to your left. If you continue the hike, the trail heads southeast, curving through the woodlands, with intermittent glimpses of the lake. It eventually ends at the southern trailhead in East Fork Park, 9 miles from Brockdale. If you decide to loop back as I've suggested, you'll bear left at this junction and head down the narrow trail toward the lake's edge then take another left onto the grassy road returning northwest. This route is an almost straight line and is significantly shorter than the outbound trip—you'll find yourself back at the trailhead in only 0.79 miles. Be sure to take your time beachcombing on your return—there are tons of empty clamshells. You're likely to spot other hikers at the water's edge collecting them too.

When you find yourself just below the rise where the parking lot is, look for a narrow single-track path heading back up. The path will be hard to see because

The trail winds through grasslands adjacent to the lake.

of the band of shrubs growing parallel to the shore; however, if you check the sand, you can see hikers' footprints. Once you get through the brush, you'll be back on the open, grassy plain, where you'll have no problem spotting the narrow dirt trail winding uphill to end in the parking lot.

NEARBY ACTIVITIES

Southfork Ranch, the famous home of the fictional Ewing family on the old TV show *Dallas,* lies just to the west of Plano. Its magnificent white mansion served as the home of the show's infamous J. R. Ewing from 1978 to 1991. It was opened to the public in 1985 and continues to offer daily tours of the mansion and ranch grounds. Visit **www.southfork.com** for more information.

To get there from the trailhead, go back to the light at the Lucas Food Mart, and turn left onto FM 1378 (Southview Drive). After about 2.3 miles, turn right onto FM 2514 (Parker Road) and drive 2.5 miles. Turn left onto FM 2551 (Hogge Road/Murphy Road) The entrance is about 0.5 miles down on the left.

PARKHILL PRAIRIE TRAIL **36**

IN BRIEF

This reconstructed and restored native prairie is inspiring in the springtime when the wildflowers bloom.

DESCRIPTION

Those who are familiar with the opening sequence of the old TV series *Little House on the Prairie*—where the girls skip and frolic through a wide, open prairie dotted with flowers—will have a good idea of what the Parkhill Prairie Preserve is like. The beautiful 436-acre preserve is very similar to the one in that unforgettable shot, offering a gently rolling, sunny, grassland that is at its best in the spring, when the wildflowers bloom. The colorful display begins with prairie flowers, such as the bright red Indian paintbrush and the violet-colored wine cup; late spring brings the wild petunia and Mexican hat, and late summer and fall sees the bright-yellow goldenrod and the soft hues of the purple coneflower. The prairie has a remnant tract of blackland prairie, most of which is disappearing throughout the country as land is converted to farmland.

The prairie is 60 miles northeast of Dallas in Collin County, making it one of the farthest hikes in this book, but it's certainly

KEY AT-A-GLANCE INFORMATION

LENGTH: 1.88 miles
CONFIGURATION: Loop
DIFFICULTY: Easy
SCENERY: Prairie, wildflowers
EXPOSURE: Sunny
TRAIL TRAFFIC: Light
TRAIL SURFACE: Grass
HIKING TIME: 40 minutes
ACCESS: Daily; free
FACILITIES: Toilets, picnic tables, water fountain
WHEELCHAIR TRAVERSABLE: No
SPECIAL COMMENTS: Wear long pants and insect repellent if you visit in the summer—ticks love the long prairie grasses.

Directions ⟶

From McKinney, take US 380 east toward Farmersville, then turn north onto 78 and go approximately 9.4 miles toward Blue Ridge. At CR 825, turn right and drive 4.4 miles, then turn left onto CR 668. The entrance to Parkhill Prairie is about 2 miles down on the left. Park in the second parking area.

GPS Trailhead Coordinates

UTM Zone (WGS84) 14S
Easting   751535
Northing   3684689
Latitude   N 33° 16' 19"
Longitude   W 96° 17' 58"

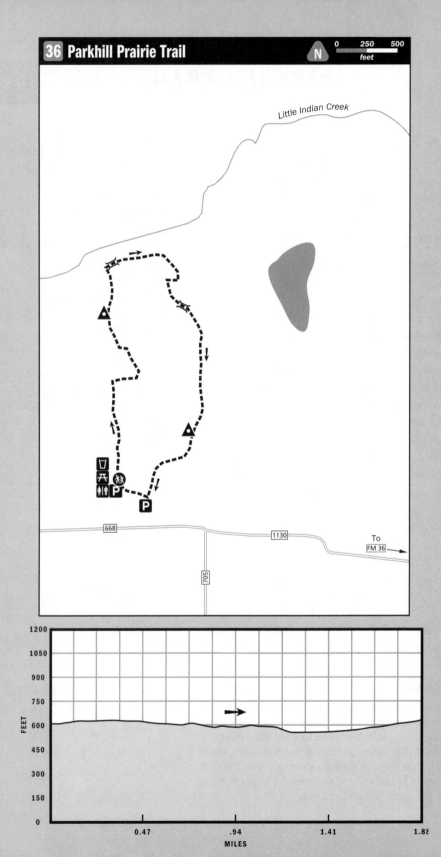

worth a visit for anyone seeking something a little different. It's fairly remote, set in the country just north of Farmersville with few other houses around. From a rocky outcropping along the trail, you'll have fantastic views of the surrounding countryside, which consists primarily of gently rolling hills dotted with trees; the view is especially beautiful in the fall, when the leaves change colors.

Each season, after the spring wildflowers and grasses come in, the trail is mowed back into the prairie. You can hike here year-round, but be advised that if you come before mowing season, you're likely to only see faint hints of the trail and will have to navigate an overgrown path. Spikes mark the trail route at regular intervals, so even if the trail is not mowed, you'll be able to find your way. Take care to avoid twisting your foot or stepping on snakes in the deep grass. Ideally, plan your visit for after the trail has been mowed, which happens sometime after Mother's Day.

Collin County has been working with the Nature Conservancy to restore the prairie. Some of these efforts include undertaking prescribed burns, which serve to control the intrusive, nonnative plants, which can take over the prairie if left unchecked. Recent drought conditions have limited the number of burns allowed here; however, as conditions improve, more burns are planned. On your hike, you're likely to notice the charred remains of trees and shrubs.

Park in the spaces in front of the restrooms; the trailhead is located opposite them and is marked by a kiosk. At the time of my visit, everything had been removed from the kiosk because they were in the middle of an improvement project. Follow the mowed lane north past the kiosk straight through the open prairie land. It's a gentle walk up and down some rolling hills, over a long wooden bridge, and through some shrubby tree growth to reach the overlook at 0.9 miles. A half-circle stone wall marks the spot atop a small rise and frames a lovely view of the rural countryside stretching out toward the horizon to the north and west.

Head back onto the trail, following it north. As you enter the northern section of the preserve, you'll notice clusters of shrubs and trees encroaching upon the prairie; you may also spot burn marks from the efforts to keep them from invading completely.

The path skirts the northern edge of the preserve. At 1.4 miles, you'll bear left and enter a smaller section surrounded by trees. At the marker, turn left and cross the bridge to enter another small section of grassland screened by trees. You'll pass through a tree line and into yet another natural enclosure, which abuts the eastern edge of the preserve. To your left, a fence marks the preserve's boundaries; just beyond it, you can sometimes spot Black Angus peering curiously at you as you pass. Much to my surprise, just beside the trail here, I also encountered the skeletal remains of what appeared to be one of their herd members. How it got where I found it remains a mystery to me. Don't worry, however, you won't encounter any live steer on the trail.

You'll soon traverse the tree-lined meadow and be back on the open prairie. From here, it's a short hike uphill to the eastern rock-wall overlook, which offers picturesque views of the prairie to the north and west. From here, hike back 0.35 miles to the trailhead. You'll emerge from the prairie at a kiosk and parking area just up the road from where you parked. The parking lot and restrooms are within easy view down the road a couple of hundred feet to your right.

NEARBY ACTIVITIES

Enjoy a picnic at Caddo Park on Lavon Lake after the hike. It's a day-use-only park 17 miles away and offers more than a dozen picnic sites, a handicap-accessible fishing pond, and a boat ramp. To get there, turn left back onto CR 668 (which becomes CR 1130). Go 1 mile and turn right onto FM 36. Head south 3.8 miles, then make a right onto FM 2194 and travel 6.3 miles. Bear right onto TX Business 78, then turn left onto TX 78. Turn left onto US 380. The park is about 2 miles down on your right.

A bridge connecting to a section of secluded prairie

PILOT KNOLL TRAIL

IN BRIEF

This trail, which winds alongside Lewisville Lake, is not the most scenic, but during hot, dry summers, the lake waters recede leaving a marsh and exposing gnarled trees favored by vultures. Birds dominate the woodlands adjacent to the trail.

DESCRIPTION

Lewisville Lake is very popular and is often referred to as Dallas's "party" lake. In the summer months, jet skiers, boaters, and fishermen fill the waters, while the shores overflow with swimmers, picnickers, and campers. Because of its popularity, the lake is always making the news for its rowdiness, including boating accidents. Occasionally, as happened earlier this year, alligator sightings prompt even more coverage. Game wardens advise that the gators' origins can be traced to the Trinity River. At any rate, alligators are a rarity here.

The lake dates back to the late 1920s, when the Elm Fork of the Trinity River was first dammed, creating the reservoir known as Lake Dallas. The lake was considerably smaller than today's Lewisville Lake, about a quarter of the current size. In the late 1940s, amid concerns for flood control, a new impoundment,

KEY AT-A-GLANCE INFORMATION

LENGTH: 2.55 miles
CONFIGURATION: Balloon
DIFFICULTY: Easy
SCENERY: Lake, woods, birds
EXPOSURE: Partly shady
TRAIL TRAFFIC: Light
TRAIL SURFACE: Packed dirt
HIKING TIME: 45 minutes
ACCESS: Free; daily
FACILITIES: Available in Pilot Knoll Park
WHEELCHAIR TRAVERSABLE: No
SPECIAL COMMENTS: This trail can be messy after a rainstorm.

Directions ───────────────→

Take I-35E and turn left (west) onto FM 407 (Justin Road). Go approximately 4.5 miles to Chin Chapel Road, then turn north (right). Make a right turn to head east on Orchard Hill Road, which dead-ends at Pilot Knoll Park. Parking is available just outside the park gate.

GPS Trailhead Coordinates

UTM Zone (WGS84) 14S
Easting 679385
Northing 3664972
Latitude N 33° 6' 31"
Longitude W 97° 4' 39"

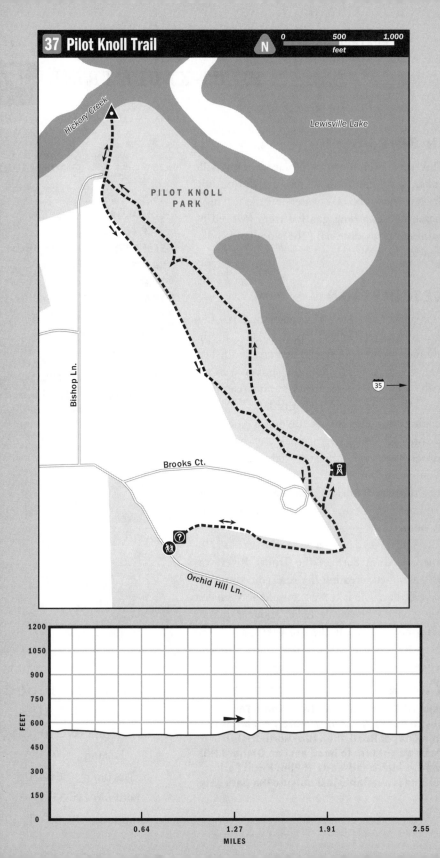

the Garza–Little Elm Reservoir, was created nearby by damming a number of creeks. About a decade later, Lake Dallas and the Garza–Little Elm Reservoir were combined to form the huge reservoir you see today, named Lewisville Lake in the 1970s.

Though recreationists are often alarmed at the low water levels on Lewisville Lake in summer, the lake's controlling authority, the Army Corps of Engineers, asserts that the lake's primary functions are flood control and water supply, which often causes low lake levels in hot, dry summers. This trail offers a unique perspective of the lake, especially when waters are below normal level. At the time of this writing, the lake was approximately 8 feet low, resulting in a severe shortage of water on this outlying side of the lake. The result is slightly reminiscent of a swamp—hundreds of gnarled, dead tree stumps were exposed as the water receded and ring the edges of huge pools of mirror-still water. Turkey vultures silently circle overhead, then glide down to the water's edge and rest on the beach's sun-baked tree stumps.

The trailhead is just outside Pilot Knoll Park, on the east side of the parking lot, just behind the map kiosk. There is a day-use fee for the immaculately maintained park, but because the trail is not maintained by the park, there is no fee to park your car or hike the trail. A sign for Hickory Creek Trail is next to the trailhead.

The wide trail winds east through the woods, following a small access road and passing RV campsites on the right and huge private homes on the left. About 0.3 miles down the trail, you'll reach a fork in the path, where you should bear right, heading north down Lake Shore Trail. The winding trail passes through a wooded area of tangled trees and then reaches another split. Head right at the junction, passing through more woods. The trail is also open to equestrian traffic—although I did not see any on my hike—so keep an eye to the ground for the occasional horse dropping.

At about 0.48 miles, you'll reach a break in the trees and get an unobstructed view of the lake on the right. When water levels are low, a wide expanse of sandy beach, dotted with old twisted tree trunks, rims the deathly still lake. On my hike, I counted at least a dozen huge turkey vultures perched at the water's edge, surveying the watery landscape.

The trail continues, with the lake coming in and out of view on the right, and a dense wood on the left. In addition to the mess of vulture feathers I found strewn across the trail, other signs of wildlife along the path are abundant, including what appeared to be deer tracks in the trail's soft dirt, and a brief glimpse of a small animal scurrying off under the trees, a raccoon, judging from the tracks. At the next junction, 1.15 miles into the hike, take the right-hand fork to head north. You'll then go straight past one more junction and at 1.2 miles find yourself at a junction where a wide road heads off toward an overlook to the right. On the left is the parking area at the end of Bishop Road, which serves as a public entrance to this overlook.

Low water levels expose tree stumps along the sandy lakeshore.

At this point, if you turn right, the trail goes about 0.1 mile and then reaches the overlook—a small hill overlooking the lake (or on a dry, summer hike—the remnants of the lake). It is important to mention that the lake's party reputation is most evident at public access points such as these. In other words, the better the access to the lake, the more likely you are to see evidence of late-night partying.

If you've ventured to the overlook, retrace your steps (or turn left if you didn't) to the Bishop Road parking area. You'll reach a junction with signs indicating that Hickory Trail is to the right and Lakeshore Trail is to the left. Go right onto Hickory Trail, heading south. The trail narrows and winds through woods. Keep an eye out for interesting birds, including some brilliant red ones, which flitted across the trail continually during my hike. At 1.78 miles, a trail heads off to the right, eventually fading out behind some private homes. Hang a left and follow the trail 0.61 more miles to close the loop. From here, turn left, retracing your steps 0.33 miles to the trailhead.

NEARBY ACTIVITIES

Pilot Knoll Park is a nice place to have a picnic lunch; their immaculate picnic area sits right on the lake's edge, affording outstanding views of the lake. Just to the southwest, Rockledge Park at Grapevine Lake also offers picnicking, swimming, and sunning options.

RAY ROBERTS GREENBELT 38

IN BRIEF

Thick woods loom over this wide, charming trail that winds north from Lewisville Lake to Ray Roberts Lake. It's a great, kid-friendly hike.

DESCRIPTION

The Ray Roberts Lake–Lewisville Lake Green-belt Corridor extends approximately 10 miles through a wooded section of land between the two lakes. It is officially part of the state park system and so requires no entry fee from those who have a state park pass. There are three trailheads along the greenbelt, one at the southern end on US 380, one at the northern end on FM 455, and one halfway through the corridor, on FM 428.

This trail starts at the southern end of the corridor, near the northern side of Lewisville Lake. Watch for the brown state park sign identifying the greenbelt. The trailhead is in front of the gravel path next to the kiosk on the north side of the parking lot. The huge lot always has at least a few cars in it, including one or two horse trailers. The horses and their riders are not permitted on the paved greenbelt but rather are restricted to an adjacent dirt path that runs parallel to the paved trail the entire length of the greenbelt.

KEY AT-A-GLANCE INFORMATION

LENGTH: 5 miles
CONFIGURATION: Out-and-back
DIFFICULTY: Easy
SCENERY: Dense woods
EXPOSURE: Partly shady
TRAIL TRAFFIC: Moderate to heavy
TRAIL SURFACE: Packed gravel
HIKING TIME: 1.75 hours
ACCESS: $5 per person; daily till 10 p.m.
FACILITIES: Recycling toilet
WHEELCHAIR TRAVERSABLE: No
SPECIAL COMMENTS: Visit the Texas Parks and Wildlife Department Web site at www.tpwd.state.tx.us/spdest/findadest/parks/ray_roberts_lake to print out a map of the entire trailway.

Directions ⟶

Follow I-35E north toward Denton and take Exit 463. Turn right onto TX 288 Loop and go about 3.5 miles. Turn right onto East University Drive. The trailhead is approximately 3 miles down on the left; keep an eye out for the brown Ray Roberts state park sign.

GPS Trailhead Coordinates

UTM Zone (WGS84) 14S
Easting 682456
Northing 3679665
Latitude N 33° 14' 26"
Longitude W 97° 2' 30"

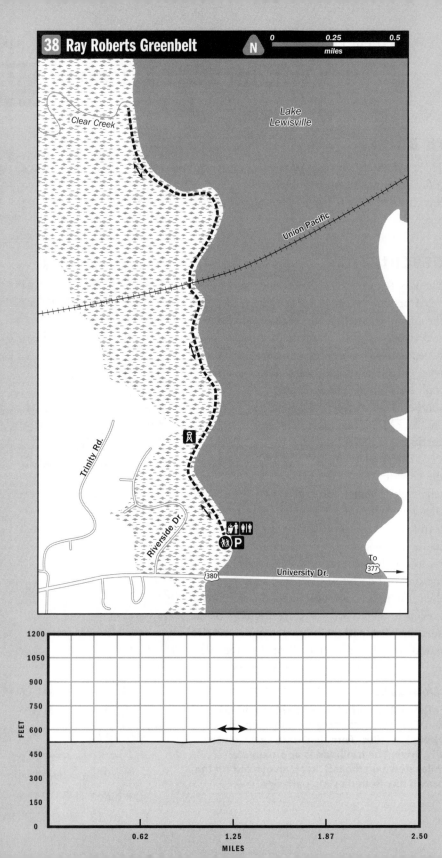

The trailhead for the dirt path is on the eastern edge of the lot. Although the dirt path is also open to hikers, it is worth your while to stick to the paved path: it provides the same scenery as the dirt trail without requiring you to step over or around horse dung.

A self-pay booth at the trailhead allows you to deposit the small trail-use fee if you don't have a state park pass. This is a great trail for youngsters because it is wide and partially shaded, has plenty of straight stretches to keep all members of the family within easy view, and is completely removed from potentially danger-ous streets and highways. Be sure to encourage younger hikers to use the toilets at the trailhead before you start down the path; the other restrooms are 6.5 miles out at the FM 428 trailhead. It's also important to note that there is no water along the trail, so be sure you've brought some along, especially if it's a hot day.

I was actually much more impressed with this trail than I expected I would be. There's something special about it that is hard to put a finger on. It might be that it feels much wilder than the typical greenbelt. The land has been left in its natural state, and as you hike along, the elegant beauty of the tall trees towering above and looming around you transports you into a different world. Ahead and behind you, the trail curves gently out of sight beneath the trees as it winds lazily north through the dense woods. Another part of its magic is that it's far removed from the ever-present hum of civilization. Deep within the greenbelt, you'll clearly hear the rustling of leaves and the creaking of limbs in the wind. The only sounds louder than this are the clear trills, whistles, and songs of birds watching you walk by. Surprisingly, the relaxing, peaceful atmosphere of the trail is not marred by the fair amount of hikers, joggers, and dog-walkers you'll find on the path. Most folks walk or jog quietly by, drinking in the calmness of the woods.

At 0.43 miles, you'll pass an overlook off to your left that offers a nice view of the Elm Fork of the Trinity River which stays hidden from view for most of the hike. The trail actually follows the river as it heads north toward Ray Roberts Lake. Occasionally, signs of civilization do temporarily invade the beauty of the greenbelt—at 1 mile into the trail, some power lines cross over the path. Just beyond, at 1.15 miles, a railway line crosses the trail, creating another brief break in the otherwise continuous belt of woods.

The trail continues for much longer than you'll probably be willing or able to hike—10 miles in one direction. The day I hiked the trail, the trail—which is just wide enough to accommodate a car—was busy with park rangers and medics winding carefully back and forth. An equestrian galloping past on her way back to the trailhead stopped to let us know that a rider had fallen farther along the trail. We turned back to stay out of the way of the medical personnel. On most days, however, the trail is clear and quiet for as long as you're willing to walk. When you're ready to head back, just retrace your steps. Be sure to reserve enough energy to make it back to the trailhead—if you're not paying attention you can easily hike farther than you intended.

Railway tracks emerge briefly from the woods.

NEARBY ACTIVITIES

Stop by downtown Denton and visit the Courthouse-on-the-Square Museum, located in the historic Denton County Courthouse at 110 West Hickory Street. Exhibits focus on African American Families of Denton County, Hispanic Families of Denton County, and Special Collections, such as Indian pottery, thimbles, and quilts. To get there, head back 5 miles down University Drive into downtown Denton, and turn left onto North Elm Street. Turn left onto West Hickory Street. You might want to check out the nearby Golden Triangle Mall, which includes department stores, gift shops, and the Silver Cinema Theater, where you can see movies for $2.

RAY ROBERTS LAKE STATE PARK, ISLE DU BOIS UNIT: Lost Pines Trail **39**

IN BRIEF

This pretty trek through hardwoods stops at interpretive signs identifying flora and leads to a pretty grove of pine trees. A spur midway through heads out to a sandy lakeshore along which you can find animal tracks and birds such as herons and egrets.

DESCRIPTION

Ray Roberts Lake, just north of Denton, is a 30,000-acre reservoir complete with boat ramps, camping, a swimming beach, trails, and a marina. The lake was originally called the Aubrey Reservoir but was renamed after a U.S. congressman in 1980. It is a big attraction for anglers, who come to fish the crappie, white bass, catfish, and flathead and is popular with nature lovers, who come to enjoy the various offerings of the state park complex on its shores.

Isle du Bois, which translates to "Island of the Trees," is part of the lake's state park complex, and sits on its southern shore. The park opened in 1993, making it a few years older than the neighboring Johnson Branch Unit, which opened in 1996. Within the park, you'll find miles of hiking, biking, and equestrian trails, all of which see good use. The main portion of these trails run slightly inland from the

KEY AT-A-GLANCE INFORMATION

LENGTH: 1 mile
CONFIGURATION: Loop with spur
DIFFICULTY: Easy
SCENERY: Lake shoreline, hardwoods, pines
EXPOSURE: Shady to sunny
TRAIL TRAFFIC: Light
TRAIL SURFACE: Packed dirt trail, sand
HIKING TIME: 30 minutes
ACCESS: Daily, 8 a.m.–10 p.m.; $5 per person for adults and children age 13 and up
FACILITIES: Restrooms, picnic area, playground
WHEELCHAIR TRAVERSABLE: No
SPECIAL COMMENTS: This hike can be extended by walking along the lake shoreline. Bring binoculars along for bird-watching.

Directions

When reading directional signs on the highway, keep in mind that there are two different state park units, one on the north side of the lake and one on the south side. To get to the Isle du Bois State Park Unit, take I-35 north to Sanger, exit at FM 455, and go east approximately 10 miles toward Pilot Point to the park entrance. Park in the first parking area, just inside the park entrance.

GPS Trailhead Coordinates

UTM Zone (WGS84) 14S
Easting 685000
Northing 3693638
Latitude N 33° 21' 58"
Longitude W 97° 0' 41"

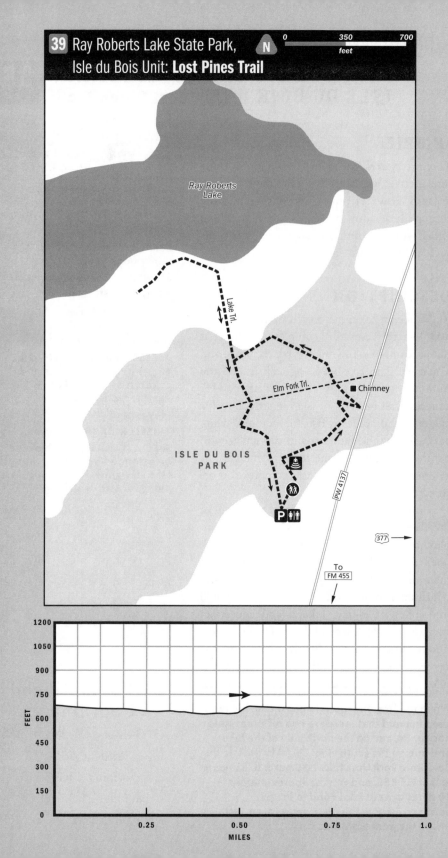

shore, traveling for miles before looping back, making them ideal for long day treks. For shorter hikes, the park offers a paved loop trail through its center and a pretty interpretive nature trail near the park entrance, highlighted below.

The trailhead is just to the north of the parking area; you can see it from the lot. Be sure to pick up one of the brochures from the box at the trailhead to help identify the flora along the trail; each plant has a numbered signpost. Heading down the trail, you'll immediately pass the first marker for Hercules' Club—or Toothache Tree—a small tree whose bark, when chewed, can cause numbness in the mouth.

In about 400 feet, you'll reach a small clearing and the amphitheater. Bear right, following the trail northeast through the woods. Here the trail is a wide path rather than a single-track dirt path, making it seem like you've stepped into another world. At some points, I half expected to see Little Red Riding Hood skipping through the woods on her way to a remote cottage.

Interpretive signs along the way will help you identify plants commonly found in this ecological woodland zone known as Eastern Cross Timbers region. Blackjack oaks and post oaks dominate the woods; bluejack oaks and live oaks are fewer. Keep an eye out for colorful birds such as the eastern bluebird and American robin in the branches of the surrounding trees.

At 0.25 miles, you'll reach a clearing amid which you'll see the remains of a chimney fenced off on the right. Elm Fork Trail, a wide path of loose dirt ideal for equestrians, intersects the nature trail here, heading west to east. Cross Elm Fork Trail and continue onto the path marked "Pedestrian Traffic Only." In the shade of a dense woodland canopy, sun filters through the trees only in small patches, keeping it cool even on a hot day. You'll pass trees such as the Chickasaw plum, gum bumelia, and eastern red cedar as you make your way northwest. As you walk along, read the interpretive brochure, which provides interesting information regarding the historical and common uses of many of these trees.

At 0.5 miles, you'll reach a split in the trail. Bear right, onto Lake Trail and toward the water. The trail breaks from the woods and winds through tall grasses growing in the sand near the lake. When the water is low, there is a huge expanse of beach to stroll along. If you feel like prolonging the hike, head right or left, following the shoreline as it curves out of sight. Binoculars are helpful—this is a great spot for bird-watching. Even novices will be able to identify egrets and gulls along the water's edge. You'll see animal tracks in the soft sand at the shoreline, including the prints of white-tailed deer, which live in the area.

When you're done exploring the shore, head back off the lake, retracing your steps to the start of Lake Trail. Once you reach the trail sign, continue straight to finish the loop. Markers along the path help you identify the American elm and cedar elm. Finally, at 0.89 miles, you'll reach the trail's namesake, a grouping of slash pines dubbed "Lost Pines." The tall pine trees, with their needles and limbs hanging in gentle arches, present a captivating display that is completely unexpected amid the hardwood forest and greenbrier thicket.

The trail offers a detour to the lake with great opportunities for beachcombing.

Continuing along the trail, you'll reach the soft dirt of Elm Fork Trail another 150 feet down. Yield to horses and riders plodding along the trail. You'll pass a few other native plants, such as the Texas prickly pear cactus, before reaching the amphitheater, where you'll retrace your steps the final few hundred feet to the trailhead.

NEARBY ACTIVITIES

Stop by Lake Ray Roberts Marina in the Sanger Unit along the lake for snacks or a fishing license and bait to enjoy the lake's renowned fishing. For a small charge, you can fish from their covered and lighted pier. For some fried catfish, stop by Huck's Catfish Restaurant, adjacent to the marina. To get there, turn right onto FM 455 and drive 7 miles. At FM 2164, turn right, go 0.5 miles, then turn right again onto FM 1190. The marina is off Marina Circle, to the right.

RAY ROBERTS LAKE STATE PARK, JOHNSON BRANCH UNIT:

40
Johnson Branch Trail

IN BRIEF

This flat, paved trail winds through the park, passing through terrain characteristic of the Eastern Cross Timbers region. You start with expansive views of the lake then trek through the park toward campsites at its northern end.

DESCRIPTION

Ray Roberts Lake, just North of Denton, is a 30,000-acre reservoir with boat ramps, camping, a swimming beach, miles of trails, and a marina. The lake was originally called the Aubrey Reservoir but was renamed after a U.S. congressman in 1980. Popular with anglers, thanks to the crappie, white bass, catfish, and flathead in its waters, it also draws nature lovers, who come to enjoy the various offerings of the state park complex on its shores.

The Johnson Branch Unit is part of the state park complex at Ray Roberts Lake and is located on its northern shore in Valley View. Nature lovers will find both biking and hiking trails. The bike trail (which is also open to hikers) is maintained by DORBA (the Dallas Off Road Bicycle Association) and is a long trail in the western section of the park offering loops through Dogwood Canyon. A long, paved trail loops through the lake, woods, and camp areas on the eastern side of the park and is the one that I've selected for this hike.

KEY AT-A-GLANCE INFORMATION

LENGTH: 3.62 miles
CONFIGURATION: Out-and-back
DIFFICULTY: Easy
SCENERY: Elms, oaks, mesquite, lake, herons, egrets
EXPOSURE: Partly sunny to sunny
TRAIL TRAFFIC: Moderate
TRAIL SURFACE: Paved path
HIKING TIME: 1.25 hours
ACCESS: Daily, 8 a.m.–10 p.m.; $5 per person for adults and children age 13 and up
FACILITIES: Restrooms, picnic area, playground
WHEELCHAIR TRAVERSABLE: Yes
SPECIAL COMMENTS: Bring your swimsuit to take a dip at the beach after the hike.

Directions

Follow I-35 north through Sanger, and take Exit 483 onto Lone Oak Road/FM 3002 and head east 7 miles to the park, entering at the Johnson Branch Unit. There are signs, but keep in mind that there are two different state park units, one on the north side of the lake and one on the south side.

GPS Trailhead Coordinates

UTM Zone (WGS84) 14S
Easting 681336
Northing 3698378
Latitude N 33° 24' 34"
Longitude W 97° 3' 0"

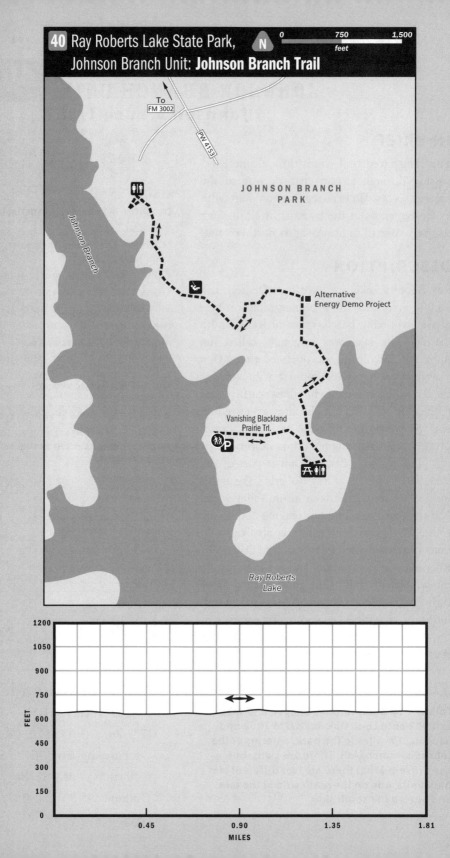

N

0   750   1,500
feet

JOHNSON BRANCH
PARK

Johnson Branch

To
FM 3002

PW 4153

Alternative
Energy Demo Project

Vanishing Blackland
Prairie Trl.

Ray Roberts
Lake

1200
1050
900
750
600
450
300
150
0

FEET

0.45   0.90   1.35   1.81
MILES

When you arrive, stop by the park headquarters for a map and information on free events. Although some of the events, such as campfire programs and stargazing parties (led by volunteer astronomers), occur during the evening, others, such as guided nature hikes, typically occur during the day.

Park in the large lot by the boat launch; the trailhead is just behind the fish-cleaning station, adjacent to the parking lot. Within a few steps, you'll turn right, following the paved trail east through the trees. At 0.13 miles, you'll reach a dirt trail turnoff on the left, with a sign identifying it as Vanishing Blackland Prairie Trail. Unfortunately, during my visit, the loop was closed. If it is open, it's worth a detour down the short trail with the interpretive guide that can be picked up at the visitor center. The small brochure describes the flora found along the trail—including trees such as honey locust, hackberry, pecan, cedar elm, and post oak, in addition to prairie grasses and wildflowers.

From the Vanishing Prairie Nature Trail turnoff, continue straight, heading east along the paved trail, which will cross the park road and pass another parking area and a picnic area before reaching a split at 0.23 miles. Head right at the split, following the trail toward the lake. The wide expanse of beach along the lakeshore is often busy with families playing ball, kids running through the sand in circles, and couples playing Frisbee. The trail does a short loop around the peninsula, allowing you to take in the lake views the whole way. Picnic tables along the trail tempt hikers to stay and enjoy the breeze.

At 0.28 miles, the trail splits; stay to the right. You'll come up behind some bathrooms, pass a playground, and then go left at 0.43 miles, looping back toward the beach. Turkey vultures can often be seen circling overhead as they search for leftover scraps of fish and other food. Also keep an eye out for water birds such as pelicans, herons, egrets, geese, and double-crested cormorants.

Turn left away from the shoreline at 0.55 miles, just before you reach the end. A few steps farther, you'll bear right, then make another right, following the trail north into some woods, which quickly obscure the lake from view. The surrounding trees are characteristic of the Eastern Cross Timbers region and include honey mesquite, blackjack oak, winged elm, and pecan.

At 0.65 miles, go right at the path split. The trail winds past some camping areas tucked into the woods then emerges again at 0.88 miles, where you'll again bear right. The trail heads straight here for one-third of a mile, following the park road, which is hidden off to your left. Birds you may spot flitting through the trees in the woods include the Carolina chickadee and the tufted titmouse. Also keep an eye out for flycatchers, swallows, woodpeckers, and bluebirds.

Turn left at 0.98 miles, next to a booth marked "Alternative Energy Demo Project." Continuing west, cross the road at 1.08 miles. Off to your right, you'll glimpse some campsites and folks pitching tents and walking dogs, and kids playing games.

At 1.28 miles, you'll cross another park road. The path heads northwest past a playground off to the left and crosses another road. You'll then enter a section

Picnic tables with lake views offer a nice spot for lunch or a snack.

of dense woods and heavy shade. After you cross a short footbridge spanning a small stream, you'll reach another park road. The restrooms are just opposite. Retrace your steps to the trailhead.

NEARBY ACTIVITIES

Stop by Lake Ray Roberts Marina in the Sanger Unit along the lake for snacks and a fishing license and bait to enjoy the lake's renowned fishing. For a small charge, you can fish from thesir covered and lighted pier. For some fried catfish, stop by Huck's Catfish Restaurant, adjacent to the marina. To get there, head 6.6 miles west on East Lone Oak Road/FM 3002 toward Morrow Road. Turn onto I-35S/US 77S and go 4 miles, then take Exit 478 toward FM 455/Pilot Point/Bolivar. Turn left onto FM 455 / West Chapman Drive, go 3 miles, then turn left onto FM 1190 and travel 0.9 miles. The marina is off Marina Circle to the right.

SISTER GROVE LOOP

IN BRIEF

This is an excellent all-around hike looping through a pretty, green woodland interspersed with open fields and inhabited by coyotes, rabbits, and armadillos.

DESCRIPTION

This remote Collin County park is located on the northeastern side of the expansive Lake Lavon, and takes an unusual drive down two interconnected bridges to reach. It's a fun trail that will suit hikers whose tastes conflict—offering both open, sunny grassland and shady lush-green woodland. Expect to find some off-road bikers here—the trail is maintained by the Dallas Off-Road Bicycle Association (DORBA). It is not as popular as many of the DORBA trails closer to the city are, so some days you might not find any bikers here at all. If you hike quietly, you might see some small wildlife along the trail—within a few minutes of starting the hike, I spotted a huge jackrabbit hopping alongside the path. Farther down the trail, I found what looked like a coyote's tracks.

The 21,400-acre Lavon Lake is operated by the U.S. Army Corps of Engineers and was impounded in 1953. More than a dozen lakeside parks dot its 83-mile shoreline.

KEY AT-A-GLANCE INFORMATION

LENGTH: 2.96 miles
CONFIGURATION: Loop
DIFFICULTY: Easy
SCENERY: Open fields, thick woodlands, wildflowers
EXPOSURE: Sunny to shady
TRAIL TRAFFIC: Moderate
TRAIL SURFACE: Dirt
HIKING TIME: 1.25 hours
ACCESS: Free; daily, sunrise–sunset (gate gets locked at sunset and hikers can get locked in)
FACILITIES: Toilet, picnic tables
WHEELCHAIR TRAVERSABLE: No
SPECIAL COMMENTS: Only the parking area, restrooms, and picnic area are wheelchair traversable.

Directions ———————————————→

Follow US 75 north toward Sherman. Take Exit 41 toward US 380 and turn right onto West University Drive/US 380 east. Travel approximately 12.5 miles. In the middle of the bridge over Lavon Lake, turn left onto a smaller bridge, CR 559. After about 1 mile, turn left onto CR 561 to reach Sister Grove Park.

GPS Trailhead Coordinates

UTM Zone (WGS84) 14S
Easting 738060
Northing 3674454
Latitude N 33° 10' 58"
Longitude W 96° 26' 48"

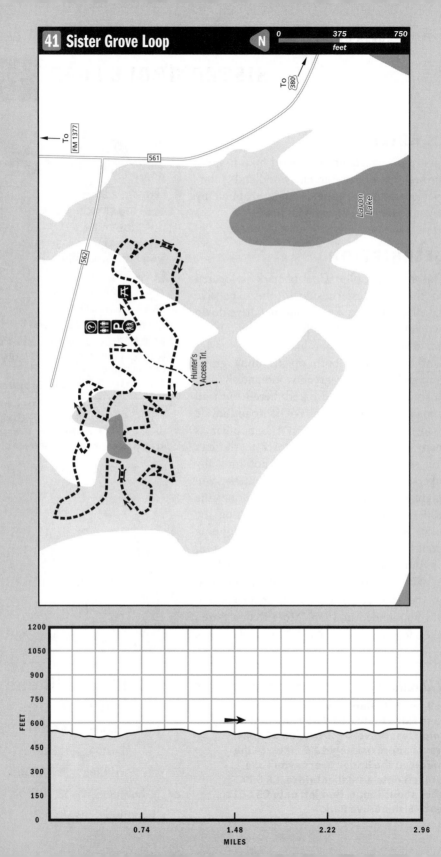

Sister Grove Park is not operated by the Corps but is part of Collin County Open Space. Its trails were started in the early to mid-90s, and have been restored and extended by DORBA volunteers continually since then. The entire trail system is approximately 6 miles long and comprises two loops—the Sister Grove Loop, which forms the northern half (and is the route for this hike), and the Lake Loop, which forms the southern half. A third trail, Hunter's Access Trail, heads south to cut directly through the two loops, directing duck hunters down to the lake. Mountain bike tires have worn a narrow groove down the middle of a couple of the softer sections of the loop trails, making it sometimes awkward to hike; wear comfortable, sturdy shoes to avoid twisting an ankle.

From the trailhead, you'll start the loop by taking the leftmost trail, which is next to Hunter's Access Trail. The path heads east past a picnic area and through a sunny, open field dotted with eastern red cedar. In the spring, small clumps of purple wildflowers grow in the grass, making for a cheery scene.

As the trail rounds a curve, you'll trade open sky for a canopy of trees as you enter a woodland filled with huge, gnarled trees with vines growing up their trunks and hanging from their branches. At 0.53 miles you'll cross a wooden bridge, then emerge from the trees and into a small pocket of wildflower-studded grassland. The trail weaves in and out of the open and wooded areas several times; it won't be long before you find yourself heading through shrubs and back into the cool green woodlands for a more prolonged hike through the shade.

At 0.88 miles, bear right at the junction, following the Sister Grove Loop west. Stay to the right at the next junction. At 1.2 miles, bear right to descend a short detour past a small pond hidden in the woods. After checking out its still, murky, green-brown waters, which are popular with birds, you'll loop back up and rejoin the main trail. A few hundred feet farther, you'll pass a wide dirt path. Bypass it, staying on the narrow single-track trail. You'll then exit yet another small pocket of grassland and find yourself entering another thick section of woodland. Tiny holes in the tree trunks provide evidence of sapsuckers and wood-peckers. Birds are plentiful; keep an eye out for the colorful plumage of the easily recognizable cardinal and an ear open for the melodic songs of warblers and thrashers. A thick understory of saplings and small trees color everything a vibrant green. The thick foliage engulfs the trail, making this a haven on a hot day.

Keep left at the junction at 1.65 miles and go another 0.2 miles to head over a wooden bridge and pass another small pond. You'll traverse a few more sections of alternating grassland and woodland pockets before you finally emerge into the main grassland near the trailhead. Look out for a springtime bluebonnets in the latter couple of grassland pockets.

Although the trailhead is just to your left, there's one last woodland section to hike before you complete the trail. Heading back into the trees, you'll work your legs on a couple of small, hilly sections before climbing back uphill and out of the woods for good. At 2.9 miles, you'll reach Hunter Access Trail, where you'll turn left to head straight back north to the trailhead.

Thick vines dangle from tree-limbs alongside the trail.

NEARBY ACTIVITIES

In nearby Greenville, visit the Audie Murphy American Cotton Museum, which includes exhibits and displays related to the cotton industry, Greenville's oldest house—the Ende-Gaillard House—a collection of historic military memorabilia, and various special collections. The museum is open Tuesday–Saturday 10 a.m.–5 p.m., and there is a small admission charge. To get there, take US 380/Audie Murphy Parkway West east toward Greenville approximately 16 miles. Bear right onto US 69, then turn right onto I-30E. The museum is located at 600 I-30.

WALNUT GROVE TRAIL 42

IN BRIEF

This trail appeals to hikers looking for a quiet, peaceful walk with plenty of solitude. Although frequented by local horse owners, trail traffic is very light. Several loops to the water's edge offer opportunities to explore the wild shoreline.

DESCRIPTION

Certified as a National Recreation Trail in 1991, this pleasant trail follows the southern shoreline of Grapevine Lake, offering almost a continuous view of the water. Unlike the northern side of the lake, where waters are a little rougher and trails more crowded, this side is calm and serene, with plenty of opportunity to be alone. The gentle waters on this side of the lake do little more than lap at the shoreline, and even the view is relaxing—only the occasional fishing boat can be seen sitting out in the tranquil waters. The trail is considered a hiking and equestrian trail, and you are likely to run across a few horseback riders clopping down the path. The horses add to the bucolic mood, though you'll want to keep an eye out for the occasional horse dropping.

The best feature of this trail is the constant beach access. The main path traverses the shoreline slightly inland, but if you're in

KEY AT-A-GLANCE INFORMATION

LENGTH: 4.76 miles
CONFIGURATION: Balloon
DIFFICULTY: Easy
SCENERY: Lake, wild beach
EXPOSURE: Sunny to shady
TRAIL TRAFFIC: Light
TRAIL SURFACE: Dirt path
HIKING TIME: 2 hours
ACCESS: Free
FACILITIES: None
WHEELCHAIR TRAVERSABLE: No
SPECIAL COMMENTS: The closest restrooms are at nearby Bob Jones Park.

Directions

Take TX 114 west into Southlake, and then head north (right) onto White Chapel Boulevard. Follow the road about 3 miles past Bob Jones Park to the very end, where you'll dead-end in a small parking lot. The trailhead is located on your right.

GPS Trailhead Coordinates

UTM Zone (WGS84) 14S
Easting 672168
Northing 3653300
Latitude N 33° 00' 16"
Longitude W 97° 09' 25"

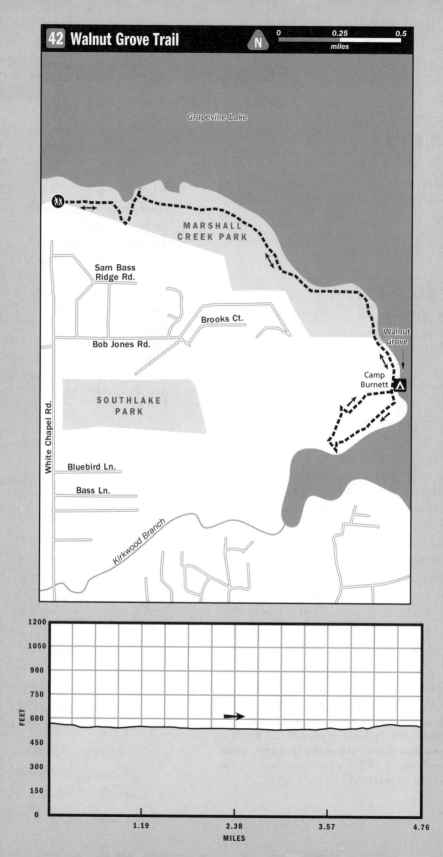

N

0   0.25   0.5
miles

Grapevine Lake

MARSHALL
CREEK PARK

Sam Bass
Ridge Rd.

Brooks Ct.

Bob Jones Rd.

Walnut
Grove

SOUTHLAKE
PARK

Camp
Burnett

White Chapel Rd.

Bluebird Ln.

Bass Ln.

Kirkwood Branch

FEET

1200
1050
900
750
600
450
300
150
0

1.19   2.38   3.57   4.76

MILES

the mood for beachcombing, you'll find a number of paths branching off the main trail toward the lake that loop back to rejoin the main trail. At 0.25 miles into the hike, reach the first of these, branching off to the left. Bear right to stay on the main trail.

The dirt trail winds along past glimpses of the lake on your left and woods and shrubs on the right. At 0.3 miles, encounter the next junction, where you'll stay to the right as the trail winds through some dense shade then reemerges into the sun. At 0.5 miles, look for another loop heading out to the shoreline. If you decide to make a brief detour down the side trail on the left, as I did, you'll find a narrow, sandy beach with tall beach grass here and there—a completely wild and unmanicured shoreline. On my hike, I saw what is probably most typical—a couple of shorebirds standing along the water's edge and a lone woman and dog picking their way down the shoreline. I did not see anyone else on the shore the entire hike, until my way back, when a couple of horseback riders slowly clopped toward me then disappeared down a lake loop, presumably for a slow horseback ride along the beach.

When you're done beachcombing, rejoin the loop, heading up and to the left through the tall grass back toward the main path. The next four junctions are more loops down to the water; just stay on the main path going straight to bypass them.

As you hike along, keep an eye out for wildlife, including fox, deer, coyote, opossum, armadillo, and rabbit. While hiking, an instructor leading a group of horseback riders passed me. She stopped to chat, commenting that on a couple of recent visits here she had spotted what she believed to be a large cougar just off the trail. She notified the Army Corps of Engineers, who told her they had already received reports of a large cat on the trail. Chances of an encounter are probably rare, but be aware of the possibility. Although I sighted few animals on my hike, I found plenty of scat and tracks on the trail. If you're interested in identifying animals that recently traipsed through, bring along an animal scat and print identification book. Prints are best sighted after rain (though if it's rained too hard, the trail may be too muddy to hike).

At 1.2 miles into the hike, turn left at a fork and you'll soon reach a clearing overlooking a sandy beach strewn with driftwood. Adjacent to the trail, about a half a dozen structures that resemble bat houses have been installed. At the next fork, stay to the left; at the next two forks, continue straight, following the main trail as it winds over grassy knolls with nice lake views.

At 2 miles into the hike, reach a fork with a sign marking Bob Jones Park/ Walnut Grove/Camp Burnett. Continue straight, following the trail as it twists uphill away from the lake. At 2.4 miles, the path forks again; a sign directs hikers to Bob Jones or White Chapel. Continue straight toward Bob Jones. A couple hundred feet farther, you'll reach the next trail sign. From here, the return loop begins, so follow the trail to the right in the direction of White Chapel. At the next fork, at 2.5 miles, bear right and follow the trail through a field spotted with

A hiker beachcombing along the lakeshore.

prickly pear cactus. At 2.65 miles, turn right at the split and follow the fence
as the trail winds back and rejoins the main trail. You'll find yourself back at the
Bob Jones Park/Walnut Grove/Camp Burnett sign, where you'll turn left to head
back toward the trailhead.

NEARBY ACTIVITIES

The huge Grapevine Mills Mall—an outlet mall with more than 190 shops and
a 30-screen AMC movie theater—is only a short drive away. You'll also find a
selection of restaurants both within and around the mall. To get there, take
TX 114 south 2 miles and exit Northwest Highway/East Southlake Boulevard.
Turn left onto Northwest Highway and go about 5 miles; you'll see the signs for
Grapevine Mills on your left.

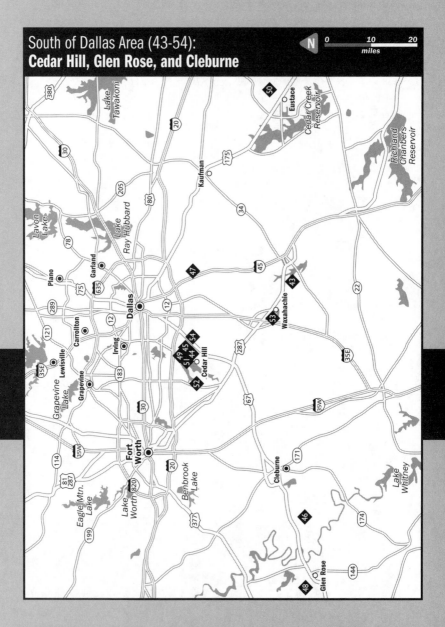

N

0   10   20
miles

UTH OF DALLAS/FORT WORTH (INCLUDING CEDAR HILL, GLEN ROSE, AND CLEBURNE)

43 BARDWELL LAKE MULTIUSE TRAIL

KEY AT-A-GLANCE INFORMATION

LENGTH: 2.34 miles
CONFIGURATION: Loop
DIFFICULTY: Moderate
SCENERY: Grassland, wooded thickets
EXPOSURE: Sunny
TRAIL TRAFFIC: Moderate
TRAIL SURFACE: Dirt
HIKING TIME: 45 minutes
ACCESS: Daily, 6 a.m.–10 p.m.; free
FACILITIES: Toilets, picnic tables
WHEELCHAIR TRAVERSABLE: No
SPECIAL COMMENTS: Trail etiquette gives equestrians the right-of-way.

IN BRIEF

Grassy meadows and sunny fields take center stage on this flat hike along Bardwell Lake. The second half of the trail loops back through wooded thickets. More than 13 miles of trails offer unlimited options for those seeking a longer hike.

DESCRIPTION

Located on Waxahachie Creek in Ellis County, the 3,570-acre Bardwell Lake is about 40 miles south of Dallas and 60 miles southeast of Fort Worth. It was impounded in 1965 to facilitate flood control and supply water, and today it also serves as a recreational spot. It offers a half dozen parks along its perimeter, including Waxahachie Creek Park, on the southwestern shoreline—the starting point for this hike. In addition to the hiking trails, the park also offers boating, picnicking, and camping.

Many folks familiar with Bardwell Lake have heard of it while visiting nearby Ennis— the "Bluebonnet City of Texas." The city's driving routes, known as the Bluebonnet Trails, lead visitors through the best of the springtime display. If you intend to tour the driving trails after you've done some hiking, you'll want to plan your visit around the end of April, when the bluebonnets should be in full bloom.

GPS Trailhead Coordinates

UTM Zone (WGS84)   14S
Easting   716859
Northing   3575588
Latitude   N 32° 17' 46"
Longitude   W 96° 41' 49"

Directions

Take I-45 south toward Corsicana. In Ennis, you'll take Exit 251A and turn left onto Creechville Road/FM 1181. Creechville Road becomes TX 34. Continue approximately 4.5 miles and turn right onto Bozek Road to reach Waxahachie Creek Park. The entrance to the park is approximately 1.5 miles down Bozek. Park in the westernmost parking lot, adjacent to the boat launch.

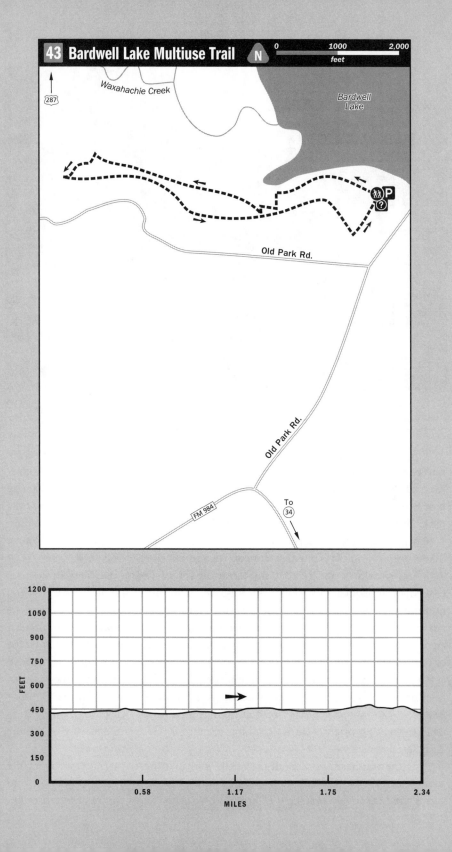

43 Bardwell Lake Multiuse Trail

N

0　　　　1000　　　2,000
feet

Waxahachie Creek

Bardwell Lake

287

Old Park Rd.

Old Park Rd.

FM 984

To
34

FEET

1200
1050
900
750
600
450
300
150
0

0.58　　　　1.17　　　　1.75　　　　2.34
MILES

The wide trail traverses sunny grasslands?

At the park entrance, you'll pass through a gate; let the park worker there know you'll be hiking, and you should receive a general map of the trails. Admission is free for hikers; however, if you plan to camp, you'll need to pay. Once you pass through the gate, turn left and park in the lot on the westernmost side of the park, near the boat launch. Although the huge parking lot can easily accommodate a large number of cars, on my visit it was completely empty because most hikers were primarily campers who just walked over.

You should be aware that the Army Corps of Engineers Web site advises that this trail is located within a hunting area, and hikers should be wary during hunting season. I did speak with a park ranger regarding safety issues, and he advised me that the trail receives a fair amount of traffic from campers, hikers, equestrians, and bikers year-round and that they have never encountered any type of a problem, even during hunting season. I felt very safe and would readily visit again at any time of year. Those still concerned, however, can check the dates of hunting season for Ellis County available in the Texas Parks & Wildlife *Outdoor Annual.* Also, some general tips for hiking close to or within a hunting area include wearing bright-colored clothing unnatural in nature, and staying on the designated trail.

At the trailhead, you should take the path that heads straight out from the gate toward the west. A couple hundred feet down, bear right at the junction, and you'll wind through a grassland clearing dotted with cactus and eastern red cedar.

The path winds up and down a couple of low grassy hills where butterflies and dragonflies come to greet you as you hike past. Off to your right, thick woodlands surround the lake to the north, forming a shield preventing any glimpse of the water.

At 0.48 miles, you'll reach a wide, grassy lane running through the center of a long stretch of grassland meadow. Bear right onto the flat, sunny route, heading west. This is an excellent trail to hike with the family because the comfortable width of the trail allows you to walk three or four abreast. With the woodlands still off to the far right, tree-dotted hillsides to the far left, and nothing but a grassy corridor before you, you'll be able to take in the peaceful scenery while still maintaining a conversation. Equestrian riders love the trail for just this reason, and you're likely to pass some along this portion of the hike.

Bear left at 1.1 miles, leaving the grassland and heading south onto the narrow path through the short trees and berry-laden shrubs. The path winds slightly uphill and curves back east through the gently rolling, shrubby woodlands. You'll eventually emerge from the woods and back into the grassland, hiking parallel to the trail you came in on, which is hidden by the tall, dry grasses on your left.

You'll merge back onto the wide path at 1.9 miles, where you'll turn right, following the trail uphill. It's a pleasant walk through more open grassland until you reach 2.2 miles, where you'll see an alternate trailhead intended for equestrians. Bear left at the junction, and follow the trail back to the final right turn at 2.3 miles, where you'll find the trailhead.

For hikers wanting a longer trail, instead of turning off the wide, grassy path at 1.1 miles, continue straight. The trail heads northwest past the Ennis Rotary Club, then turns east, leading all the way out to Mustang Point on the edge of the lake; in total there are more than 13 miles of trail.

NEARBY ACTIVITIES

For lunch, don't miss Bubba's Bar-B-Q & Steakhouse in Ennis, spotlighted in a 2006 article in *USA Today* as an excellent roadside eatery. Bubba's is located right off I-45 at Exit 251.

If you're here in spring, don't miss Ennis's Bluebonnet Trails driving routes, which take you past fields of wildflowers. Springtime also brings the Bluebonnet Trails Festival, where you'll find arts, crafts, food, and music. Visit the city's convention and visitor bureau for the exact dates, or check online at **www.visitennis .org.**

44 CEDAR HILL STATE PARK:
Talala–Duck Pond Loop

KEY AT-A-GLANCE INFORMATION

LENGTH: 4.23 miles

CONFIGURATION: Loop with spurs

DIFFICULTY: Easy

SCENERY: Native plants, wildflowers, pond

EXPOSURE: Partly shady

TRAIL TRAFFIC: Light

TRAIL SURFACE: Packed dirt

HIKING TIME: 2 hours

ACCESS: $5 per person; daily 8 a.m.–10 p.m.

FACILITIES: Restrooms, water fountain, picnic area

WHEELCHAIR TRAVERSABLE: No

SPECIAL COMMENTS: Bring insect repellent in spring and summer. Pack a picnic to enjoy at a lakeside table.

IN BRIEF

This pleasant hike winds along an interpretive trail where markers help you identify native plants and grasses then loops around a small pond. A couple overlooks along the trail provide peaceful spots to enjoy the scenery.

DESCRIPTION

Since Cedar Hill State Park's opening in 1991, it has become one of the most visited state parks in the state of Texas, in large part because it is so close to both Dallas and Fort Worth (about 20 miles from the former, and about 25 miles from the latter). Located adjacent to Joe Pool Lake, the park's expansive 1,826 acres attract millions of outdoor enthusiasts each year. Although it is not the most scenic lake, it is justifiably popular as a spot to get outside and enjoy the park's endless variety of activities, which include hiking, camping, biking, fishing, picnicking, and boating.

The park's several miles of trails include some open to both mountain bikers and hikers, and a couple open only to hikers. Before the hike, stop by the visitor center at the park's entrance and ask for the interpretive brochure for the Talala Trail. The small booklet is not usually out with the other park maps and information, but the park rangers do have

GPS Trailhead Coordinates

UTM Zone (WGS84) 14S

Easting   689392

Northing 3610556

Latitude N 32° 36' 59"

Longitude W 96° 58' 53"

Directions

Take I-20 to exit FM 1382 toward Cedar Hill. Cedar Hill State Park is about 4 miles south on the right. The trailhead is on the south side of the park. From the park entrance, turn left at the first intersection, onto South Spine Road. Continue straight, past some campsite turnoffs on the right, before reaching the trailhead parking lot, also on the right.

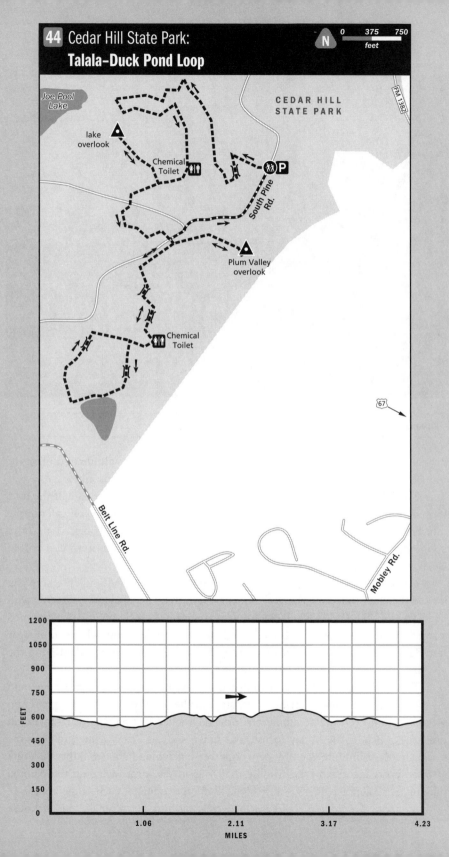

Wildlife, such as the bobcat, call the wild terrain home.

brochures if you ask. The pamphlet, which describes native wildlife and plants at numbered posts along the trail, is useful at the beginning of this hike.

You'll find the trailhead adjacent to the parking lot. The first part of the hike is along the Talala Trail, which loops through a hilly terrain where you can use the interpretive brochure to identify points of interests. This trail is best done on a cooler day because much of the trail is exposed; small trees and brush cast partial shade on only some portions.

Starting down the trail, you'll reach a split in the path at 0.13 miles, where you should turn left, following the trail as it curves south through a grassy meadow with a few trees. At 0.18 miles you'll reach a wooden bridge (which, on my hike, spanned a dried-up creek), across which you'll find another trail junction, where you'll bear left. The next junction is at 0.21 miles and has the first marker, identifying the clasping coneflower, a yellow annual with a long, cone-shaped head.

The trail slopes slightly downhill, crosses another small, wooden bridge, and passes through some hackberries. A few steps farther on is the marker for giant ragweed, which flowers in late summer. For the next mile, the trail winds slightly uphill past trees, such as the honey locust, and grass, such as Texas wintergrass. In the spring, markers indicate you can see wildflowers, including Indian paintbrush. You'll also see posts identifying the wildlife that lives in the area, including the painted bunting, red-tailed hawk, and cattle egret, and larger animals, such as the bobcat.

At about 1.1 miles, you'll reach a clearing and see a small red outhouse intended for primitive campers, and a trail split, where you'll bear right. Watch for a marker identifying the mesquite tree, recognizable by its spiny branches. About 150 feet farther is the next junction, where you'll go right. Continue straight until you reach 1.18 miles, where the path splits. Head right to reach Lake Overlook, which offers a view of the glistening waters of Joe Pool Lake in the distance. This is a nice spot to rest for a minute on the bench and take in the scenery. Retrace your steps to the overlook turnoff, and this time take the left split, to resume the trail. The path widens, still winding through the trees. You'll see a campground over to the left, and then you'll cross over a small road that heads past the campsites. Cross the street and pick up Duck Pond Trail at the yellow gate just to the left of some restrooms. The path winds downhill through the trees, crosses a bridge, and then starts to wind back uphill through grassy terrain.

At 1.88 miles, cross South Spine Road and resume the trail on the other side. A couple hundred feet farther, you'll reach the next junction. To the left, the trail dead-ends at Plum Valley Overlook, where a bench is tucked away beneath some vine-covered trees and you can relax and enjoy the views of the surrounding hillsides.

When you're ready, head back to the overlook turnoff, then follow the trail to the right, which curls downhill through trees and native grasses and over a couple of long, wooden bridges spanning ravines. The path slowly winds uphill, and then at 2.63 miles, reaches a junction marked by another red outhouse, indicating this is another area for primitive camping. When I was here, however, I saw no evidence of any such adventurers.

Turn right, onto a wide gravel trail peppered with cacti. At 2.7 miles you'll reach the loop junction. Turn left onto the loop. The trail crosses a wooden bridge and then heads through some tall trees before passing two more bridges and finally reaching Duck Pond. The small pond is like an oasis amid the woods. There's only one small vantage point between the trees, however, discouraging anything more than a short rest.

Continuing past the pond, you'll cross a bridge and turn right at the split at 3.18 miles. At 3.25 miles, you'll have completed the pond loop. From here, retrace your steps to South Spine Road. Turn right onto the road and walk along the grassy shoulder. The trailhead and parking lot are about 0.29 miles down on the left.

NEARBY ACTIVITIES

Within the park, you can explore Penn Farm Agricultural History Center, a restored farm exhibit. Ask at the visitor center for a self-guided interpretive booklet.

About 8.5 miles northwest of the park, you can visit Trader's Village, open weekends from 8 a.m.–sundown. The largest weekend flea market in the state, thousands of booths sell all manner of products. To get there, take I-20 west to Exit 454 and turn right onto South Great Southwest Parkway. After 1 mile, turn left onto Mayfield Road. Trader's Village is about 0.3 miles down on the right.

45 CEDAR MOUNTAIN TRAIL

KEY AT-A-GLANCE INFORMATION

LENGTH: 1.2 miles
CONFIGURATION: Balloon
DIFFICULTY: Easy
SCENERY: Woodlands, cedar trees
EXPOSURE: Mostly shady
TRAIL TRAFFIC: Light
TRAIL SURFACE: Packed dirt
HIKING TIME: 45 minutes
ACCESS: Free; daily,
6 a.m.–sundown
FACILITIES: None
WHEELCHAIR TRAVERSABLE: No
SPECIAL COMMENTS: Caution
younger hikers on what they should
do if they see a snake. Bring insect
repellent. Bikes are not allowed on
this trail.

IN BRIEF

This pleasant trail winds slowly uphill through a dense woodland. It is a nice hike for kids just getting interested in hiking because the size and terrain are easy to manage, but it is still wild and secluded enough to feel like an accomplishment.

DESCRIPTION

The Cedar Mountain Preserve, a 110-acre section of hilly woodland next to Joe Pool Lake, draws a fair number of visitors, despite its proximity to larger trail systems, such as the Cedar Ridge Preserve (AKA the Dallas Nature Center) and Cedar Hill State Park. This is in part due to its convenient, appealing location. The small parking lot is adjacent to the main road and is easy to stumble upon. If you happen to be driving by on a sunny day and see a couple of parked cars and a few folks disappearing down one of the trails, you'll undoubtedly want to pull over and investigate. Many of the hikers lured in to the preserve are on their way to or from the lake, a man-made reservoir named after a 1960s congressman instrumental in its establishment. The lake lies just to the west of the preserve. Organized events are always happening somewhere along the lake and include bike rallies, fishing tour-

GPS Trailhead Coordinates

UTM Zone (WGS84) 14S
Easting 690295
Northing 3610455
Latitude N 32° 36' 55"
Longitude W 96° 58' 19"

Directions

Take I-20 and exit onto FM 1382 toward Cedar Hill. The trail is located in Cedar Mountain Preserve, about 5 miles south on the right, just past Cedar Hill State Park.

45 Cedar Mountain Trail

0   375   750
feet
N

entrance to woods

FM 1382

John Penn Branch

CEDAR HILL STATE PARK

P

To 67

service rd.

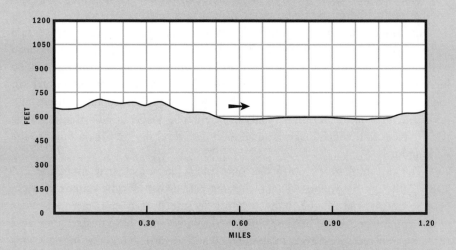

The trail winds through thick woodlands.

naments, outdoor club meet-ups, and activities such as camping, picnicking, and bird-watching.

Because the trails in the preserve are not incredibly lengthy, visitors do not stay long, and parking is plentiful. It's popular with folks walking their dogs and families with children, who appreciate its manageable size.

In front of the parking lot, a kiosk displaying a map of the preserve gives you a chance to get oriented before the hike. To get to the trailhead from here, head to the right, following the sidewalk north. The trail curves away from the parking lot, and at about 0.1 mile, reaches the trailhead—a dirt path branching north off the paved trail. A sign here advises that bicyclists are prohibited and cautions hikers of the presence of poisonous snakes. (Many folks just continue straight on the wide, paved trail, which makes a small loop over level terrain back around to the parking lot.)

The dirt trail heads northwest onto the wide, grassy strip alongside FM 1382. Although the sounds of cars whizzing past drown out the sounds of crickets, the trail is well off the roadway and feels safe. Just as you start to wonder where you are going and become concerned that you may have missed some vital turn, the trail veers west away from the road and toward an opening in the woods at about 0.27 miles. A rustic sign mounted between two tree trunks marks the entrance where the trail disappears into the trees.

The trail heads slightly uphill and then back downhill, twisting and turning as it makes its way through the woods. The closely packed trees do an excellent job of shrouding the trail in shade. Although we did pass a couple of folks on the trail—one group with children and one couple, the trail still had a feeling of solitude and remoteness to it.

You'll soon reach a grove of trees where an intoxicating scent hangs thick in the air. A few deep breaths will help you identify it as the rich smell of cedar. In the summer, flying insects buzz regularly around the path. Be sure to apply plenty of insect repellent for your walk through this wooded hillside. I also found it impossible to ignore the thick spider webs that stretched across the ground and between trees, bridging gaps between logs, across branches, amid leaves, and in every trunk's knothole. Fortunately, most of the spiders stay in the woods and, unless you are one of the first hikers on the trail, their webs don't obstruct the path. The woodlands are also home to raccoons, coyotes, and armadillos.

At about 0.55 miles, head right onto the beginning of the trail loop, which continues a slow, mild, uphill climb. The path passes an interesting section, where a number of old, dead trees litter the ground, then bypasses a dried-out ravine. After you duck under a low-hanging branch that spans the trail, you'll reach the top of a hill. Although you have not climbed high enough to get above the trees for any kind of a view, the surrounding wilderness rewards you with a sense of being deep in the woods.

The trail then loops east, heading back downhill before rejoining the trail. At about 0.88 miles, you'll be back at the loop junction. From here, just retrace your steps to the trailhead. To extend the hike, you can detour onto the paved pathway loop through the woods and back to the parking lot.

NEARBY ACTIVITIES

Just up FM 1382, Cedar Hill State Park, which lies along Joe Pool Lake, is popular with fishermen, boaters, picnickers, campers, and birders. Inside the state park you'll also find the Penn Farm Agricultural History Center, a restored farm exhibit.

46 CEDAR RIDGE PRESERVE TRAIL

KEY AT-A-GLANCE INFORMATION

LENGTH: 3.25 miles
CONFIGURATION: Double loop
DIFFICULTY: Moderate
SCENERY: Pond, creek, abundant birdlife
EXPOSURE: Open to shady
TRAIL TRAFFIC: Light
TRAIL SURFACE: Dirt, rock
HIKING TIME: 2 hours
ACCESS: Donations
FACILITIES: Restrooms, benches and water fountains
MAPS: Online at www.audubondallas.org/cedarridge.html
WHEELCHAIR TRAVERSABLE: Yes
SPECIAL COMMENTS: Bring sunscreen.

IN BRIEF

This rigorous hike takes you through varied terrain on what is one of the most enjoyable hikes in the area. You'll hike up a modest hill, trek down a fossil trail, traverse a pond enclosed by hundreds of cattails, and meander down excellent bird-watching footpaths.

DESCRIPTION

A 10-mile network of paths of varying difficulty keeps the Cedar Ridge Preserve—a park that can be fairly busy on weekends—uncrowded and even desolate in parts. In spring the preserve is a great place to see butterflies, migrating and breeding birds, and beds of bluebonnets. In addition to hawks circling overhead, you may see a snake or two, as I did on another recent hike here. Signs clearly posted at several points along the trail warn of copperheads, rattlesnakes, water moccasins, and coral snakes; obviously, sticking to the defined trail is a must.

Formerly known as the Dallas Nature Center, Cedar Ridge Preserve is managed by the Dallas Audubon Society, which has done an excellent job of maintaining the park. The amenities in particular are excellent and include picnic tables, restrooms, well-marked

GPS Trailhead Coordinates

UTM Zone (WGS84) 14S
Easting 691467
Northing 3612842
Latitude N 32° 38' 12"
Longitude W 96° 57' 32"

Directions

From I-20 west, take Exit 458, then turn left onto Mountain Creek Parkway and follow it 2.8 miles to the Cedar Ridge Preserve. Access the reserve via a turnoff on the right where there is a small sign—keep an eye out for it. Follow the road into the preserve and turn right at the fork to enter the main parking lot; the left fork terminates at a smaller lot reserved for persons with disabilities.

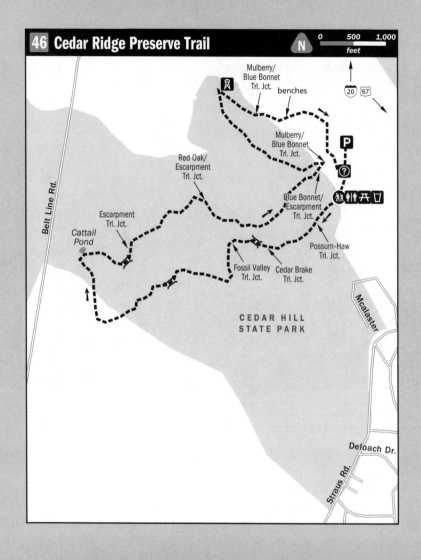

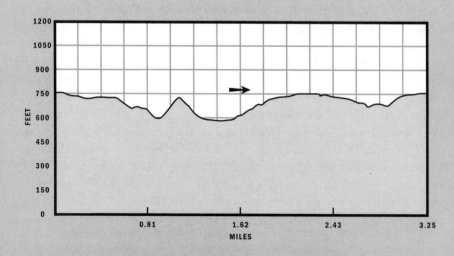

A view of Cattail Pond

trails, and water fountains . . . even one at ground level for those who hike with their pets!

From the parking area, head into the preserve, and stop to orient yourself at the visitor kiosk. The trailhead starts just behind the kiosk, so once you're ready to go, follow the main trail a few steps until you see a sign for Cattail Pond Trail. The trail is well kept, and you'll note that much of the first half mile is strewn with mulch, which makes walking fairly easy. You will, however, want to keep an eye out for low branches and exposed roots, especially as you venture farther down the trail and deeper into the preserve. Most of this section is enclosed by trees and shrubbery, keeping hot sun to a minimum. But you should expect it to be warm, even on an otherwise cool day because trees tend to block the wind.

Continue following the trail past prickly pear cactus and signs warning of poison ivy, until you reach a trail split at about 300 feet into the hike, where Possumhaw Trail branches off to the left. Continuing straight on Cattail Pond Trail, a short hike quickly leads you to another junction, where you can access Cedar Brake Trail (a 1.7-mile loop). For this hike, stay to the right on Cattail Pond Trail, which will briefly descend down a rocky path then up a gentle incline. The path meanders through low trees and brush, past the spot where Cedar Brake Trail rejoins Cattail Pond Trail, and then over a small wooden bridge that spans a dry ravine. The preserve is particularly well known among birders; many birds visit and live here, particularly in the spring, including warblers, flycatchers, buntings, vireos, bluebirds, and hawks. The bridge is a good vantage point to catch sight of one of these residents, the Carolina wren—a small rust-colored bird distinguished by a thin white stripe over its eye, further described on a plaque adjacent to the bridge.

A little more than 0.5 miles into the hike, turn left onto the path marked Fossil Valley Trail. The trail will curl downhill, before starting a steep ascent. As you begin the uphill trek, scan the ground for fossils, which you may find embedded in rocks along the trail if you have a keen eye. The next 0.25 miles is the most challenging part of the hike—the trail climbs steeply to the summit of a small hill, passing a couple of benches, some grassy patches with dragonflies buzzing past and butterflies darting about, a wide shallow creek, and another wooden bridge. When you reach an unmarked trail split, with both paths continuing steeply uphill, take the path to the right for a more moderate climb. A short climb later, you'll reach a small clearing that marks the hill's summit. Although trees obstruct the view of the surrounding terrain, there are several viewpoints on the descent, which make the climb worthwhile. This is an excellent spot (with a conveniently placed bench) to take a breather before starting the downhill trek.

Your route downhill winds its way past a couple more benches before emerging into a small meadow teaming with purple wildflowers and offering excellent views of the surrounding hills and the surprisingly close highway. When you reach the bottom of the hill, you'll find yourself on the other side of Cattail Pond, which is hidden by hundreds of 6-foot-tall cattails. As you wind your way around the pond, take time to enjoy the scenery. You may discover animal tracks or sight the elegant great blue heron. This portion of the trail is much more exposed to the sun, so be prepared.

At the next trail split, look for signs marking Escarpment Road Trail to the left and Cattail Pond Trail to the right. Head left down Escarpment Road Trail, which quickly widens and follows the remnants of an old wagon trail. This portion of the trail has a few scenic overlooks on its way slowly up another hill.

At about 1.85 miles into the hike, you'll reach the intersection of Red Oak Trail and Escarpment Road Trail. Continue right, up Escarpment Road Trail, then bear left onto Bluebonnet Trail. The past couple of summers have seen few bluebonnets, but if you're hiking in spring, you should see at least some bordering the trail. At the next trail split, take a hard left, continuing along Bluebonnet Trail. At the next unsigned junction, bear right. A few steps up this trail, at 2.75 miles into the hike, you'll find an observation tower that is an excellent vantage point to take in the surrounding hills and woodlands. A few steps up the trail from the tower, turn left onto Mulberry Trail, where you'll find yourself at the top of a set of steep stairs built into the trail, overlooking what is one of the most striking parts of the hike. Tall trees, threaded with vines, rise out of a small valley and tower overhead, casting deep shadows on the trail and the surrounding dense, green vegetation. This little section of trail makes you feel as though you're deep inside a forest. The most curious feature—an old tree that has somehow curled in

Signposts help direct visitors onto the preserve's many trails.

upon itself to form a "C" before reaching for the sun—is definitely worth a closer look. A few benches tucked next to the trail offer a spot from which to enjoy the unique beauty of this portion of trail. At this point, you're close to 3 miles into the hike.

The final portion of the hike follows the trail until it reaches an unmarked split, where you'll turn left. The trail then emerges into an open meadow, where the trail splits, strategically circling the meadow—ideal for bird-watching. Turn left at the split to reach the trail's end, located behind the restrooms; head toward and around them, and you're back at the trailhead.

NEARBY ACTIVITIES

Just 3 miles away, Cedar Hill State Park, which lies along Joe Pool Lake, is popular with fishermen, boaters, picnickers, campers, and birders. Inside the state park you'll also find the Penn Farm Agricultural History Center, a restored farm exhibit. To get there, head north on Mountain Creek Parkway for 1 mile, then turn left onto Eagle Ford Drive. About 0.8 miles down, turn left onto South Beltline Road; the park entrance is about 1.7 miles down on the right.

CLEBURNE STATE PARK LOOP TRAIL 47

IN BRIEF

This rocky trail loops through the woods of the park's outer perimeter, offering a few steep sections that will raise your heart rate. Its highlight is an overlook with a view of an elaborate masonry spillway adjacent to the park's small Cedar Lake.

DESCRIPTION

The 528-acre Cleburne State Park was opened in 1938 thanks in part to the hard work done by the Civilian Conservation Corps, whose efforts are apparent in the elaborate masonry spillway they constructed adjacent to the park's spring-fed Cedar Lake. The park's amenities include camping and fishing (though at only 116 acres, the lake is quite small), and more than 5 miles of hiking trails. These trails, with names such as Whispering Meadow Trail, Fossil Ridge Trail, and Spillway Hiking Trail, can be combined to form an exhilarating loop circumnavigating the park.

To get to the trailhead for the loop, you'll enter the park, pass the bathrooms on the left, and pull off into the first small parking area on the right, just off the park road. The trail curls downhill through trees and brush and crosses a creek. Across the creek bed, continue straight,

KEY AT-A-GLANCE INFORMATION

LENGTH: 5.86 miles

CONFIGURATION: Loop

DIFFICULTY: Difficult

SCENERY: Spillway, lake, woods, meadow, fossils

EXPOSURE: Partly shady

TRAIL TRAFFIC: Light

TRAIL SURFACE: Packed dirt

HIKING TIME: 2.75 hours

ACCESS: $3 per person; daily, 7 a.m.–10 p.m.

FACILITIES: Restrooms, benches, and picnic tables in nearby day-use area

WHEELCHAIR TRAVERSABLE: No

SPECIAL COMMENTS: Bring a walking stick and wear good hiking shoes.

Directions

Take US 67 south toward Cleburne. Approximately 6 miles past Cleburne, follow the brown state park signs left onto Park Road 21. Cleburne State Park is about 6 miles down on the right. When you enter the park, you should park in the first lot on the right, just after the restrooms.

GPS Trailhead Coordinates

UTM Zone (WGS84) 14S

Easting 636292

Northing 3570082

Latitude N 32° 15' 33"

Longitude W 97° 33' 11"

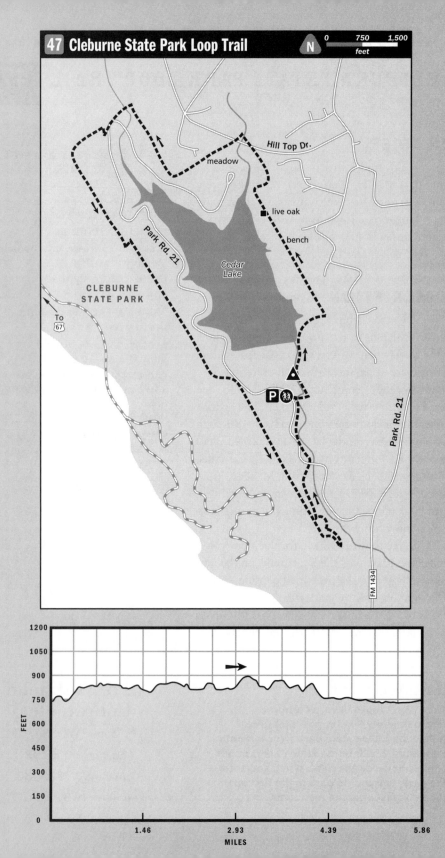

heading east. The trail starts to ascend along a rough, rutted path strewn with small rocks.

At about 0.1 mile, you should bear left at the trail split. The path heads parallel to the creek you crossed and climbs uphill toward an overlook. Be prepared for uneven footing; this ragged section of trail resembles a gully more than a path. Small bushes adjacent to the path cling to the hillside, offering little by way of scenery.

After a short climb, you'll reach the overlook at 0.3 miles, from which you'll have an exceptional view into the ravine and spillway below. When I first reached this overlook, I was unprepared for the spillway's massive size and beauty and so was awestruck. Masonry built onto the sides of the bluff on the far side of the ravine accentuates a matching spillway that rises gradually in three massive tiers, appearing almost to resemble an ancient pyramid rather than a common spillway. You can pick your way along the bluffs for a couple of great lookout spots.

When you're ready, continue down the trail, following the sign reading "To Overlook and Lake Loop," and bear right at the 0.35 mile junction. The path makes another short, strenuous climb up a rock-strewn stretch before reaching an old, gnarled tree clinging precariously to the edge of the bluff, beyond which is another fantastic view of the lake and spillway.

The trail continues, heading into the piney woods, where you should keep an eye out for exposed tree roots. Bear to the right at the next couple trail splits. You'll then begin a downhill trek through woods of mesquite, ash, oak, and elm. From here, the trail runs along the state park's outer perimeter, marked by a barbed-wire fence. It is useful to note that, when in doubt at a trail split, keeping the fence to your right will keep you on the correct trail. The fence is almost invisible at most points, thanks to an overgrowth of vines and trees, and does not detract from the scenery.

Stay to the right at the next two junctions, continuing through terrain characterized by short, steep, rocky hills. The trail will eventually flatten somewhat; however, it will remain rocky and uneven for almost the entire hike. The path winds through the shade of the woods, keeping the sun from overheating you on hot, sunny days.

You'll pass a sign marking a beautiful, huge, old live oak tree, before reaching a junction at 1.25 miles, where you should bear right. Continue across a babbling brook, then turn right at the next junction, where you'll trek through a small, cheery meadow. You'll have a brief glimpse of some private houses off to the right before the next split at 2 miles, where you should continue straight. When you get 0.35 miles farther down the path, you'll reach a paved road in Shady Spring's camping area, where, if you've brought your lunch, you might stop at one of the shaded picnic tables for a rest and a quick bite to eat.

To resume the trail, head southwest along the road and look for a narrow dirt trail disappearing into the woods off to the right. It will be the first trail you see, only a few hundred feet from where you emerged. It is unmarked, so watch

A short climb offers outstanding views of the spillway below.

for it: it is easy to miss. You'll know you're on the correct trail by the familiar barbed-wire fence, which reappears a few feet down the trail on the right.

The trail continues straight, adjacent to the park's southwestern boundary and along a rocky slope appropriately named Fossil Ridge Trail. I spotted a couple of excellent imprints of ammonites (an extinct mollusk with a spiral shell) embedded in the trail's rock bed. Stay to the right at the next few junctions.

The property to the southwest of the park is being developed for its natural resources, and at various points along this section of the park's boundary, you'll see signs advising you not to cross out of the state park and into the adjacent property. A barbed-wire fence continues along this section, clearly demarcating the boundary; however, be sure youngsters don't get too curious and try to explore—the adjacent property is a lime quarry and can be dangerous. As you hike farther south, you'll also start to hear the rumbling growl of heavy machinery, the source of which is a huge natural-gas rig on the next property off to the right.

Continue past the rig, bearing right at the next junction, at 4.3 miles, where the path reaches the park road. The sound of machinery will fade. The trail continues straight, stretching out toward the southern park boundary before looping back through the woods and along a narrow creek. At 5.53 miles, it intersects the park road again, where you'll cross over and resume the trail on the far side. You'll continue another 0.33 miles alongside the densely wooded creek before finally emerging at the trailhead from which you started.

The hard-packed trail can be rough on the feet.

NEARBY ACTIVITIES

Dinosaur Valley State Park, where you can explore dinosaur footprints fossilized in the park's riverbed, can be found in nearby Glen Rose. The Fossil Rim Wildlife Center, an 1,800-acre drive-through park where animals such as antelopes, rhinos, giraffes, ostriches, and zebras roam through the fields and hillsides, is also close by. You can drive through the 10 miles of road in your own vehicle. Guided tours are available with advance booking. To get there from Cleburne State Park, return to US 67 and head west about 15 miles. You'll see a brown state park sign for Dinosaur Valley on your right. The wildlife center is about 3 miles beyond it, down County Road 2008, on the left. Hours vary by season. For more information, call (254) 897-2960.

48 COTTONWOOD CREEK TRAIL

KEY AT-A-GLANCE INFORMATION

LENGTH: 2.17 miles
CONFIGURATION: Loop
DIFFICULTY: Easy
SCENERY: Pecan grove, creek
EXPOSURE: Shady to sunny
TRAIL TRAFFIC: Light
TRAIL SURFACE: Grass
HIKING TIME: 40 minutes
ACCESS: Free; daily, year-round
FACILITIES: Picnic tables
WHEELCHAIR TRAVERSABLE: No
SPECIAL COMMENTS: Watch your step if you leave the trail; there are some patches of poison ivy along the creek.

IN BRIEF

This peaceful trail winds alongside a creek toward a tall pecan grove. Interpretive signs along the way identify the flora, and a pretty bridge at the far end crosses the creek to take you back to the beginning.

DESCRIPTION

Hidden down a small, bumpy road behind an old neighborhood in Wilmer, the 220-acre Cottonwood Creek Preserve was private land before it was given to the city. Its original owner planted the land with pecan trees. The pecan grove, which remains, comes as a pleasant surprise halfway through the hike.

During your visit, you'll probably see only one or two other hikers, more because of the hidden location than anything else. We arrived to an empty parking lot and empty trails and took our time enjoying the scenery before having a leisurely lunch at the picnic table. It was not until we were about to leave that others arrived—one local who quietly let his dog out for some romping, and then left shortly thereafter, and another local couple who arrived with pecan pie in mind; they headed down the trail to quietly collect a few pecans from the thousands strewn through the grove.

GPS Trailhead Coordinates

UTM Zone (WGS84)   14S
Easting   718368
Northing   3609642
Latitude   N 32° 36' 10"
Longitude   W 96° 40' 23"

Directions

Follow I-45 south toward I-30 and take Exit 270 onto Beltline Road. Turn left onto East Beltline Road and go 0.4 miles, then make a left onto North Goode Road and travel 0.3 miles. Turn right onto Cottonwood Valley Road to reach Cottonwood Creek Preserve.

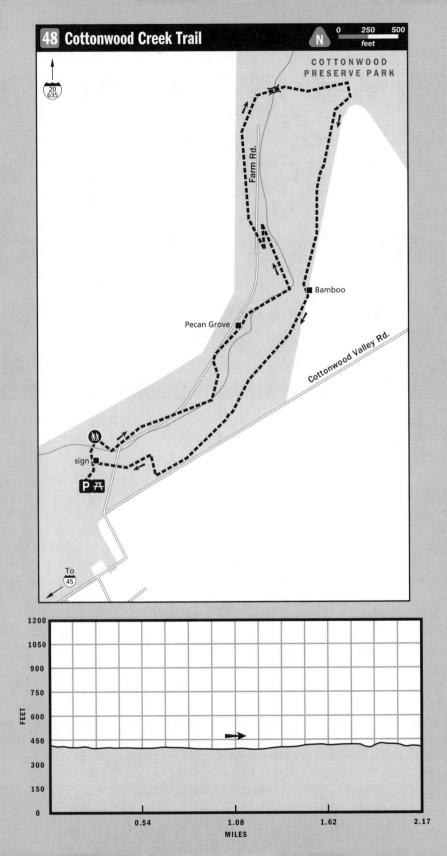

A quiet pecan grove

From the parking lot, head down the road past the entrance gate toward the creek. Initially, it can be difficult to determine where the trail is. On your right, a low cable strung between some posts cordons off the road from the rest of the landscape. A small wooden sign reading "Creek Trail" sits in the grass against the creek, with seemingly no trail in sight. This is in fact the end of the trail loop. In many places along the hike, the trail—though marked with regular wooden signs pointing the way—is not well defined, being nothing more than a mowed strip in the tall grass. You do not need to worry about getting lost, however, because the trail simply follows the creek out, crosses a bridge, then comes back along the other side. Helpful signs along the way identify trees and point to the trail.

The trailhead is down the road and over the creek a few hundred feet past the Creek Trail sign. Turn right onto the mowed, grassy strip, and you'll see a sign identifying the trail as the Green Trail, which is where the hike starts. A sign next to it advises that archaeological remains, which you may sight in the preserve, are not to be disturbed. The trail heads northeast. To your right, between the trees, you'll catch sight of the wide creek running along the bottom of a deep gully. Trees loom on either side, forming a shady canopy over the water. To your left, a small treeless meadow soaks in the sun, stretching alongside the path. Lime-green, softball-sized fruits known as horse apples (or sometimes referred to as "green brains" because of their mottled appearance) litter the trail. An old farm road, now mostly grass, runs a couple dozen feet off to the left along the length of the trail. It stays mostly hidden from view, except at 0.2 miles, where the trail curves to join the road temporarily before veering east back toward the creek.

Along the trail, you'll spot a number of wooden signs in front of various plants and trees. The signs identify the honey locust, a thorny tree identifiable by its long brown seedpods; the grapevine, a climbing vine; the saw greenbrier, a vine that can form thick thickets; and poison ivy. Other signs along the trail advise that the area is a poisonous-snake habitat.

The trail continues along the creek, offering a couple of nice overlooks with views of the water on the right. You'll pass more signs identifying native plants, including coralberry, chittamwood, and privet. The meadow ends as you enter a large grove of pecan trees where the creek curves. In the fall, leaves litter the ground, hiding the trail.

Continue alongside the creek, traversing the outskirts of the grove. Along the banks, you'll spot trees such as chinaberry, dogwood, cedar elm, and hackberry. At various points, the trees open a little and you can peer into the creek and see the intricate patterns of exposed tree roots clinging to the sides of the steep bank.

The preserve narrows into a lane with the creek on the left and a fence on the right. The trail then merges onto the park road, overgrown and barely discernible, before it curves toward a wooden bridge. The bridge, built atop two huge logs that bounce with each step, mark the hike's halfway point. Cross the bridge and follow the trail signs on the opposite side of the creek for Creek Trail. The path winds through another grove and then curves back south along the creek. In the fall, the grove's small leaves turn a brilliant yellow. When they fall in the breeze, the sun glints off them, in an entrancing snow-like effect.

At 1.5 miles, you'll traverse a patch of bamboo. At 1.6 miles, the trees recede and the trail is exposed to sun as it passes through a small meadow of tall grass. Droves of crickets and grasshoppers, including some up to two inches long, live along this section. With your every step, they spring up and fly out of the way in a wide spray. Stay in the mowed area alongside the creek. Before long, you'll pass another Creek Trail sign and find yourself back at the trailhead.

NEARBY ACTIVITIES

The Rogers Wildlife Rehab and Farm Sanctuary is in Hutchins, only 6 miles away. The facility is a nonprofit organization that rehabilitates injured birds and farm animals. Visitors are welcome to roam the property free of charge; donations are accepted. On the grounds, you'll find dozens of outdoor cages serving as temporary homes for rehabilitating hawks, owls, blue jays, vultures, and herons, among others. Geese and pheasants wander around unfettered. To get there, follow I-45 north 2 miles and take Exit 274 (Dowdy Ferry Road). Stay on the service road about 0.5 miles, then turn right onto East Cleveland Street.

49 DINOSAUR VALLEY TRAIL

KEY AT-A-GLANCE INFORMATION

LENGTH: 4.31 miles

CONFIGURATION: Loop

DIFFICULTY: Moderate to difficult

SCENERY: Hills, valley, river, dinosaur tracks

EXPOSURE: Partly sunny

TRAIL TRAFFIC: Light

TRAIL SURFACE: Packed dirt

HIKING TIME: 2 hours

ACCESS: $5 per person; daily 8 a.m.–10 p.m.

FACILITIES: Restrooms, picnic area, store

WHEELCHAIR TRAVERSABLE: No

SPECIAL COMMENTS: If the water level is not low, be prepared to ford a couple shallow rivers. Bring your swimsuit for a dip in the swimming hole after the hike.

GPS Trailhead Coordinates

UTM Zone (WGS84)   14S

Easting   611870

Northing   3568723

Latitude   N 32° 14' 59"

Longitude   W 97° 48' 45"

IN BRIEF

This hike gains a little altitude to offer excellent overlooks of the park then winds down to the riverbed, where you trek along million-year-old fossilized dinosaur tracks.

DESCRIPTION

Dinosaur Valley State Park is known internationally for the well-preserved dinosaur tracks in the riverbed that runs through the park. The tracks date back approximately 110 million years to the Cretaceous period. It is believed that, at that time, this area was an ancient shoreline along which the dinosaurs may have been migrating or feeding. The mud tracks of these huge creatures eventually fossilized and were buried by limestone and sandstone in what is now the Paluxy riverbed. Today, the river cuts through these sheets of rock, exposing the tracks buried within. In summer, the river dries out and many of the tracks are exposed on the dry, stony riverbed. The park allows you to roam freely around these sites, and in summer, you'll find hoards of visitors closely examining the imprints left by these prehistoric reptiles.

Directions

Take US 67 south to Glen Rose and Dinosaur Valley State Park. Just before you leave Glen Rose, turn right onto FM 205 (Barnard Street); the Dinosaur Valley sign is small, so keep an eye out for it. At about 3 miles, bear right at the fork onto Park Road 59. The park entrance is about 1 mile farther. When inside the park, take the first two right turns, following the signs toward the camping area. The parking lot is on the right, just before the campsites.

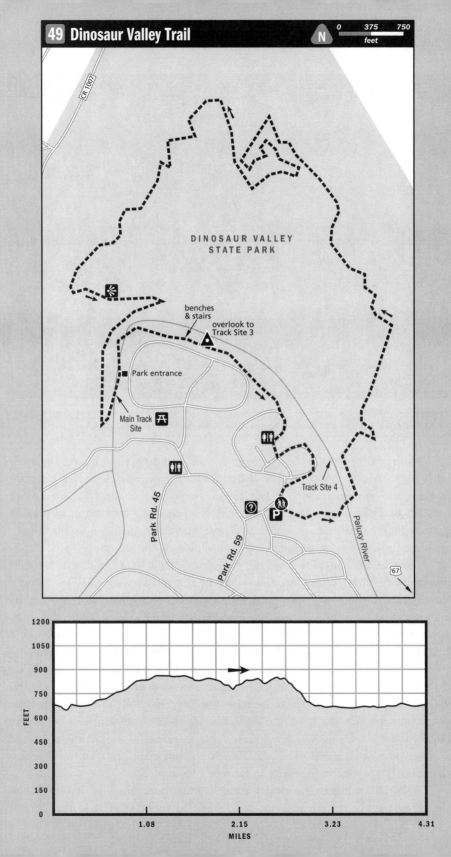

N

0   375   750
feet

CR 1007

DINOSAUR VALLEY
STATE PARK

benches
& stairs

overlook to
Track Site 3

Park entrance

Main Track
Site

Track Site 4

Park Rd. 45

Park Rd. 59

P

Paluxy River

67

1200
1050
900
750
600
450
300
150
0

FEET

1.08   2.15   3.23   4.31

MILES

A 45-foot tall T-Rex and a 70-foot tall Apatosaurus guard the entrance to the park.

Although the park is heavily visited, you'll find that the hiking trails are fairly empty because most folks head straight for the main track sites or for a dip in the nearby swimming hole. In fact, the day we set out on this hike, we did not pass any other hikers on the trail, although footprints and bike marks in the dirt indicate that the trails do see some use. Those who don't venture onto the hillside trails are missing out on one of the more fun hikes in the area.

The hike I've selected starts with a decent workout as it climbs into the hills alongside the river, offers inspiring views of the surrounding hillsides midway through, and finally rewards you with the excitement of discovery as you reach the ancient dinosaur tracks at its end. When you arrive, stop by the park's headquarters at the main entrance to pick up a trail map, check out the interpretive display, and find information on any ranger-led talks or events happening during your visit.

Parking is a short drive from the main entrance; you'll find the trailhead on the east side of the parking lot, adjacent to a kiosk with a map displaying the various trails. Take a moment to examine the map; you'll see the trails are referenced by color. On the hike, the trail's corresponding color appears every few hundred feet on a tree. Watch for these color markings to ensure you're on the correct route—it is easy to get lost. The park's trail maps are a good reference, though they are slightly outdated and can be confusing.

Follow the trail past the kiosk through a grassy field dotted with trees. When the path splits at 0.18 miles, stay to the left to follow the main trail. You'll descend a brief switchback and a few steep stairs before reaching the riverbed. Hop across the rocks or wade through the shallow river to resume the trail on the opposite bank. If you've come late in summer, as I did, chances are that the river will be dry, allowing you to stop and investigate Track Site 4, which is in the riverbed about 500 feet to the left. Look for the three-toed tracks, which are about a foot long, on the left bank of the river. Many of them are so well defined that it's hard to believe they're not freshly made and that one of the huge beasts isn't waiting around the bend for you.

After you cross the river, you'll be on White Trail, which heads steadily up through a wooded hill, paralleling the river. Continue straight, following this trail and ignoring any secondary paths branching into the woods, until you reach a pole marking junction "A," at about 0.36 miles. The trail to the right heads southeast into the primitive camping area; you'll want to take the left branch, following the trail downhill into the Denio Creek riverbed. Cross the shallow river and pick the trail up across the river, slightly to the right. You'll head back uphill until you reach another junction at about 0.43 miles, where you'll bear left. Stay on this path, following it as it slowly climbs into the hills, through woodlands peppered with grassy clearings and cacti; you should see paint on the trees marking this as the Green Trail. During the summer months, dragonflies, crickets, and, curiously enough, flies, buzz across the trail often, so you'd be well advised to bring insect repellent along. As for animals, in the early morning, you can hear movement in the brush adjacent to the trail as they clear out of your way. The area is home to deer, armadillos, coyotes, and skunks. Though we spotted nothing more than lizards (of which there are many), we came very close to seeing a raccoon, as indicated by the fresh scat on the trail.

The trail passes a barbed-wire fence marking the boundary of the park then switchbacks downhill. You'll pass a small pool on the right, followed by some excellent unobstructed views of the surrounding valley, before reaching the next junction at 2.41 miles. To the right, you can catch glimpses between the trees of the park's entrance down below. A better overlook is not far off; just stay to the left, and at 2.61 miles, you'll reach another junction, with a path heading steeply downhill to the right. Again, stay to the left, and at 2.81 miles you'll reach an overlook where you'll have a bird's-eye view of the Main Track Site below and the scores of visitors bending over to examine the ground.

Continuing on the trail, you'll see yellow markings on the trees, indicating you have reached the Yellow Trail. The trail descends, and then, at 2.96 miles, reaches a pole (which, during my visit, had a huge vulture perched atop it), marking yet another junction. Head right, onto the Blue Trail. The trail descends steadily toward the river peeking through on the left. At 3.29 miles, just past a field on the right, you'll see the turnoff on the left to get to the river; a small sign marks it as the continuation of the Blue Trail. Turn left here and, at 3.36 miles, you'll reach the edge of the river, and the Main Track Site, where you can see the tracks of theropods (three-toed prints from large carnivorous dinosaurs) and

Only a couple of inches tall, these small cacti can be seen growing along some parts of the trail's edge.

sauropods (elephant-like prints from gigantic herbivorous dinosaurs, resembling brontosaurs).

The trail resumes on the left, adjacent to the entrance steps, on the other side of the river. In summer you probably won't have to ford the river to get there but can simply walk across the dried-out riverbed, examining the tracks as you go. You might even catch one of the park rangers giving an impromptu presentation there. When you're done exploring, continue on the trail. At about 3.69 miles, you'll reach some benches and stairs climbing up out of the riverbed, and at about 3.71 miles, you'll pass a parking lot and an overlook to the theropod tracks at Track Site 3. The trail continues along the sidewalk through the woods and to the camping area. At about 3.96 miles, you'll reach the camping area, where you'll turn left onto the road, following it 0.35 miles past the restrooms and back to the trailhead.

NEARBY ACTIVITIES

The nearby Fossil Rim Wildlife Center is an 1,800-acre drive through a park where animals such as antelopes, rhinos, giraffes, ostriches, and zebras roam the fields and hillsides. You can drive the 10 miles of road in your own vehicle. Guided tours are also available but require advance booking. To get there from Dinosaur Valley, take US 67 southwest 3 miles and turn left onto CR 2008; it is about 1 more mile to the park. Hours vary by season. For more information, call (254) 897-2960.

PURTIS CREEK TRAIL 50

IN BRIEF

This shady trail loops through the woods in an area used for primitive camping. Several access points to the water and a photo blind make it a good morning hike for bird-watchers.

DESCRIPTION

Located almost exactly 60 miles from Dallas, Purtis Creek State Park is known specifically for its excellent fishing. The waters are stocked with largemouth bass (catch and release), catfish, and crappie and attract anglers from throughout the metroplex. The lake has speed limits and permits only 50 boats on the water at a time, resulting in a quiet, mellow atmosphere. The park was acquired in 1977 and opened to the public in 1988. It includes a 355-acre lake with a swimming area, fishing pier, boat ramp, and bait shop. If you're interested in getting out on the water after the hike, you can rent a canoe or a kayak.

Information from the Texas Parks and Wildlife Department indicates that the Caddo and Wichita tribes originally inhabited the area and that some petroglyphs have been found nearby. When I visited, I inquired with the park ranger on site, who said the petroglyphs could not be viewed from the park because they are on private land. She did,

KEY AT-A-GLANCE INFORMATION

LENGTH: 1.73 miles
CONFIGURATION: Balloon
DIFFICULTY: Easy
SCENERY: Woods, lake
EXPOSURE: Shady
TRAIL TRAFFIC: Light
TRAIL SURFACE: Packed dirt
HIKING TIME: 40 minutes
ACCESS: 7 a.m.–10 p.m.; $2 per day for adults and for children age 13 and older
FACILITIES: Restrooms, playground, water fountain
WHEELCHAIR TRAVERSABLE: No
SPECIAL COMMENTS: Pets are allowed but must be leashed. A couple days a year, in the winter, are for hunting only. Check the park's Web site before your visit, www.tpwd.state.tx.us/spdest/findadest/parks/purtis_creek. Canoe and kayaks are available for rent.

Directions

From Dallas, take US 175 to Eustace. Follow the signs to Purtis Creek State Park, exiting left (north) onto FM 316 to travel 3.5 miles. From the park entrance, take the first left, pass the fish ponds, and head into the camping area. Take the left fork and park in the small parking lot on the left.

GPS Trailhead Coordinates

UTM Zone (WGS84) 14S
Easting   782035
Northing 3584722
Latitude N 32° 21' 50"
Longitude W 96° 0' 10"

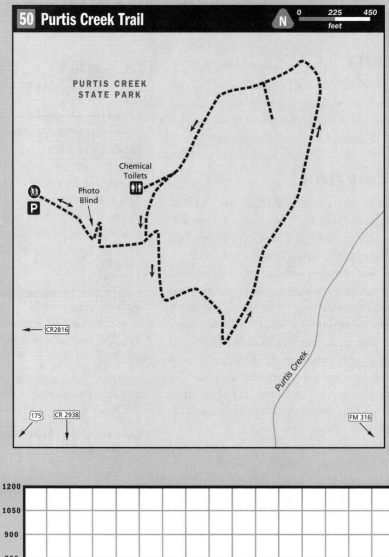

0   225   450
feet
N

PURTIS CREEK
STATE PARK

Chemical
Toilets

Photo
Blind

P

CR2816

175   CR 2938

Purtis Creek

FM 316

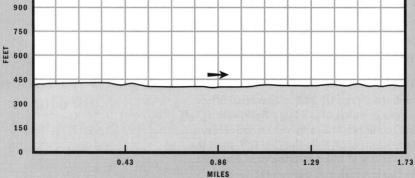

1200
1050
900
750
600
450
300
150
0

FEET

0.43   0.86   1.29   1.73
MILES

however, have a pamphlet that provided a little more information on the park's history. You can also pick up a park map and an interpretive brochure from the park headquarters. The brochure, in conjunction with numbered signposts along the trail, will help you identify the local flora.

The trailhead is adjacent to the parking area. You'll head southeast down a narrow dirt path bordered by dense thickets. Plants you'll spot along the trail include the American beautyberry, which bursts with purple berries in the fall. Also look for the flowering dogwood. In the fall, this short tree produces small red fruits that look like berries; in the spring, they sport hundreds of pretty, small, white flowers.

The trail continues, winding its way through the woods before reaching a lookout over a swampy inlet of the lake. Across the water, you can sometimes spot hikers peering out of the narrow slats of a wooden photo blind on the opposite bank.

Back on the trail, you'll cross a couple bridges spanning small streams, before reaching the first trail junction. Bear right at the path split and right again at the next split. This portion of the trail loops through the woods and around a primitive camping area. As you venture onto the loop trail, you'll first reach the photo blind you glimpsed earlier on the hike. When waters are low, the narrow inlet in front of the blind is very shallow, exposing numerous tree stumps. The main portion of the lake is farther off to the left. This is a nice spot for spying some of the park's birds. More than 200 species inhabit the area, including the downy and hairy woodpeckers, the warbling and red-eyed vireos, the belted kingfisher, and the yellow-billed cuckoo. I lingered in the photo blind a while and spotted a turkey vulture, an egret, and some mallards. Farther down the trail, a fellow hiker glimpsed what he believed to be a red-tailed hawk, before it disappeared behind the trees. Birders can pick up a complete list of all bird species found in the area, at the park headquarters.

Continue along the loop, which follows the shoreline. The trail stays inland, offering only brief glimpses of the water through the trees. You'll pass a number of shorter side trails shooting off to the right from the main trail. These trails lead down to primitive camping spots on the water's edge and provide nice overlooks and access to the water. Investigate as many of these trails as you'd like; each gives a different view of the lake. Just be sure no campers are settled into the sites you explore. You'll notice that each of these sites is designed for boat (and pedestrian) access. Trails lead from the campsite itself out to small beaches along the adjacent shoreline. Small, numbered signposts on the water's edge allow boaters to float up to their site from the lake.

The trail continues through dense woods that close in on both sides. If you've failed to spot any birds, you won't fail to hear the cawing of crows as you walk along. Old, gnarled trees in a couple spots along the trail add interest to the mass of woodlands.

If you enjoy geocaching—using a GPS unit to locate items hidden in various

Looking through the photo blind for birds

public places—you can pick up a handout from the park headquarters that describes a few caches hidden here.

You'll pass some chemical toilets then find yourself back at the beginning of the loop. From here, just retrace your steps to the trailhead.

NEARBY ACTIVITIES

If you're interested in getting on the lake after the hike, rent a canoe, kayak, or paddleboat. Outside the park, stop by the Texas Freshwater Fisheries Center, which has a hatchery, an aquarium, a wetlands trail, and a 1.2-acre lake, where rods and bait are provided. They are closed on Mondays. To get there, turn left onto US 175 heading south, then take Loop 7 east to FM 2495, where you'll turn left and go about 3 miles.

VISITOR'S OVERLOOK: 51
Joe Pool Lake Dam Trail

IN BRIEF

This flat trail runs across the top of Joe Pool Dam, rewarding you with unobstructed views of the lake. The trail is kid-friendly, dog-friendly, and bike-friendly.

DESCRIPTION

Though not the prettiest lake in the metroplex, since its recent completion in 1989, Joe Pool Lake has been surprisingly popular, and for good reason. The lake is ideally located about 20 miles southwest of Dallas and about 25 miles southeast of Fort Worth. A state park and several city parks border the lake, making it a natural choice for summer outings. Large and sprawling amid nondescript tree-filled terrain, the lake is not likely to drop your jaw. But what it lacks in beauty, it makes up for in activities: the parks offer everything from camping and hiking to boating, fishing, and swimming. Organized events are always happening somewhere along the lake and include bike rallies, fishing tournaments, and outdoor-club activities.

Named after a 1960s congressman instrumental in its establishment, the lake is a huge man-made reservoir created by impounding creek waters with a long embankment dam. The dam is of earth fill, composed of

KEY AT-A-GLANCE INFORMATION

LENGTH: 3 miles
CONFIGURATION: Out-and-back
DIFFICULTY: Easy
SCENERY: Lake, spillway
EXPOSURE: Sunny
TRAIL TRAFFIC: Moderate
TRAIL SURFACE: Paved
HIKING TIME: 1.5 hours
ACCESS: Free; sunrise–sunset, year-round
FACILITIES: Restrooms
WHEELCHAIR TRAVERSABLE: No
SPECIAL COMMENTS: Be sure to bring plenty of water, a hat, and sunscreen because there is no shade on this trail. Restrooms are at the trailhead.

Directions ———————➤

From I-20, head west toward Fort Worth. Exit onto FM 1382, and turn left (south). The entrance is 3 miles down on the right and has a small sign identifying it as Visitor's Overlook.

GPS Trailhead Coordinates

UTM Zone (WGS84) 14S
Easting 689846
Northing 3613o2
Latitude N 32° 38' 28"
Longitude W 96° 58' 34"

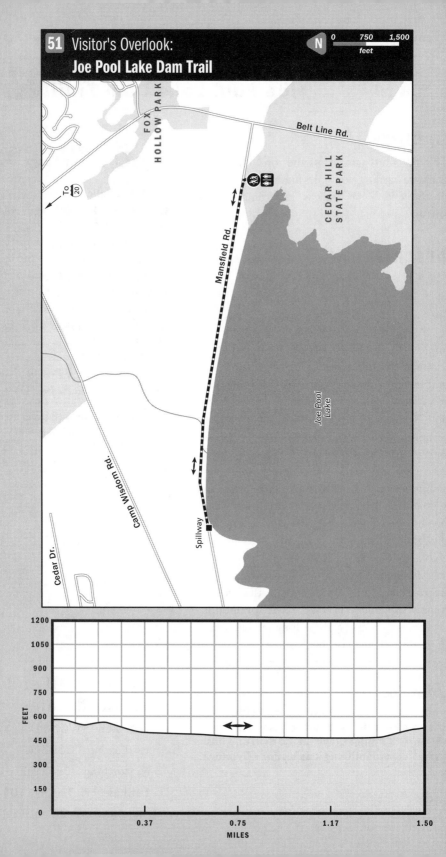

compacted soils that form a raised wall on the northern side of the lake. An old road that runs along the top of the dam and over the lake is popular with cyclists and joggers and is the route for this hike.

The trail is flat and there is little nature along the route, but that's why it is an excellent spot for hikers who want to bring their dogs and those looking for an easy walk. From any point along the trail, you have unparalleled views of all lake activity, and thanks to nearby Cedar Hill State Park, which is just 1 mile south on FM 1382, there is always something to see on the waters, including kayakers, sailors, fishermen, and seabirds. Be sure to bring plenty of sunscreen— the trail is completely sun-drenched, though a strong breeze helps keep the trail cool on even the hottest day.

Adjacent to the parking area, a long walkway twists back and forth, leading to the restrooms and ending at a very nice overlook, which curiously enough looks out onto nothing but grass and shrubs. Several trails disappear off into the brush from this area, heading toward the lake. This hike starts at the trailhead just to the right of the restrooms and is marked by a sign advising that all pets must be leashed. The trail heads into the trees and within 100 feet ends at a service road, where you'll turn left toward the lake. This road serves as the trail for the duration of the hike and is open only to pedestrian and bicycle traffic. At 0.25 miles, the trail meets the lake's edge and continues straight along the top of the dam to head to the far side of the lake.

The day I hiked this trail, I expected to reach the other side of the lake fairly quickly; on a clear, sunny day the opposite bank looks so close. The distance, however, is greater than it appears, and as much as I walked, the far side of the lake stayed just out of reach. As I later discovered, the trail continues along the dam for an extensive 1.5 miles before reaching the far side of the lake, where it continues another couple miles inland.

As you hike along the dam, enjoy unobstructed views of the lake on the left and a vacant, low-lying floodplain on the right. A pair of binoculars comes in handy—the vastness of the lake makes it hard to see much detail along the shoreline. Without binoculars you'll be able to make out little more than some of the closer tents pitched by state park visitors.

Wildlife along the route consists of only a few butterflies fluttering across the trail and birds soaring over the lake, although nearby Cedar Hill State Park's Web site (**www.tpwd.state.tx.us/spdest/findadest/parks/cedar_hill**) identifies more than 200 types of birds that have been found here, including several varieties of hawks, herons, and pelicans, and more than a dozen types of sparrows. The bald eagle even makes the list, although on my hike I saw only a few gulls swooping over the water.

At 2 miles, you'll reach the far side of the lake and the end of the dam, marked by a tower and a concrete spillway. This is a good place to turn around because, from here, the trail quickly heats up as you leave the water and lose the breeze coming off it.

The spillway

NEARBY ACTIVITIES

The Visitor's Overlook is adjacent to Cedar Hill State Park, which is only 1 mile south down FM 1382. The state park visitor center is a good place to get maps and brochures. Check with the staff for events information; the park also regularly schedules nature walks and talks.

WALNUT CREEK TRAIL   52

IN BRIEF

A shady trail with multiple overlooks for bank fishing, this hike follows the creek through the woods. After the hike, enjoy a picnic overlooking Joe Pool Lake; the picnic area is just down the road in the northern section of the park.

DESCRIPTION

This scenic park on the northwest banks of Joe Pool Lake in Grand Prairie is operated by the city of Grand Prairie Parks and Recreation Department. The lake is a man-made reservoir named after a 1960s congressman instrumental in its establishment. Cedar Hill State Park sits on the shores on the opposite side of the lake.

At Loyd Park, aside from the hiking and equestrian trails, you'll find more than 200 campsites, eight cabins, a beach, a designated swimming area, a boat ramp, fishing piers, and an assortment of picnic areas along its shoreline. The park sometimes appears empty; however, a quick drive from end to end reveals considerable activity; the amenities are fairly spread out and so, too, are the visitors. From the hiking trailhead on the west side of the park, you would never know how many boaters are coming and going at the easternmost

KEY AT-A-GLANCE INFORMATION

LENGTH: 2.16 miles
CONFIGURATION: Out-and-back
DIFFICULTY: Easy
SCENERY: Woods, lake
EXPOSURE: Shady to sunny
TRAIL TRAFFIC: Light
TRAIL SURFACE: Sections of loose-dirt and packed-dirt trail
HIKING TIME: 45 minutes
ACCESS: Open 24 hours, quiet time after 10 p.m.; $10 per vehicle/day
FACILITIES: Restrooms, picnic area, fishing pier, swimming beach
WHEELCHAIR TRAVERSABLE: No
SPECIAL COMMENTS: Up to 6 people per car for the one entrance rate. There is a special senior citizen's rate of only $2 per person.

Directions

Follow I-20 west toward Fort Worth and take Exit 453B onto TX 360 south toward Frontage Road/Watson Road. Go about 3 miles and turn left onto Arlington Webb Road/CR 2017, which becomes Ragland Road. The entrance to Loyd Park is on your right at 3401 Ragland Road. The trailhead is on the western side of the park; to reach it, turn right after you enter the park.

GPS Trailhead Coordinates

UTM Zone (WGS84) 14S
Easting 681277
Northing 3608345
Latitude N 32° 35' 52"
Longitude W 97° 4' 6"

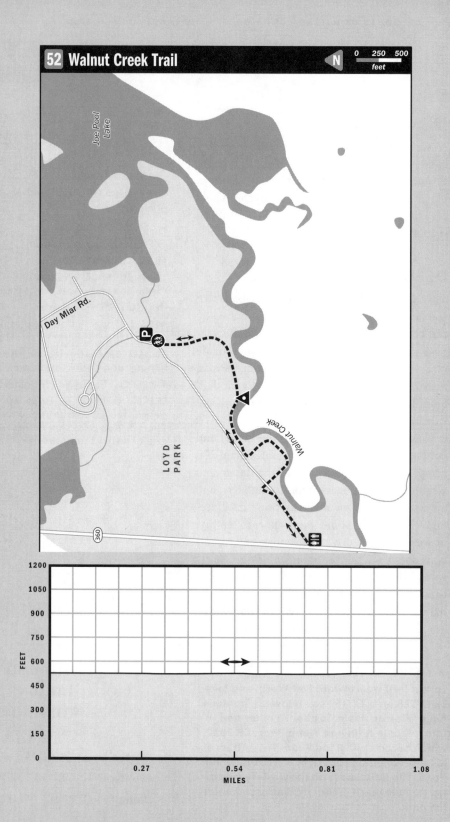

52 Walnut Creek Trail

0 250 500
feet

N

Joe Pool Lake

Day Miar Rd.

LOYD PARK

Walnut Creek

360

FEET

1200
1050
900
750
600
450
300
150
0

0.27   0.54   0.81   1.08

MILES

side or how many kids are romping on the beach just to the west. Leashed pets are allowed in the park, except for at the swimming beach and playgrounds.

There is an admission fee, which may seem a bit high for just a day hike, considering the other options. However, you'll find this park spotlessly clean and the trail well maintained. And after the hike you can enjoy the roped-off swimming beach and other amenities. Another tip—come with a couple of friends: the charge per car is the same whether you have two people in the car or six.

The trail starts on the park's west side. A small wooden sign marking Walnut Creek Trail welcomes you onto a wide path that disappears into the trees. Tall grasses beneath the towering trees provide good cover for snakes. I did not spot any, and you are unlikely to have a problem, but it's always a good idea to watch where you step. The trail is easily wide enough to walk two abreast and allow you to step around anything you might see. Because the trail also welcomes equestrians, you'll want to keep an eye out for horse manure, although I found little evidence of horses.

The trail winds through the woods and heads south along a creek connected to the lake. There are a couple of pretty water overlooks at the beginning of the hike; after that, the water is hidden from view behind the trees to your left. There are, however, plenty of paths which head over to the water, and you'll pass a number of spurs from the main trail heading off to the left toward the bank. The spurs, which are marked with "Bank Fishing" signs, attest to the trail's popularity with fishermen. I ventured down some of these trails and found a father fishing with his son at one, a young teen fishing alone at another, and only the soft rustling of leaves at the third. It comes as no surprise that fishermen like the area— most of the trail has a quiet, mellow feel, the only sounds being the wind rustling in the leaves and the occasional bird chirp.

Because most of the trail winds through the woods, the fall is an excellent time to hike here. The reds, yellows, and greens of the changing leaves add to the trail's beauty. This is also a good hike on a bright, sunny day because the trees cast most of the trail in deep shade, protecting you from the harsh rays of the hot, summer sun. Pick a different trail if it's rained the day before your hike; some sections of the trail are loosely packed soil, making for a muddy walk if the trail is even slightly wet.

At 0.63 miles, the trail emerges from the woods onto a grassy maintenance road. Head left and pick up the trail that disappears back into the woods on the left. You'll wind through more woods before finally reemerging onto the maintenance road at 0.9 miles. Head left down the service road. You'll hear the sounds of cars coming from US 360, which you'll see ahead, beyond the park's boundary. At 1.08 miles, within view of the highway, you'll reach a small building—the Walnut Creek Restroom. This is a good turnaround spot; just retrace your steps to the trailhead. If you'd like to extend the hike, you can pick up the trail just beyond the restroom, where it continues its peaceful meander through the woods.

A sign points the way at the trailhead.

NEARBY ACTIVITIES

The nearby Lone Star Park, site of the 2004 Breeder's Cup, is a huge horse race track that offers horse racing in the spring, early summer, and fall. The park also hosts special events such as live music, throughout the spring and fall. To get there, follow **TX** 360 north 6 miles and take the exit to I-30/Six Flags Drive toward Dallas. Go 3 miles and take Exit 34. Turn left onto Belt Line Road. Lone Star Park will be on your right.

WAXAHACHIE CREEK & BIKE TRAIL

IN BRIEF

A surprisingly charming hike down a rural path running alongside Waxahachie Creek and ending at the remnants of the historic Interurban Railway. The lush, green setting and abundance of bird boxes make this trail a must-visit for birders.

DESCRIPTION

Dubbed "Gingerbread City," thanks to the ornate carpentry on some of its Victorian-style homes, Waxahachie is the seat of Ellis County. It also has the distinct honor of being associated with the Texas state shrub, having been designated the Crape Myrtle Capital of Texas. A third nickname refers to the city as the Movie Capital of Texas, thanks to a number of feature films' having done location shooting here. Located about 30 miles south of Dallas and 40 miles southeast of Fort Worth, the city is easy to reach from anywhere in the metroplex.

The Texas Parks and Wildlife Department helped fund the trail, which currently offers approximately 6 miles of paved path. The trailhead is hidden just outside downtown Waxahachie in Lion's Park, a small city park dominated by soccer and softball fields. As you enter the park, you'll see a huge field with

KEY AT-A-GLANCE INFORMATION

LENGTH: 5.54 miles
CONFIGURATION: Out-and-back
DIFFICULTY: Easy
SCENERY: Historic bridges, rail tracks, creek, birds
EXPOSURE: Partly sunny
TRAIL TRAFFIC: Moderate
TRAIL SURFACE: Paved
HIKING TIME: 1.75 hours
ACCESS: Daily, sunrise–10 p.m.; free
FACILITIES: Restrooms, picnic tables, benches
WHEELCHAIR TRAVERSABLE: Yes
SPECIAL COMMENTS: This trail is a good option if it's recently rained.

Directions

Follow I-35E south toward Waxahachie and take Exit 408 onto US 77 south. Go approximately 9 miles, then turn left onto Howard Street. -Lion's Park is about 1.3 miles down on the left. Park in the lot next to the pavilion at the northeast end of the road.

GPS Trailhead Coordinates

UTM Zone (WGS84) 14S
Easting 703826
Northing 3583296
Latitude N 32° 22' 5"
Longitude W 96° 50' 1"

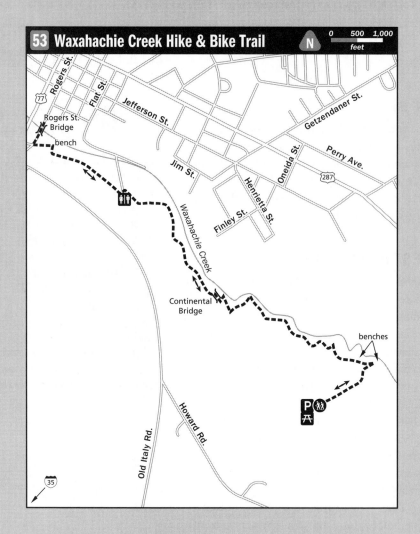

Rogers St.

Flat St.

Jefferson St.

Getzendaner St.

77

Rogers St.
Bridge

bench

Jim St.

Perry Ave.

Oneida St.

287

Finley St.

Henrietta St.

Waxahachie Creek

Continental
Bridge

benches

P

Old Italy Rd.

Howard Rd.

35

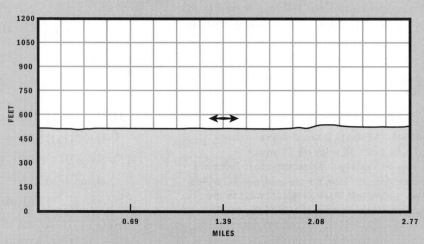

FEET

1200
1050
900
750
600
450
300
150
0

0.69   1.39   2.08   2.77

MILES

a pavilion at the northeastern end. Park in the small lot adjacent to the pavilion, where you'll find the trailhead.

The trail heads a few hundred feet northeast away from the park until it meets up with Waxahachie Creek then turns left, following the curves and bends of the creek as it heads northwest. For the duration of the hike, the creek gurgles and babbles just beyond the hardwoods off to your right. As you hike along, Lion's Park soon disappears from view and is replaced by fenced-in pastures where horses graze and trot lazily through sunny fields. The trail is very well maintained, and in addition to trash bins placed discreetly at various points along the trail, you'll find handsome large stone mile markers at quarter-mile intervals, which helps you keep track of where you are on the trail.

As you hike, you'll hear the near-constant chirping and whistling of birds, many attracted by the wooden bird boxes that have been set up at various points along the trail. Benches at key spots overlooking the creek offer opportunities for you to rest and pull out your binoculars. Especially in spring, this trail is so full of life that even if you don't have any binoculars, you won't leave disappointed—the birds swoop and flit across the trail, disregarding hikers. Keep an eye out for the colorful cardinals, bluebirds, robins, and warblers. If you're lucky, you'll even spot a few hummingbirds—as I stood taking a swig from my water bottle, a couple of them buzzed boldly past me, seeming to ignore my very existence.

At 0.38 miles, a small clearing offers a scenic overlook where you can view the creek. Trees loom on either side, partially shading its clear waters. If you look carefully, you're likely to spot turtles warming themselves in the small patches of sun that filter through the tree branches. Just ahead, environmentalists have built a bat house. Just beyond it and behind the trees across the river, you'll glimpse some railroad tracks paralleling the creek.

At 1.53 miles, you'll reach the short, wooden Continental Bridge. Beyond it, the trail continues to curl lazily through the lovely rural setting, framed by pastures on the left and a dense clustering of hardwood trees growing up against the creek on your right—a combination that is utterly peaceful and entirely relaxing without being boring.

The trail crosses Mathews Street at 2.15 miles; if you glance to the right as you cross the street, you'll glimpse the top of the Ellis County Courthouse towering in the distance. Continuing along the trail, you'll cross the railroad tracks and hike another 0.3 miles to the Interurban Park, named for the Interurban Railway (AKA Texas Electric Railway), which ran from Dallas through Waxahachie to Waco until December 31, 1948. Signposts show old photographs of the 1,442-foot trestle bridge that spanned Waxahachie Creek here. Though the bridge is long gone, the supports are still intact. The scenery has not changed much since the photographs were taken, and with a little imagination you can almost see the bridge disappearing north toward downtown.

Continue northwest down the trail until you reach Rogers Street, at 2.58 miles. Cross the street and turn right toward the old, metal, red truss bridge,

Horse-filled pastures line this pretty trail.

known as the Rogers Street Bridge. This Texas Historic Bridge, now only open to pedestrians, was built in 1889 when the area was first settled; vehicles used it until 1990, when a newer bridge replaced it. Across the bridge and to your right, you can cross back over Rogers Street and explore the old depot, sitting just in front of the rail tracks. Adjacent to the depot, an old feed store reminds you of the city's agricultural roots. This is an ideal spot to turn and retrace your steps to the trailhead. If you want to extend the hike, the trail continues northwest to Getzendaner Park.

NEARBY ACTIVITIES

Stop by Waxahachie's Downtown Historic District, where you can browse antiques shops and boutiques, visit the Ellis County Museum, and admire the Ellis County Courthouse, which dates to 1895. To get downtown, turn right onto Howard Street, then right onto South Elm Street (US 77).

WINDMILL HILL PRESERVE TRAIL   54

IN BRIEF

This shady trail loops through a small, heavily wooded preserve, making it an excellent spot for hiking on a hot, sunny day. Though not especially scenic, the trail is appealing to those who enjoy exploring because the myriad trail junctions allow you to digress with little risk of becoming too lost.

DESCRIPTION

The local community lobbied to get this plot of land set aside, and now, thanks to their efforts, it is part of the Dallas County Trail and Preserve Program. The 72-acre nature preserve has a large network of trails criss-crossing the woods and is well used by those in the area.

On my hike, the Plano Search and Rescue Team was there for the day training their dogs. As my friend and I approached the trailhead, one of them playfully called over that if we got lost, they'd come search for us. While that was a comforting thought, as I started the hike I quickly realized how unnecessary that would be. Though unmarked trails split off in different directions every few hundred feet, it is almost impossible to get lost for long because almost all trails eventually lead back to the center of the preserve, where a trail runs

KEY AT-A-GLANCE INFORMATION

LENGTH: 1.8 miles
CONFIGURATION: Double loop
DIFFICULTY: Moderate
SCENERY: Woodlands, bridge
EXPOSURE: Mostly shady
TRAIL TRAFFIC: Light
TRAIL SURFACE: Packed dirt
HIKING TIME: 50 minutes
ACCESS: Free; open daily, year-round
FACILITIES: None
WHEELCHAIR TRAVERSABLE: No
SPECIAL COMMENTS: Leashed dogs and mountain bikers are welcome on this trail.

Directions

Take US 67 south toward Cleburne, and exit at Duncanville Road/Main Street, turning left. Head south on Main approximately 0.75 miles; the parking lot is at Windmill Hill Preserve on the left at the corner of Wintergreen Road.

GPS Trailhead Coordinates

UTM Zone (WGS84)   14S
Easting   696291
Northing   3610754
Latitude   N 32° 37' 1"
Longitude   W 96° 54' 29"

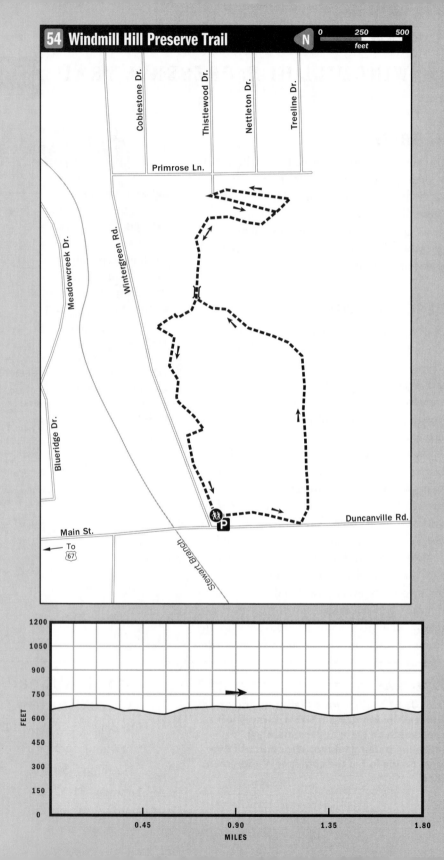

west–east through its center. All trails funnel into this central trail and go across the Stevie Ray Vaughan Memorial Bridge, which divides the western side of the preserve from the eastern side. The bridge honors the famous 1980s blues rock guitarist, Stevie Ray Vaughan. Vaughan played lead guitar on David Bowie's *Let's Dance* album and became very popular with his own band, Double Trouble. The guitarist died in a tragic helicopter crash following a concert on August 26, 1990. Vaughan is memorialized here because he was born and raised in Dallas.

The trail I've mapped out is a rough loop around the preserve and has lots of small ups and downs through hilly terrain, providing a nice workout. If you miss a turn (highly possible with so many trails branching out), don't be overly concerned—explore as you like, and you'll eventually find yourself back at the bridge, which is a good reference point.

There are two main entrances from the parking lot. Take the trailhead on the right (the one on the left is where you'll come out at the trail's end). Immediately, you'll be on a somewhat rocky trail. The scenery for most of this hike is what you see here—dense woods that shade much of the trail. About 250 feet into your trek, the trail will split; take the right branch. At the next trail split, at 0.13 miles, bear left. At this point, the trail has some small steep uphill and downhill climbs. The ruggedness here appeals to mountain bikers, who maintain the trail. On my hike, however, I did not see a single biker, just a couple of hikers whose dogs were thoroughly enjoying the workout.

At the next junction, 0.28 miles into the hike, continue straight, heading downhill. The preserve abuts some backyards, and through the trees you'll catch glimpses of houses before the trail returns to the woods. Finally, at 0.55 miles into the hike, you'll come to the Stevie Ray Vaughan Memorial Bridge, a very pretty brick-red truss bridge that spans a dry creek bed.

Cross the bridge and a small gully, then turn right at the next split, at about 0.65 miles. This will take you on a half-mile loop through the eastern half of the preserve. Hang a right at the path split at 0.8 miles, and the trail will loop through a piney grove and emerge into a small field with a few pine trees. Bear right at the next turnoff to climb up and down some small hills before yet another turnoff, where you'll continue straight. The trail then curls around a small field, meets up with a creek, and then puts you back at the Stevie Ray Vaughn Bridge.

Cross back over the bridge and turn right, heading down a concrete trail. A picnic table sits off to the left, and a little farther down, at 1.45 miles, is a small clearing to the right, where you'll see some large, dirt ramps for mountain bikers.

Turn left right before the dirt mounds onto the trail heading west; the path switchbacks down a small, steep hill. A couple hundred feet farther, you'll reach the next turnoff, where you should go right.

To exit the preserve, follow the right split at the next three turnoffs. If you prefer a little more exercise, do as I did and head left and uphill, staying to the left at the next couple of turnoffs. The trail emerges into a small field on the eastern side of the parking lot.

A hiker enjoying the trail's shady path.

NEARBY ACTIVITIES

Joe Pool Lake, along which lies Cedar Hill State Park, is nearby and is popular with fishermen, boaters, picnickers, campers, and birders. Inside the state park, you'll also find Penn Farm Agricultural History Center, a restored farm exhibit. To get there, take US 67 south. After about 1.5 miles, exit to the right, onto Pleasant Run Road. Turn right onto South Belt Line Road (FM 1382). The park is about 2 miles down on the left.

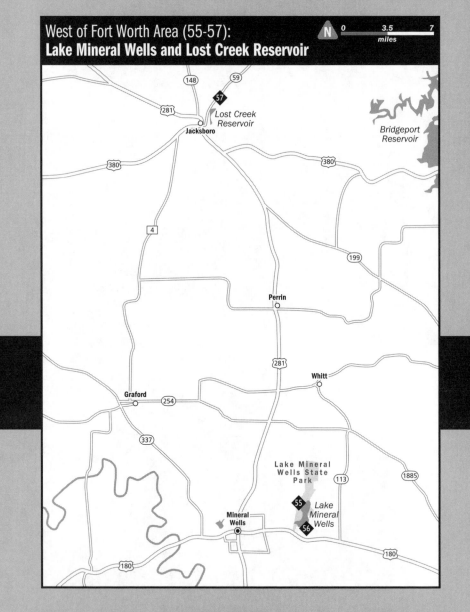

148   59

57

281   Lost Creek
       Reservoir
Jacksboro

Bridgeport
Reservoir

380   380

4

199

Perrin

281

Whitt

Graford   254

337

Lake Mineral
Wells State
Park   1885

113

55   Lake
      Mineral
Mineral   Wells
Wells
       56

180   180

180

WEST OF FORT WORTH

55 LAKE MINERAL WELLS STATE PARK:
Cross Timbers Trail

KEY AT-A-GLANCE INFORMATION

LENGTH: 4 miles
CONFIGURATION: Balloon
DIFFICULTY: Easy
SCENERY: Rocks, cactus, grasslands
EXPOSURE: Sunny
TRAIL TRAFFIC: Light
TRAIL SURFACE: Packed dirt, rock
HIKING TIME: 1.5 hours
ACCESS: $5 per person entrance fee; daily 6 a.m.–10 p.m.
FACILITIES: Restrooms, picnic tables
WHEELCHAIR TRAVERSABLE: No
SPECIAL COMMENTS: Bring along an animal track and scat identification book.

IN BRIEF

This wide trail is great for spotting animal tracks after a rainstorm, just be sure to check with the park to ensure the path has dried out enough to hike. The route starts in a wooded area then loops through some sunny cactus-dotted grasslands.

DESCRIPTION

Located about 46 miles west of Fort Worth, Lake Mineral Wells State Park is popular among outdoor enthusiasts for good reason—not only does it have a generous trail system, which welcomes bikers, hikers, and equestrians, it also has a fishing pier, which attracts anglers; beach access for lake swimming; and, most uniquely, a section of canyons and boulders open to rock climbers. The park, which opened in 1981, covers more than 3,200 acres, which includes the 646-acre Lake Mineral Wells. The lake was originally designed to supply water for the expanding city of Mineral Wells. It served its purpose for 40 years before an alternate water supply was found in 1963.

On the northwest side of the lake, you'll find the park's camping areas and the backcountry trail this hike traverses. On the southeast

GPS Trailhead Coordinates

UTM Zone (WGS84) 14S
Easting   590212
Northing 3633345
Latitude   N32° 50' 4"
Longitude W 98° 2' 10"

Directions

Follow I-20 west toward Abilene. Take Exit 414 onto Fort Worth Highway/US 180 west toward Mineral Wells. Continue approximately 21 miles (about 14 miles past Weatherford), then turn right onto Park Road 71, following the brown state park signs. To get to the trailhead, enter the Lake Mineral Wells State Park and make a sharp left, crossing over the spillway. Bear left at the next juncture. The parking lot is at the end of the road.

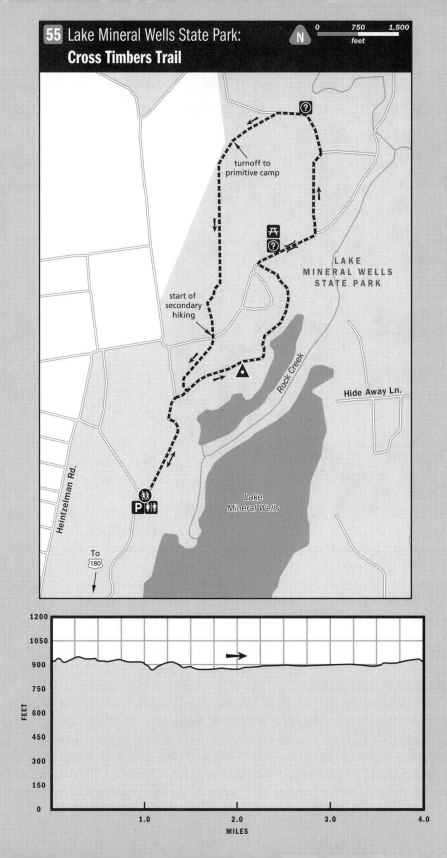

Animal tracks criss-cross the path the day after a rainstorm.

side of the lake, you'll find the trailhead for the Lake Mineral Wells State Trailway and the rock climbing area, known as "Penitentiary Hollow." Its narrow rocky canyons are a stark contrast to the wide, open grasslands of the trail; before or after the hike, be sure to stop by for a look. There is a trail that runs down a stone stairway to the canyon floor, which rock climbers and rappellers use to access climbing spots with names such as "Scrambled Egg Boulder," "The Cave," and "Pee Wee's Playhouse." If you're interested in exploring (or rock climbing) you can pick up a map at the entrance to Penitentiary Hollow. Rock climbers bring their own equipment, are required to sign a liability release, and must pay a $3 climbing fee. If you're not up for another hike and just interested in taking a look, there is a scenic overlook only a couple dozen feet down the rock-climbing trail that offers fantastic views of the canyon and lake. You're likely to see a rock climber or two scaling the far walls.

To get to the trailhead from the park entrance, take a sharp left at the first road juncture, then follow the road across the spillway. At the next intersection, stay left. The road dead-ends at the parking area, and you'll find the trailhead on the northeast side of the lot.

You'll find the trail is very wide, and it does stay this way for most of the hike, easily accommodating both hikers and equestrians. You'll also find that the combination of partially rocky surface and sunny exposure allows for the trail's quick drying after rains. I encountered few problems with mud or puddles, even though I visited at the end of a very rainy week. And because I hiked it just after it had rained, I was rewarded with some of the best animal tracks I've ever encountered on a trail—clear prints from raccoons, opossums, white-tailed deer, coyotes, and birds zigzagged all across the path throughout the entire length of the hike. Though I did not spot any of the animals themselves, I had a lot of fun reconstructing the scenes of skirmishes, crossings, and encounters that I imagined had occurred the night before my visit. A sign at the trailhead does indicate that the trail is closed when wet, so be sure to call ahead to check on trail conditions and possible closures.

The trail is bordered by cactus to your right, beyond which the woods shroud all but brief glimpses of Lake Mineral Wells in the distance. To your left, a chain-link fence marks the boundary of the state park.

The trail soon curls away past the fence, and at 0.5 miles, you'll find yourself at a split, where you should veer right. You'll soon pass the juncture to a small single-track hiking trail that heads off to the primitive camping area. Bypass this, staying on the wide trail as it heads slightly uphill through rocky terrain. Close examination of the ground will reveal the rocks to be varying shades of pink, glittering with flecks of mica or some other mineral.

Off to the right you'll catch glimpses of the surrounding hillsides through breaks in the trees. You'll find a better vantage point at 0.83 miles, where a small path off to the right leads to an overlook.

Continuing on, you'll bypass a turnoff heading back the way you came. A few dozen feet beyond, a trail forks; veer right to continue north. Rest areas have been placed at each of the major trail junctures, and at 1.68 miles you'll reach the first one, which has both a kiosk with a map of the entire backcountry trail and a shady picnic table just off the trail.

At 1.85 miles, veer left at the next trail fork. The trail passes through a sun-baked grassland dotted with the occasional tree. In the winter, the flatlands can be uninspiring; however, in the spring, wildflowers peak from amid tall grasses, adding interest and beauty to the setting. At 2.28 miles, you'll reach another juncture and rest area with a kiosk. Turn left (south), to begin the trek back toward the trailhead. If you wanted to extend the hike another few miles, you could instead turn right (north) to follow the trail onto another loop.

The trail back continues through grassland another 0.8 miles, passing the turnoff to the primitive camping area and another split, where you'll continue straight. Finally, at 3 miles, you'll reach a juncture with a smaller, single-track hiking trail. For a change of scenery, veer right into the trees and onto the narrow trail; it winds slightly uphill through dense woods. The path will cross over the wide trail once, disappearing into the woods on the far side. At 3.5 miles, it crosses back onto another section of the main trail you just left. This time you should veer right, back onto the main trail, to retrace your steps to the trailhead. Alternatively, if you're enjoying the woods, you can cross the wide trail and pick the single-track path where it runs through the woods back toward the trailhead parallel to the main trail.

The wide trailway curls through grasslands.

NEARBY ACTIVITIES

You can buy bottled mineral water and souvenirs at Mineral Wells' Famous Mineral Water Company. The company was founded in 1904 by the pharmacist Edward Dismuke, who believed the town's mineral waters could cure ailments—including his own. At the age of 40, he was told he had only a short time left to live; he ended up dying at the age of 97, attributing his longevity to the mineral waters. The Texas Historical Commission has honored the building with a historical marker.

To get to Mineral Wells, follow US 180 west 4 miles. Turn right onto Northwest Sixth Street; the building is number 209. They are open Tuesday through Friday, 8 a.m.–5:30 p.m., and Saturday 9 a.m.–5 p.m. If you have more time, take US 180 west 15 miles to Palo Pinto, where you can visit the Palo Pinto Museum, located in a jail from the mid-1800s just off US 180 in Palo Pinto.

LAKE MINERAL WELLS STATE TRAILWAY 56

IN BRIEF

This packed-gravel trail runs atop an old railway bed and connects the cities of Mineral Wells and Weatherford. It will appeal most to folks looking more for exercise than for scenery.

DESCRIPTION

With four access points along its 20-mile route, Lake Mineral Wells State Trailway stretches between Mineral Wells and Weatherford along a converted railway line. The multiuse trail, which opened in 1998, runs through countryside peppered with ranches. Because of its length, it is well suited to joggers and to walkers looking for a good section of uninterrupted trail upon which to stretch the legs. Access points for bicyclists, hikers, and equestrians are located (from east to west) just outside Weatherford, in Garner, and at Lake Mineral Wells State Park. The fourth access point at the far western end of the trail is in the Mineral Wells; access here is restricted to hikers and bicyclists.

Besides the trailway, you'll find an excellent backcountry trail within the park, which I've also highlighted. The park's more unusual

KEY AT-A-GLANCE INFORMATION

LENGTH: 3.16 miles
CONFIGURATION: Out-and-back
DIFFICULTY: Easy to moderate
SCENERY: Hills, grass, chaparral, old railway bed
EXPOSURE: Sunny
TRAIL TRAFFIC: Light to moderate
TRAIL SURFACE: Packed gravel
HIKING TIME: 1 hour
ACCESS: State park open 6 a.m.–10 p.m., trail open sunrise–sunset; adults $2; senior citizens over age 65, and children under age 12, $1; state park admittance fee $5
FACILITIES: Restrooms, benches
WHEELCHAIR TRAVERSABLE: Yes
SPECIAL COMMENTS: You can extend this hike for just about as long as you like—there are about 20 miles of trail.

Directions

Follow I-20 west toward Abilene, then take Exit 414 onto Fort Worth Highway / US 180 west toward Mineral Wells. Follow the highway about 21 miles (approximately 14 miles past Weatherford), then turn right onto Park Road 71, following the brown state park signs. To get to the trailhead parking, enter the Lake Mineral Wells State Park and stay right at the road juncture. The parking lot is on the right.

GPS Trailhead Coordinates

UTM Zone (WGS84) 14S
Easting 590649
Northing 3631008
Latitude N 32° 48' 48"
Longitude W 98° 1' 54"

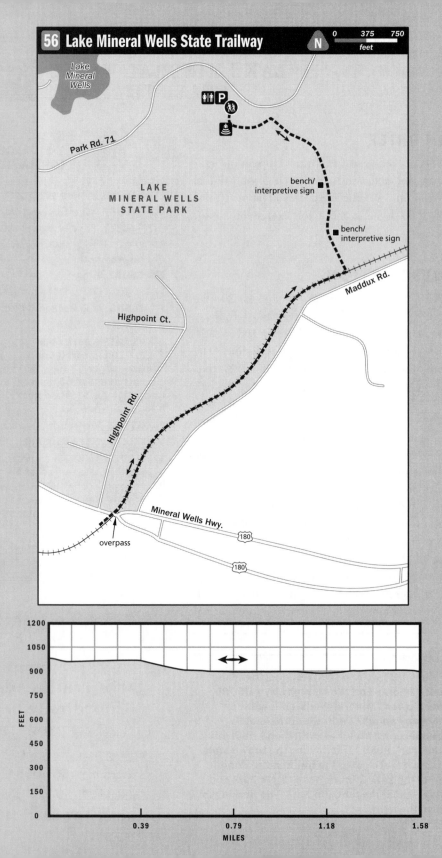

attraction, however, is a rock-climbing area known as "Penitentiary Hollow"—a section of narrow canyons on the eastern side of the lake near the trailhead for this hike. See the description for hike 55, Cross Timbers Trail, for more details about the area.

To get to the trailhead, stay to the right at the first fork after you enter the park. A short drive down on the right, you'll find the huge parking lot. There is a small trail fee, and a self-pay box has been set-up adjacent to the trailhead for hikers' convenience.

As you head down the paved trail, the path immediately starts to switchback down a steep hill. You'll pass an open outdoor amphitheater off to the right, then the trail turns into packed gravel. This section of trail is actually a small spur that connects the state park with the trailway itself, which is 0.6 miles to the southeast. The spur curl towards the main trail, cutting through grassy fields peppered with cactus and the occasional isolated tree.

At 0.38 miles, you'll pass a bench alongside an interpretive sign identifying native wildflowers of the area. The sign advises you to keep an eye out for the vivid hues of more than a dozen wildflowers, including the Texas bluebonnet, the standing cypress, and the Texas yellow star. Unfortunately, when I visited (in the middle of winter), the dry grasses were all devoid of all color but brown. Although in winter it's not at its most picturesque, it is at its most pleasant, temperature-wise. Sections of this little-shaded trail—which would normally be baking midday in summer—are mild and gentle, even on a late-winter afternoon.

Continuing on, the trail switchbacks down another hill. As you descend, you'll have a charming view of the trail snaking away into the distance against a backdrop of small wooded hills. The path cuts through grasslands and passes another interpretive sign identifying the red-tailed hawk, a common resident. Finally, at 0.63 miles, you'll reach the main juncture with the trailway. The trail splits here, extending 14 miles to the left (east) to Weatherford, and 6 miles to the right (west) into Mineral Wells.

I opted for a shorter hike, by heading right toward Mineral Wells. Both directions are equally pleasant, offering wide, paved trails atop an old railway bed, suitable for comfortable walking shoes, strollers, or bikes. The trail runs parallel to a road, so expect the sound of cars occasionally passing as folks head to and from their ranches. Traffic is light, however, and not distracting. The section of trail between Garner and Weatherford on the far eastern portion of the trailway does not run near any roads, something to consider if you're looking for a more remote feel.

Turn right (west) onto the trailway. The scenery along the trail is mostly trees and shrubs, and, unlike the hilly spur from the state park, this section is fairly level. As you near US 180, the trail starts to climb gradually to cross the highway via an overpass. The other side of the bridge marks exactly 1.5 miles into the hike and is the point where I turned around. If you're interested in continuing on, the trail stretches another 4.5 miles west into downtown Mineral Wells.

Cactus and isolated trees dot the grasslands along the trail.

NEARBY ACTIVITIES

You can buy bottled mineral water and souvenirs at Mineral Wells' Famous Mineral Water Company. See Nearby Activities for hike 55, Cross Timbers Trail, for more information.

LOST CREEK RESERVOIR STATE TRAILWAY 57

IN BRIEF

Located in an area rich with history of the North Texas frontier settlement, this peaceful, sunny hike winds through grasslands and over the dam of the Lost Creek Reservoir toward Fort Richardson State Park. Ranchlands abut the trailway, and you'll sometimes be greeted by the curious stares of bulls or livestock as you hike along.

DESCRIPTION

Located in Jacksboro along the banks of Lost Creek, the Fort Richardson State Park, Historic Site, and Lost Creek Trailway's amenities include fishing, hiking, and camping. The trailway portion opened in 1998 and is about 10 miles long (one way), connecting the state park with the Lost Creek Reservoir. Trailheads are located at both the park and the reservoir. On my visit, a park ranger at the fort advised me it's best start from the reservoir end, which he said was more scenic. The reservoir trailhead is a few miles away from the state park and historic site, a short drive northeast.

If you want to explore Fort Richardson itself, it will require a separate stop before or after the hike but is well worth it. Consider making a weekend of this trip—not only is

KEY AT-A-GLANCE INFORMATION

LENGTH: 5.35 miles
CONFIGURATION: Balloon
DIFFICULTY: Easy
SCENERY: Grassland, ranches, reservoir, dam
EXPOSURE: Sunny
TRAIL TRAFFIC: Light
TRAIL SURFACE: Pavement and crushed rock
HIKING TIME: 2 hours
ACCESS: $3 per person; daily
FACILITIES: Composting toilet and picnic tables near the swimming beach
WHEELCHAIR TRAVERSABLE: No
SPECIAL COMMENTS: This trail can be very hot in summer; bring a hat, suntan lotion, and plenty of water—there are no fountains along the route.

Directions

Take Jacksboro Highway/TX 199 west toward Jacksboro. Fort Richardson State Park is located on the left, just off the highway, approximately 1 mile outside Jacksboro. To get to the trailhead itself, you'll bypass the state park and continue straight into downtown Jacksboro. Turn right onto East Belknap Street; the road will curve left and become Bowie Street/TX 59. The parking lot is about 2 miles down on the right.

GPS Trailhead Coordinates

UTM Zone (WGS84) 14S
Easting 580272
Northing 3678779
Latitude N 33° 14' 42"
Longitude W 98° 8' 18"

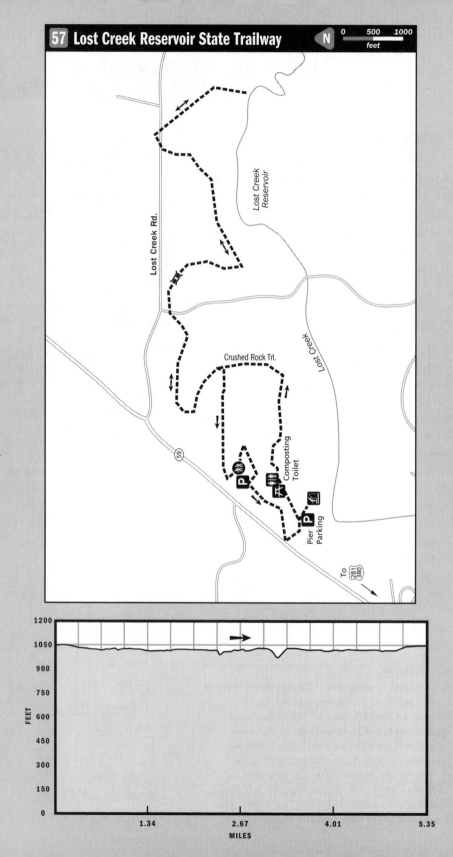

N

0   500   1000
feet

Lost Creek Reservoir

Lost Creek Rd.

Lost Creek

Crushed Rock Trl.

Composting Toilet

Pier Parking

To 281 380

1200

1050

900

750

600

450

300

150

0

FEET

1.34   2.67   4.01   5.35
MILES

there a lot to explore, but the state park has been named one of the top 100 family campgrounds among U.S. federal and state parks.

The fort was established to protect frontier settlements against raids from Southern Plains Indian tribes after the Civil War. Named after Civil War general Israel Bush Richardson, it is associated with many battles, including the Salt Creek Massacre (AKA Warren Wagon Train Massacre). The massacre involved a bloody raid against a wagon train by a group of Kiowa and Comanche. The chiefs were eventually arrested and tried for murder—the first trial of its kind. In 1878, 11 years after its establishment, the unsettled frontier plains were secured and the fort was finally abandoned.

In 1963 the fort was named a National Historic Landmark. In 1968 the Texas Parks and Wildlife Department claimed it, opening it to the public as a state park and historic site a few years later. A few of the buildings from the fort's original complex have been restored or preserved, including the commanding officer's quarters, the post hospital, and the magazine. You can pick up a walking-tour pamphlet at the visitor center to guide you around the entire site. The tour starts at the Interpretive Center, where you'll find displays and information about the fort's history.

This hike starts at the trailhead at the reservoir. If you want to pick up a map or other park information, be sure to stop by the state park visitor center before heading to the trailhead; the trailway is unmanned. A self-pay booth allows you to pay the marginal trail fee; state park pass holders should just hang their pass inside their car. Park rangers do patrol the area, so be sure you've paid your dues. The trail is open to hikers, bikers, and equestrians, though on the gorgeous weekend day I visited, I encountered no one.

When you arrive, you'll find a huge parking area with trailheads on both the east and west sides of the lot. Start by heading down the trail on the west side; facing the back of the lot, it'll be the trail at the back on the right. The path is actually a paved one-way park road bordered by woods and shrubs, which loops downhill toward the reservoir. Within a few hundred feet of starting down the path, you'll see the waters come into view and will pass a charming wooden fishing pier stretching out into the still blue-green waters; anglers come here to fish for channel and blue catfish. Looking across the reservoir, the opposite shoreline is dotted with trees and shrubs and is pleasantly devoid of development or construction.

Just past the pier, you'll pass a huge day-use area replete with a long pavilion and picnic tables overlooking the water. Just before and below it, a swimming beach with a wide stretch of sand beckons visitors on hot days. The park road continues its loop then splits at 1.45 miles; follow the crushed-limestone multiuse trail. (Continuing to the left—on the road—would take you back to the parking lot and the opposite trailhead.) To the right, the reservoir's water will still be visible, glinting in the sunlight just beyond the tall prairie grasses.

The trail winds around a small inlet of the reservoir and heads east through flat prairie lands dotted with the occasional tree. To the left, a fence marks the boundary of a local ranch. On the sunny day of my visit, I was greeted here by the steady gaze of a couple of huge bulls eyeing me through the fence.

A wooden fishing pier attracts anglers.

At 2.1 miles, you'll reach a large old metal bridge nestled among the prairie grasses, mysteriously spanning nothing more than flat grassland. Cross the bridge and continue following the trail east. The scenery is mostly trees and rocks to the right, blocking the nearby reservoir from view, and ranchland to the left. Eventually, the eastern edge of the reservoir will come into view between the trees to the right, and you'll have a glimpse of the dam. The trail winds toward then atop the dam. From the middle of the dam, you'll have a fabulous view of a lush green valley to the left. I spotted some type of livestock grazing there (though from the height of the dam, they looked like nothing more than white dots). To the right, the reservoir spreads out before you, shimmering in the sunlight. This is a great spot to take a break and enjoy lunch atop the dam before retracing your steps to the trailhead. If you wanted to extend the hike, you can follow the trail approximately 6 more miles across the dam, around the southern side of the reservoir, past the local airport, and to the state park.

NEARBY ACTIVITIES

If you're hiking the trailway, be sure to stop by Fort Richardson itself before or after the hike to explore the old buildings on the fort grounds. Within Jacksboro, you can visit the Jack County Museum, a historical house with period furnishings. It is near the town square, at 237 West Belknap.

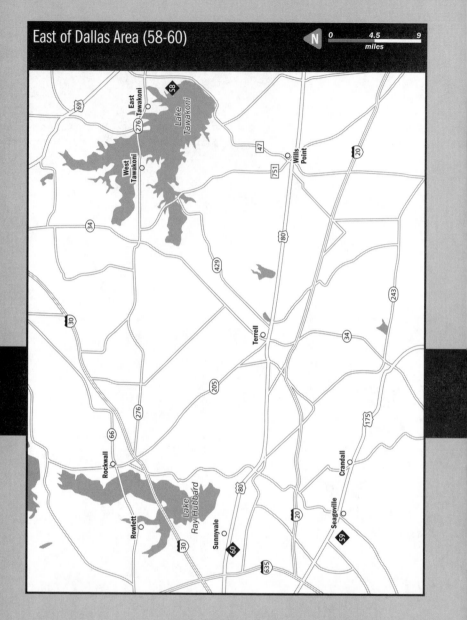

East of Dallas Area (58-60)

EAST OF DALLAS

58 LAKE TAWAKONI NATURE TRAIL

(i) KEY AT-A-GLANCE INFORMATION

LENGTH: 1.72 miles

CONFIGURATION: Balloon

DIFFICULTY: Easy

SCENERY: Hardwood forest, birds

EXPOSURE: Partial shade

TRAIL TRAFFIC: Light

TRAIL SURFACE: Packed dirt

HIKING TIME: 45 minutes

ACCESS: $3 per person; daily 7 a.m.–10 p.m.

FACILITIES: Restrooms, picnic area, benches

WHEELCHAIR TRAVERSABLE: No

SPECIAL COMMENTS: Look for the unusually knobby bark of a couple of trees along the first half of the trail.

IN BRIEF

Located near the "Bluebird Capital of Texas," this trail winds through the woods near Lake Tawakoni and is great for bird-watching.

DESCRIPTION

The 36,700-acre Lake Tawakoni (tuh-wock´-o-nee) is a huge reservoir on the Sabine River occupying the corners of three counties—Hunt, Van Zandt, and Rains. Its dam (the Iron Bridge Dam) and spillway are 5.5 miles long. The reservoir serves as a municipal and industrial water supply and a recreational spot. Along its 200-plus-mile shoreline, boaters will find half a dozen boat ramps, hunters will find three units of the Tawakoni Wildlife Management Area, and hikers and campers will find a state park. It is also known among anglers as an excellent spot for catfishing in particular; striped, largemouth, and white bass can also be found in good numbers.

At only 376 acres, Lake Tawakoni State Park sits like a tiny speck on the reservoir's southern shoreline. Opened in 2002, the state park is refreshingly remote, being just a 20-minute drive down a secondary road. Even the closest town—Wills Point—has a

GPS Trailhead Coordinates

UTM Zone (WGS84) 15S

Easting 219759

Northing 3638139

Latitude N 32° 50' 44"

Longitude W 95° 59' 39"

Directions ———————————————→

Take US 80 east toward Terrell. When you reach Wills Point, turn left onto FM 47/North Fourth Street, then bear right and go approximately 5 miles. Turn left onto FM 2475, then travel approximately 4 miles, following the brown state park sign to enter Lake Tawakoni State Park. You can pick up a map of the park at the headquarters as you drive in. As you head into the park, stay to the left at the first junction, and you'll reach the day-use area on your left, where you should park in the first parking lot.

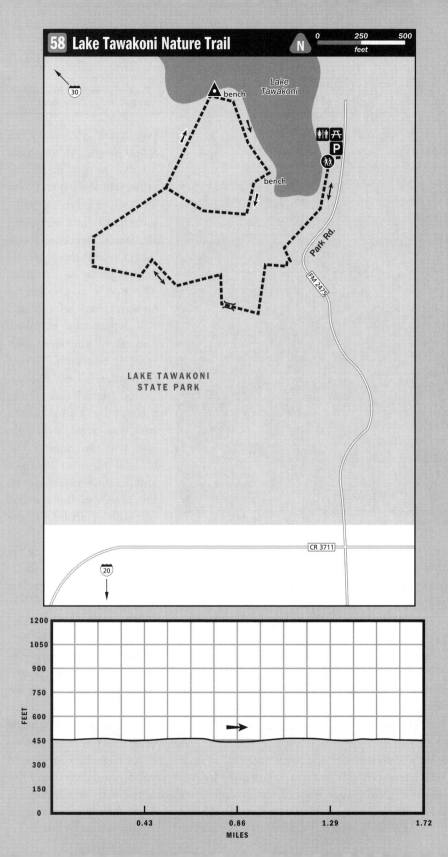

N

0   250   500
feet

Lake
Tawakoni

30

bench

bench

Park Rd.

FM 2475

LAKE TAWAKONI
STATE PARK

CR 3711

20

1200

1050

900

750

FEET

600

450

300

150

0

0.43   0.86   1.29   1.72
MILES

The curious bark of a tree trunk on the trail invites closer study

population of fewer than 5,000 people. Although it's a drive to get there, the effort will reward you with a couple of charming trails, including a short loop along the lake's shoreline, and a longer trail through woodland adjacent to the lake. The park's atmosphere is laid-back and relaxed and will appeal most to hikers looking for a mellow, quiet hike. If you come during the winter, it's not unusual to find yourself one of only a handful of visitors in the park, and certainly the only one on the trails. The unusual name of the lake and park are a reference to the Tawakoni Indians that originally inhabited the area.

The trailhead is in the far left corner of the parking lot, marked with a "Nature Trail" sign and a notice that it is only open for use when dry. The single-track path winds southwest through the woods. A thick mixture of American elms and post oaks provide a pleasant canopy of shade as you hike.

At 0.3 miles, you'll reach a split in the trail, where you should turn right, heading west through more hardwood forest. Vines hang thick from the surrounding tree limbs, shrouding any wildlife in the vicinity from view. Occasionally, however, a rustling in the leaves indicates something is nearby—typically birds hopping through the underbrush. As you continue, keep an eye out for poison ivy.

The trail continues west, crosses a bridge spanning a small creek, heads slightly uphill, then reaches a juncture at 0.57 miles. The entire trail is open to both bike and foot traffic, with one section exclusively for bikes. If you were to head left at this juncture, you'd reach the loop reserved for mountain bikes. You should therefore veer right at the juncture, following the path 1 mile farther, where you will reach a three-way juncture. The first trail, to the right, loops to the south, from where you just came. The second trail, straight ahead, loops north toward the lake, curls around, and comes back out onto the third trail to your right. You should continue straight, following the second (middle) trail north, where you'll find the hardwood trees starting to mix with junipers such as eastern red cedar. The elevation is slightly higher than that of the lake, and as you reach the farthest point of the loop, you'll catch glimpses of the water to the left through the trees. If you've brought your binoculars, you'll find a couple of benches at 0.83 and 0.93 miles, just before you loop back. Just off the trail, beneath the trees, the benches provide ideal shade-covered spots for bird-watching. Keep an eye out for the eastern bluebird, which is commonly found in the park; the nearest town of Wills Point, is called the "Bluebird Capital of Texas." State park materials indicate more than 200 species of birds have been identified here.

At 0.93 miles, veer right, following the red arrow, and after about 500 feet, you'll be back at the start of the loop. From here, retrace your steps to the trailhead. If you're interested in extending the hike, you can drive to the northern end of the park and pick up the trailhead just to the right of the swimming beach to hike along the lake. The first half of the trail hugs the shoreline, providing inspiring views of the lake, before looping back through the woods, making it a little more than 1 mile roundtrip. Keep an eye out for bird-attracting plants such as the American beautyberry, a shrub that produces clusters of berries in the autumn, and yaupon holly, a berry-bearing evergreen shrub.

NEARBY ACTIVITIES

In 1995 Wills Point was recognized as having the most bluebirds in the State of Texas and was officially proclaimed the Blue Bird Capital of Texas. In honor of this fact, the town hosts an annual blue bird festival each spring, with food, exhibits, and live entertainment. Check the official Web site (**www.willspointbluebird .com**) to see if your visit will coincide with the April festival. Year-round, you can explore the town's historic buildings, Depot Museum, and pioneer cabin. You can also take a Wagon Tour (starting and ending at the Depot Museum) to visit the historic spots around town.

59 POST OAK TRAIL

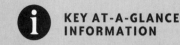

KEY AT-A-GLANCE INFORMATION

LENGTH: 1.69 miles
CONFIGURATION: Loop
DIFFICULTY: Easy
SCENERY: Pond, thickets, woods, meadows
EXPOSURE: Partly sunny
TRAIL TRAFFIC: Light
TRAIL SURFACE: Dirt
HIKING TIME: 45 minutes
ACCESS: Daily; free
FACILITIES: Picnic tables
WHEELCHAIR TRAVERSABLE: No
SPECIAL COMMENTS: Birding is excellent around the small lake.

IN BRIEF

A shady hike looping through a pretty preserve, the first half of the trail is through a predominately thickly wooded area, whereas the second half winds through smaller clearings of native grasses. A small lake midway through the hike attracts birds.

DESCRIPTION

As part of an effort to provide students with environmental learning programs, the Dallas Independent School District established the Environmental Education Center. Located in southeast Dallas County in the small town of Seagoville (named for its founder, T. K. Seago), the center was established in the 1970s and offers students an outdoor education experience; in addition, there is a museum complete with ecosystem exhibits, learning labs, and interactive video stations. Although the center is mainly intended for students, it also manages the Post Oak Preserve, which is just across the street, where this hike begins. The preserve's namesake—the post oak—is a small, acorn-producing, drought-resistant tree, commonly used to make fence posts.

Open to the public, the preserve offers nature trails winding through a small remnant of post oak savannah. The 334-acre preserve

GPS Trailhead Coordinates

UTM Zone (WGS84) 14S
Easting 728058
Northing 3614118
Latitude N 32° 38' 28"
Longitude W 96° 34' 8"

Directions

Take US 175 east toward Kaufman. In Seagoville, take the exit for Simonds Road/ Kimberly Drive. Turn right onto Simonds Road and travel 2 miles to Bowers Road, then turn left. The Post Oak Preserve is about 1.5 miles down on the right, across from the Environmental Education Center.

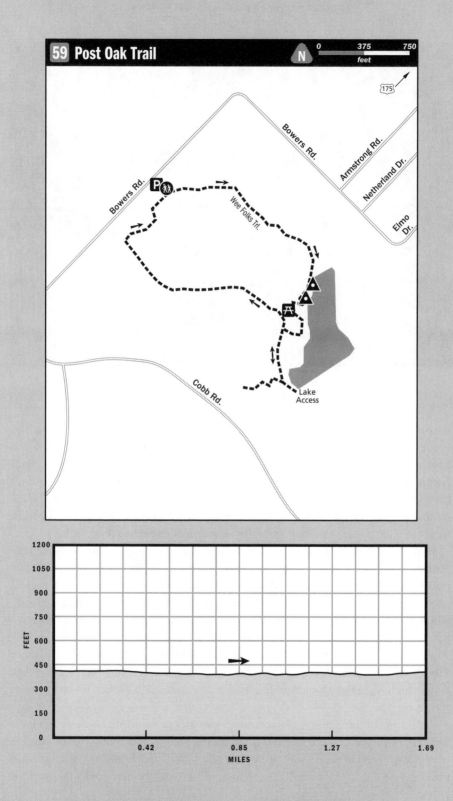

Take a brief rest on the shores of a small pond midway through the trail.

is also regularly used by the center as an extension of its outdoor classroom, and if you visit on a weekday, you may encounter students or teachers along the trail. This is an excellent trail for younger hikers because wooden signs at various points along the trail instruct less experienced hikers, providing general reminders and tips, such as to keep an eye out for snakes, be cautious of poisonous plants such as poison ivy, and keep the wildlife wild by not feeding the animals. In addition, the trail is wide and flat—easy for small, curious feet to maneuver.

Start the hike by heading past the picnic area and bearing left onto the trail heading east (the path on the left is where you'll exit at the end of the hike). The trail winds through a thick woodland dotted with cedars and sporadic clumps of prairie grasses. Faced with all these trees, many of you may wonder, as I did, where the savannah is. Interestingly, natural fires and grazing bison are the two key forces in maintaining a savannah. The former keeps the woodlands at bay, allowing the prairie grasses to thrive, while the latter spreads the seed. Without these forces, the woodlands start to take over. As you hike along, you'll pass some educational signposts, which indicate that a woodland takeover is what you're seeing here.

As you continue, the trail becomes more densely wooded. Thick vines tangle themselves in the branches of the surrounding trees, hiding all signs of wildlife from view, though occasional rustling in the leaves and branches hints at their presence. At 0.3 miles, a small sign with bright-green lettering marks the split for the easy Wee Folks Trail. Stay to the left, bypassing the turnoff. As you continue along, the trees will start to thin, and you'll catch a few brief glimpses of water sparkling in the distance before you reach a signpost marking the "moderately easy" Lake Shore Trail. Another 0.27 miles down the trail, you'll reach a quiet overlook of the preserve's 12-acre lake. A large old tree offers a shady spot for you to sit and observe the birds that frequent the small oasis. Most commonly, you'll spot teams of ducks paddling through the marshy waters or herons wading along the shoreline. If you glance up, you're likely to spot at least one slow-circling bird peering down at you—most likely a resident turkey vulture monitoring the ground for any food it can scavenge.

Back on the trail, you'll notice the scenery start to change as the woodlands thin dramatically and mix with patches of cactus and clumps of prairie grasses. At 0.92 miles, turn left onto a wide, paved road framed by short trees and shrubs. The road heads west and passes a picnic area before reaching another juncture a few hundred feet down. Bear left, following the paved path to its end, where it fades to join the soft, sandy banks of the lake. The gentle, sandy slopes offer you another chance to take a brief break and scope the pond-sized lake for waterfowl.

After exploring the short shoreline, head back up the trail and bear right at the next juncture to head northwest. The trail winds through patches of grassland dotted with small shrubs and cedar trees, markedly different from the dense woodlands characterizing the first half of the trail. You'll start to notice the shrubs and trees thin out, and then a sign advises that you've entered the Thickets and Meadow Trail. Throughout this section of trail, you'll find a couple of small, sunny meadows, framed by bright blue skies. Dragonflies and butterflies buzz and flutter around you as you round the final bend and turn back northeast toward the trailhead. From the final turn, it's a mere 0.2 miles before you emerge back at the trailhead, completing the loop.

NEARBY ACTIVITIES

The Rogers Wildlife Rehab and Farm Sanctuary is located in nearby Hutchins, about 14 miles away. The facility is a nonprofit organization that rehabilitates injured birds and farm animals. Visitors are welcome to roam the property free of charge; donations are accepted. On the grounds, you'll find dozens of outdoor cages serving as temporary homes for rehabilitating hawks, owls, blue jays, vultures, and herons, among others. Geese and pheasants wander around unfettered. To get there, turn left, heading west on Simonds Road approximately 1.6 miles, then bear left onto Beltline Road and drive 4.6 miles. Turn right onto I-45 north, and go 3.6 miles to Exit 274, Dowdy Ferry Road/Palestine St. Stay on the service road for about 0.5 miles, then turn right onto East Cleveland Street. The sanctuary is about 1 mile down on the left.

60 SAMUELL FARM TRAIL

KEY AT-A-GLANCE INFORMATION

LENGTH: 2.93 miles
CONFIGURATION: Triple loop
DIFFICULTY: Easy to moderate
SCENERY: Ponds, meadows, woods, birds, antique tractors
EXPOSURE: Sunny
TRAIL TRAFFIC: Light on weekdays, heavy on weekends
TRAIL SURFACE: Packed dirt
HIKING TIME: 1.5 hours
ACCESS: Free; Tuesday–Sunday, 9 a.m.–5 p.m.
FACILITIES: Restrooms, picnic area
WHEELCHAIR TRAVERSABLE: No
SPECIAL COMMENTS: Hike in the morning to avoid the heat of the day on this sunny trail.

IN BRIEF

This cheery hike through an old farm traverses a couple of pretty meadows and offers plenty to see, including a windmill, log cabins, and vintage tractors.

DESCRIPTION

Located just off the service road of busy US 80 in Mesquite, Samuell Farm may seem like an unlikely spot for an enjoyable hiking experience, but don't let its location mislead you. The 340-acre farm is surprisingly beautiful, with miles of hiking trails and scores of birds. The farm is often used as an educational resource for school field trips and is also a regular monthly walk on the Dallas Trekkers Walking Club agenda. The atmosphere on the farm switches easily from festive and active to quiet and peaceful, so be prepared for either. I arrived one afternoon to find the huge gravel parking lot teeming with school kids and families. I set off expecting a lively hike; however, within 30 minutes of my arrival, the school buses had packed up and driven off, leaving me almost the only visitor on the entire farm. I enjoyed a couple hours of quiet hiking and exploring and encountered only one other family, just as I was leaving.

GPS Trailhead Coordinates

UTM Zone (WGS84)   14S
Easting   726272
Northing   3630225
Latitude   N 32° 47' 12"
Longitude   W 96° 35' 2"

Directions

Take I-30 east to US 80 east toward Terrell. Exit at Belt Line Road. Cross Belt Line Road, and continue 0.3 miles on the service road. The entrance to Samuell Farm is just off the service road on the right and is marked by a huge tractor.

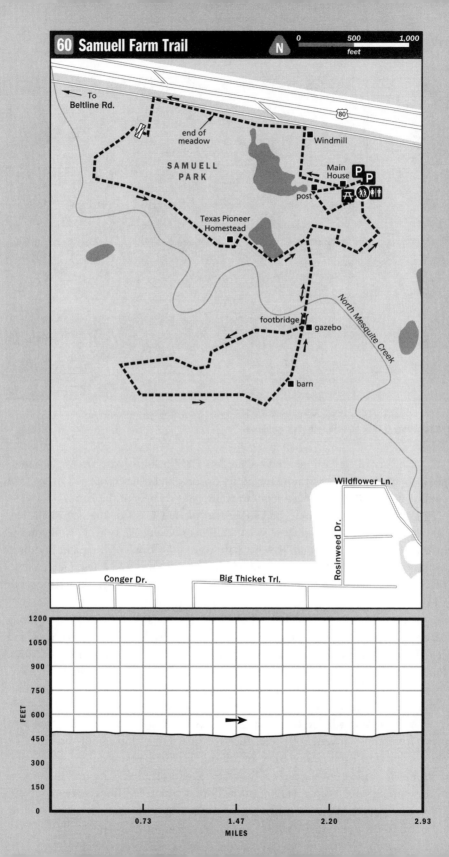

60 Samuell Farm Trail

0   500   1,000
feet

To
Beltline Rd.

end of
meadow

SAMUELL
PARK

Windmill

80

Main
House

post

P P

Texas Pioneer
Homestead

North Mesquite Creek

footbridge

gazebo

barn

Wildflower Ln.

Rosinweed Dr.

Conger Dr.

Big Thicket Trl.

1200
1050
900
750
600
450
300
150
0

FEET

0.73   1.47   2.20   2.93
MILES

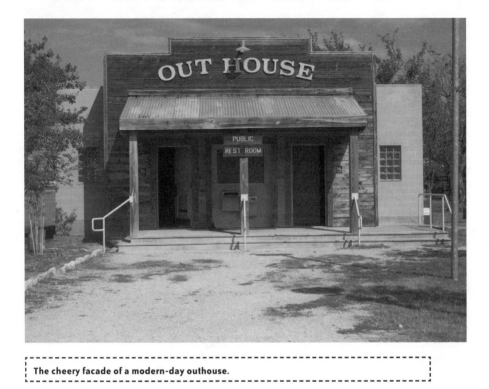

The cheery facade of a modern-day outhouse.

The City of Dallas inherited the land in 1937 from the late Dr. W. W. Samuell. In 2001, budget constraints forced its closure, and it has reopened in the past couple of years only with help from the nonprofit Friends of the Farm.

Enter the farm through the gate just to the left (east) of the main building. To your left, you'll see a small wooden building housing the restrooms. Begin the hike by turning right to take the dirt path passing in front of the main building. A cheery picnic area dotted with colorful vintage tractors and a few picnic tables fills a large expanse of grass off to your left. On your right, you'll pass a small working garden, then the trail splits in several directions.

Follow the wide, dirt path to the right as it curves back toward the highway between a small pond and the parking lot. The trail heads toward the highway and at 0.57 miles reaches a windmill, where you'll turn left. The trail then narrows, following a faint grassy trail between the highway on the right, and a pretty meadow on the left. (Although the cars are distracting, the trail is safe for all ages—there is a wide grassy expanse in addition to a fence between hikers and the roadway.)

When you reach the trees that border the meadow on the west, turn left, away from the highway, following the tree line. Hike along until the tree line ends, then turn right, away from the meadow. You'll pass through a gate and continue 0.1 mile until the next split, where you'll turn left. The trail then loops back southeast alongside a wide meadow dotted with trees. Insects are abundant, so be sure you've applied repellent. On a sunny day, you may see small yellow butterflies flitting across the trail. Crickets and grasshoppers are also abundant and are likely to smack you in the chest as they hop out of your way and back into the tall meadow grasses. The meadow also attracts birds and is a good spot to see the scissor-tailed flycatcher, easily identified by its forked tail.

Straight ahead, you'll see the Texas Pioneer Homestead, a picturesque old log cabin, whose cramped quarters and tiny rooms are open to exploration. Continue along the path past a small pond, to the next split at 1.5 miles, where you'll turn right, following the gravel trail south. The trail heads slightly downhill into a dip where a shallow creek cuts the trail and prevents further progress. Instead of wading through the water, cross the grass to your right, following the creek a few dozen feet to a small red footbridge hidden behind the trees. Rejoin the trail, keeping the gazebo to your left. Another pond off to the right sets the bucolic mood as you pass rolls of hay and approach a large barn. At 2.15 miles, follow the trail to the right, passing the barn and a picnic area. The trail continues past a huge sunny meadow with tall grasses and brilliant yellow sunflowers.

You'll soon reach the next trail split, where you'll hang a right, following the shady remnants of a wide dirt road. Stay to the right at the next path split at 2.33 miles. After about another 0.2 miles, the gazebo will pop back into view. Before you reach it, bear left back onto the footbridge and cross the creek heading back toward the entrance.

At 2.7 miles, turn right on the path just before the picnic area. If you've brought lunch, grab a table and a bite; otherwise, continue along the trail, which passes between dozens of antique tractors. Take the next two lefts to do a small loop. Another picnic area and a small log cabin to the right invite closer inspection. From here, it's just a few hundred feet back to the trailhead.

NEARBY ACTIVITIES

From spring through early fall, you can catch the Mesquite Championship Rodeo, which features bull riding, chuckwagon races, clowns, cowboys, and cowgirls. Shows typically start in the early evenings. Be sure to check their Web site (**www.mesquiterodeo.com**) for the current season's hours and rates. The rodeo is 8 miles away. To get there, take US 80E west 3 miles. Merge onto I-635 south and travel 2 miles, then exit at Scyene Road/TX 352. Stay on the service road for about 0.5 miles, then turn right onto Rodeo Drive.

60 HIKES
WITHIN 60 MILES

DALLAS/FORT WORTH
INCLUDES
TARRANT, COLLIN, AND DENTON COUNTIES

APPENDIXES
AND INDEX

APPENDIX A:
OUTDOOR SHOPS

Academy
www.academy.com
6101 I-20 (at Bryant Irvin Road)
Fort Worth, TX 76132
(817) 361-1240
(See Web site for more locations
throughout the metroplex.)

Backwoods
www.backwoods.com
3212 Camp Bowie Boulevard
Fort Worth, TX 76107
(817) 332-2423

Bass Pro Shops
www.basspro.com
2501 Bass Pro Drive
Grapevine, TX 76051
(972) 724-2018

Bass Pro Shops
www.basspro.com
1800 East I-30 Freeway
Garland, TX 75043
(469) 221-2600

Cabela's
www.cabelas.com
12901 Cabela Drive
Fort Worth, TX 76177
(817) 337-2400

Camping World
www.campingworld.com
10100 South Freeway
Fort Worth, TX 76140
(866) 393-6441
(817) 568-1991

Camping World
www.campingworld.com
5209 I-35 North
Denton, TX 76207
(800) 527-4812
(940) 898-8906

Mountain Hideout
www.mountainhideout.com
14010 Coit Road
Dallas, TX 75240
(972) 234-8651

Mountain Hideout
www.mountainhideout.com
5643 Lovers Lane
Dallas, TX 75209
(214) 350-8181

Mountain Sports
www.mountainsports.com
2025 West Pioneer Parkway
Arlington, TX 76013
(800) 805-9139
(817) 461-4503

REI
www.rei.com
4510 LBJ Freeway
Dallas, TX 75244
(972) 490-5989

REI
www.rei.com
2424 Preston Road
Plano, TX 75093
(972) 985-2241

APPENDIX A: (CONTINUED)
OUTDOOR SHOPS

Sports Authority
www.sportsauthority.com
1244 Green Oaks Road
Fort Worth, TX 76116
(817) 731-8578
(See Web site for more locations
throughout the metroplex.)

Sports Authority
www.sportsauthority.com
15490 Dallas Parkway
Dallas, TX 75248
(972) 991-3533
(See Web site for more locations
throughout metroplex.)

Sun & Ski Sports
3000 Grapevine Mills Parkway
Grapevine, TX 76051
(972) 355-9424

Whole Earth Provision Co.
www.wholeearthprovision.com
5400 East Mockingbird Lane
Dallas, TX 75206
(214) 824-7444

APPENDIX B:
PLACES TO BUY MAPS

Mapsco
www.mapsco.com
11811 Preston Road
Dallas, TX 75230
(972) 960-1414
(800) 796-6277

Mapsco
www.mapsco.com
6353 Camp Bowie Road
Fort Worth, TX 76116
(817) 731-1666
(800) 388-1201

Mapsco
www.mapsco.com
8300 Gaylord Parkway #7
Frisco, TX 75034
(972) 668-MAPS
(866) 627-7261

Mapsco
www.mapsco.com
4181 Centurion Way
Addison, TX 75001
(972) 450-9380
(800) 950-5308

One Map Place
www.onemapplace.com
3128 Forest Lane, Suite 212
Dallas, TX 75234
(972) 241-2680

Texas Parks & Wildlife
www.tpwd.state.tx.us
Free download of many
Texas State Park maps

U.S.D.A. Forest Service
www.fs.fed.us/r8/texas/maps

APPENDIX C:
HIKING CLUBS

Adventure Team DFW
www.adventureteam.com

American Hiking Society
www.americanhiking.org

Dallas Sierra Club
texas.sierraclub.org/dallas

DFW Outdoors
www.dfwoutdoors.com

Fort Worth Sierra Club
Burleson, TX
texas.sierraclub.org/fortworth

Texins Outdoor Club
www.outdoorclub.org
Dallas, TX

INDEX

HIKERS' AND BACKPACKERS' GUIDE FOR TREATING MEDICAL EMERGENCIES

by Patrick Brighton, M.D.
ISBN 10: 0-89732-640-7
ISBN 13: 978-0-89732-640-7
$9.95
116 pages

By keeping descriptions and remedies for injury and illness simple, this book enables participants in a particular sport to be informed, stay calm, and appropriately treat themselves or fellow participants. Reading this book before initiating the activity also enhances awareness of potential problems and fosters prevention of accidents and disease. With a refreshing splash of humor, this guide is as informative as it is entertaining.

GPS OUTDOORS

by Russell Helms
ISBN 10: 0-89732-967-8
ISBN 13: 978-0-89732-967-5
$10.95
120pages

Whether you're a hiker on a weekend trip through the Great
Smokies, a backpacker cruising the Continental Divide Trail,
a mountain biker kicking up dust in Moab, a paddler running
the Lewis and Clark bicentennial route, or a climber
pre-scouting the routes up Mount Shasta, a simple
handheld GPS unit is fun, useful, and can even be a lifesaver.

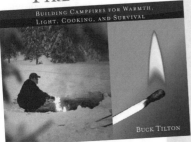

AMERICAN HIKING SOCIETY

Because you hike.

We're with you every step of the way

American Hiking Society gives voice to the more than 75 million Americans who hike and is the only national organization that promotes and protects foot trails, the natural areas that surround them and the hiking experience. Our work is inspiring and challenging, and is built on three pillars:

Volunteerism and Stewardship: We organize and coordinate nationally recognized programs – including Volunteer Vacations, National Trails Day® and the National Trails Fund –that help keep our trails open, safe and enjoyable.

Policy and Advocacy: We work with Congress and federal agencies to ensure funding for trails, the preservation of natural areas, and the protection of the hiking experience.

Outreach and Education: We expand and support the national constituency of hikers through outreach and education as well as partnerships with other recreation and conservation organizations.

Join us in our efforts. Become an American Hiking Society member today!

American Hiking Society

1422 Fenwick Lane · Silver Spring, MD 20910 · (301) 565-6704
www.AmericanHiking.org · info@AmericanHiking.org

DEAR CUSTOMERS AND FRIENDS,

SUPPORTING YOUR INTEREST IN OUTDOOR ADVENTURE, travel, and an active lifestyle is central to our operations, from the authors we choose to the locations we detail to the way we design our books. Menasha Ridge Press was incorporated in 1982 by a group of veteran outdoorsmen and professional outfitters. For 25 years now, we've specialized in creating books that benefit the outdoors enthusiast.

Almost immediately, Menasha Ridge Press earned a reputation for revolutionizing outdoors- and travel-guidebook publishing. For such activities as canoeing, kayaking, hiking, backpacking, and mountain biking, we established new standards of quality that transformed the whole genre, resulting in outdoor-recreation guides of great sophistication and solid content. Menasha Ridge continues to be outdoor publishing's greatest innovator.

The folks at Menasha Ridge Press are as at home on a white-water river or mountain trail as they are editing a manuscript. The books we build for you are the best they can be, because we're responding to your needs. Plus, we use and depend on them ourselves.

We look forward to seeing you on the river or the trail. If you'd like to contact us directly, join in at www.trekalong.com or visit us at www.menasharidge.com. We thank you for your interest in our books and the natural world around us all.

SAFE TRAVELS,

Bob Sehlinger

BOB SEHLINGER
PUBLISHER